WALKS AND TALKS

OF

AN AMERICAN FARMER IN ENGLAND

Walks

and Talks

of an American Farmer
in England

FREDERICK LAW OLMSTED

Ann Arbor
The University of Michigan Press

To
GEORGE GEDDES, Esq.,
of Onondaga County, New York,
this volume is respectfully inscribed.

INTRODUCTION
By Alex L. Murray

On April 30, 1850, the "Henry Clay" slowly left New York harbor bound for Liverpool. On her decks watching the city slip away were three excited young men on their first trip to Europe. One of them was Frederick Law Olmsted, who was destined within a decade to become a widely published commentator on the American South and, within two decades, the father of American landscape architecture. During his thirteen-week tour of England Olmsted kept a record of what he saw and thought. Later, he turned the notes into the *Walks and Talks of an American Farmer in England,* published in two editions, 1852 and 1859.

Travel books of this kind are almost invariably unsystematic and wide-ranging in their subject matter. Olmsted's was no exception; if anything, his account was more all-embracing than most, for he discussed the arrangement of farm buildings, kitchen utensils, the dress and posture of fellow travelers, the condition of various social classes, agricultural techniques, religious and political arrangements, architecture, the natural and man-made landscape, penal methods, dock facilities, and the rigging of ships. Although he had little to say about factories or industrial workers he was much interested in how new industrial cities coped with the problems of providing civic amenities for their inhabitants. Thus, this ostensibly modest "Memoir of a Farmer's Visit to England [written] . . . for Farmers and Farmer's Families" is in reality much more. It is a balanced, incisive, and entertaining look at rural and urban England in 1850 through the eyes of a New Englander peculiarly well equipped for the job.

Olmsted was born in 1822 in Hartford, Connecticut, the son of a prosperous and generous merchant. Despite such a start in life, Olmsted, as he later put it, was "strangely un-educated—mis-educated." As eye trouble prevented him from attending school regularly, he was "let run wild . . . roaming afield and day-dreaming under a tree" (*Frederick Law Olmsted, Landscape Architect, 1822-1903*, F. L. Olmsted, Jr. and T. Kimball, eds. (New York, 1922), p. 69). He acquired enough self-discipline, however, to study topographical engineering privately for almost three years. This led to nothing by way of a career, and in August 1840 he went to work for a French dry goods importer in New York City. After eighteen months he decided that business was not for him. He attended lectures at Yale briefly before resorting to a classic escapist solution for ennui. He shipped out to China as an ordinary seaman on the bark "Ronaldson." After a year before the mast he re-turned to Connecticut as uncertain about his future as ever. For the next three years he alternated unofficial attendance at Yale with the study of farming in Connecticut and New York. Early in 1848 he settled down on his own farm on Staten Island. From all accounts he quickly proved himself to be an enthusiastic and progressive farmer, and a most unusual one. His letters from that time show that while concerning himself with pear-tree grafts and manures, he was also buying prints, drawings, and books. He was reading Ruskin's *Modern Painters*, as well as studying "Landscape Beauty and the Beauty of all Nature, . . . the Theory of Language and the Theory, Economy etc. of Love" (*ibid.*, p. 73).

Two years after Olmsted acquired his Staten Island farm, he again felt the need to travel, this time in Europe, ostensibly to learn more about advanced agricultural methods. He de-cided to join his brother John and a college friend on a walk-ing tour of the British Isles and Germany.

The *Walks and Talks* reveals Olmsted as a man of wide-ranging interests with an omnivorous appetite for details. He had an eye for those special qualities which determine the style of a situation, a person, or an object, and this sensitivity was reinforced by a talent for vivid description. Whether his subject was a proud but alcoholic fellow passenger, a tavern keeper, a farm kitchen, or a landscape, Olmsted captured it in a pithy verbal sketch. As his wife commented seventy years later, "Frederick had a very pretty talent for caricature, not of a grotesque kind but full of quiet humour. . . ." (*ibid*, p. 80).

Another trait which much affected his writing was that despite his advanced religious views he was still a Puritan at heart. He had a deep moral sense which often gave a transcendent significance to an otherwise unimportant event or scene. Upon seeing some elegant rooms in an aristocratic mansion his first reaction was to daydream about living there for a few months, but his reverie was interrupted by the question: "Is it right and best that this should be for the few, the very few of us, when for many of the rest of us, there must be but bare walls, tile floors and everything besides [a] harshly screaming scrabble for life." This was followed by similar rhetorical questions as to the moral appropriateness of the style of life which these rooms symbolized. His New England heritage was also reflected in his preference for simple and unostentatious furniture and architecture. Though he could enjoy richness and good design, he particularly admired objects and spaces which contributed to a restful and domestically scaled environment. But there was nothing pinched or blunted about his capacity for taking pleasure in the world around him—quite the reverse. Olmsted reacted with uncomplicated enthusiasm to whatever was beautiful, grand, or picturesque. There was something very immediate and direct about the way he became totally absorbed in a storm or in the green English countryside. In his perception of the world around him, however, Olmsted had one weakness—he unshamedly searched for and enjoyed whatever was picturesque or quaint. When not looking for advanced farming techniques he tended to prefer a storybook England of thatched cottages, jolly innkeepers, and medieval walls. "Such a scene I had never looked upon before and yet it was in all its parts as familiar to me as my native valley. Land of our poets! Home of our fathers! Dear old mother England it would be strange if I were not affected at meeting thee at last, face to face."

As one might expect, this book contains a great deal of information about the condition of English agriculture in the 1850's. There was hardly an aspect of rural life which he did not touch upon. He was specially interested in unfamiliar farming methods. He took a particularly close look at the drainage systems used in the heavier English soils, citing examples of moderate investment in tiles improving the value of land many times over. Perhaps because he "heard nowhere anything but gratification and satisfaction expressed with the operation of the thorough-drains," Olmsted about 1850 established the first cylindrical drainage tile works in the United States (*ibid.,* p. 61). He was not enthusiastic about English agricultural implements, which generally seemed "unnecessarily cumbersome and complicated." He was equally unimpressed by English fruit-growing methods.

Olmsted was much interested in the condition of farm laborers. He made a careful study of their wages, their working conditions, their housing and their food. White bread, potatoes, and bacon, he discovered, formed the diet of the majority, along with unbelievable amounts of beer and cider —as much as ten quarts a day. Although the farmers he met were as varied as one might expect, Olmsted was shocked at the uniformly degraded condition of the rural laborers in certain counties. He had never seen, not even in the Orient, "men whose tastes were such mere instincts or whose purpose of life and whose mode of life was so low, so like that of domestic animals altogether, as these farm labourers." He was saddened to find that most influential Englishmen ignored the condition of the rural laborers, accepting their plight as ordained by God and the laws of economics. He was quick to see the parallel between this assumption and the assumptions held by the supporters of American slavery. Although the solution for slavery was not in "Abolitionism," he believed that if slaves were assumed to have to remain slaves forever, Americans were as much "tyrants and insolent rebels to humanity" as were indifferent Englishmen. He was optimistic, however, that a love of justice and freedom in both countries would overcome the inertia of established institutions.

After he returned to the United States Olmsted was encouraged to take up the problem of slavery. The first edition of *The Walks and Talks of an American Farmer in England* was well received (*Harpers New Monthly Magazine*, 6 (1852), p. 138), and he was asked by the New York *Daily Times* to write a series of articles on the South and slavery. The series also was very successful, being published in 1856 as a book—*A Journey in the Seaboard Slave States*. Thereupon, he sold his farm and took a brief, financially unsuccessful try at journalism. Then almost by chance, in 1857, he was appointed superintendent of the new Central Park in New York City.

Within a year he and his friend Calvert Vaux submitted a prizewinning design for Central Park. Olmsted was appointed architect-in-chief. Thus, he was launched as a landscape architect and city planner. Over the next thirty-five years, he made a greater visual impact on the North American continent than any other single person. He designed dozens of parks, many college campuses, private estates, city plans, and subdivisions. In 1892-93 at the age of seventy he capped his career with the site plan for the Columbian Exposition in Chicago, thus providing a link between the Romantic Suburb of the nineteenth century and the City Beautiful of the twentieth.

An interruption in Olmsted's career as a landscape architect occurred between 1861 and 1863 when he became secretary of the United States Sanitary Commission, the Civil War precursor of the Red Cross. He took this position not only because of a sense of moral responsibility but because he was fascinated by anything that affected human welfare. He had a sociologist's interest in people as members of groups, yet he did not attempt to stuff them into procrustean molds. Sensitive to individuality, he was tolerant of what some might term aberrant behavior. This characteristic is evident in *Walks and Talks,* in which, despite his New England upper middle-class background, he showed that he could appreciate and reproduce in a superb piece of narrative description the witty banter of a group of London factory boys. He also drew a surprisingly sensitive portrait of prostitutes in Liverpool. Well aware of their "degradation" and involvement in "vice, shame and misery," he sympathized with their search for "a short space of jollity, excitement and forgetfulness," with some sailors.

Olmsted was much interested in English religious life. Like any tourist he visited the Anglican cathedrals and attended services, but he also became familiar with the Nonconformist side of English religion through a number of introductions from Congregationalist, Unitarian, and Methodist friends. Interested in the differences between the Anglican and Nonconformist *style*, he was impressed that nearly all men carry out public religious exercises in "a very different tone and mode of utterance from that which is usual or natural with them." He did not condemn this *"intoned"* or *"sing-song"* manner, but found it expressive not of the meaning of the words but of "a sense of dependence on a superior being—of love, of gratitude, and of reverence." He deplored what he considered to be the excessive interdependence of political and religious authority in England. Crown and Church were merged together in "an abominable masquerade of words . . . on all public occasions, clothing government with antiquated false forms of sacredness." Thus, he discovered, when Englishmen grew sceptical about the Crown, they lost faith in the religious creed associated with it.

By the end of his tour Olmsted was convinced that there was very little patriotism among the lower classes of Englishmen—it seemed "to have been starved out." The lower classes did not identify themselves with the greatness or the prosperity of their country; that all belonged to somebody else. They would, he believed, "see it become a dependency of France or Russia with entire indifference, certainly with exaltation if it were promised them that wages should be higher and bread cheaper for it."

But in comparing England and the United States, he found that the English had a greater capacity for the enjoyment of life. Americans, he wrote, "have less of pleasure and less of actual suffering than any other in the world. Hopefulness, but hope ever unsatisfied is marked in every American's face . . . most of us know but little of the virtuous pleasure God has fitted us to enjoy in this world."

Olmsted's career as a landscape architect can be seen in part as an attempt to bring joy and pleasure into the everyday lives of Americans through the influence of close contact with nature. In his later years he always insisted that he had more or less stumbled into his role. "Never the slightest thought till I was more than thirty years old had entered my mind of practicing landscape gardening except as any fairly well-to-do, working farmer may . . ." (Olmsted and Kimball, pp. 62-63). This may well have been so, but it is clear from the *Walks and Talks* that in 1850 he already had a very high opinion of landscape architecture. "What artist, so noble . . . as he who, with far-reaching conception of beauty and designing power, sketches the outline, writes the colors, and directs the shadows of a picture so great that Nature shall be employed upon it for generations, before the work he has arranged for her shall realize his intentions." He was moved to this kind of enthusiasm by the overwhelming experience of English parks and landscape design. The very first park he saw—in Liverpool, a city about which he had very mixed feelings—astonished him: "I have seen nothing so fine in America." Several weeks later he had seen nothing in England to make him change his mind: "Not a town have we seen in England but has had a better garden-republic than any town I know of in the United States." About a park in Birkenhead, which he examined very closely, he was ecstatic. ". . . Gardening has here reached a perfection that I had never before dreamed of. I cannot undertake to describe the effect of so much taste and skill as had evidently been employed." The irregular and deceptively natural design fascinated him, for its character changed as he moved through the park. He was equally interested in the technical means by which so natural an effect had been achieved. The tile system, the moving of earth, the road surfaces, and the various buildings—all were discussed with the head gardener. Despite his great interest in the design of the Birkenhead park, its usefulness to the common people was for him equally important. What impressed him was that "all this magnificent pleasure-ground is entirely, unreservedly and for ever the peoples' own, the poorest British peasant is as free to enjoy it in all its parts as the British Queen."

As for the less consciously designed landscape of the countryside, Olmsted repeatedly tried to establish what made it so different from the American landscape. Invariably, it was the long graceful lines of deep green hedgerows stretching irregularly in every direction. The practice of leaving occasional large trees in the fields for ship timber and cattle shade, he noticed, led to a "natural open growth . . . therefore branching low and spreading wide and more beautiful, much more beautiful, than we allow our trees to make themselves." The ubiquitous ivy, the overall tidiness, and the "deep, narrow, crooked gulch-like lanes" were also distinctive. Equally important, he observed qualities in the English landscape which went beyond mere specifics. There were peculiarities for which he could not satisfactorily account. English foliage, he found, was "as if the face of each leaf was more nearly parallel with all others near it, and if all were more equally lighted than in our foliage. . . ." Similarly, the smaller variety in forest foliage and the mildness of the light made the English landscape softer, "more indistinct." Thus, he saw little of what he called the "sublime or the picturesque in Nature . . . except on the sea coast." Yet at a time when picturesqueness was becoming a dominant aesthetic principle in America, he found the landscape of rural England strangely fascinating. Scenery which he called "commonplace, because there is nothing striking in it: no one point to be especially noted . . ." charmed him continually on his tour. He was beginning to understand that neither dramatic vistas nor ivied ruins were essential to a certain kind of picturesqueness.

At a time when most Americans were slowly freeing themselves from a concentration on pure historical styles in architecture, he had gone well beyond that point. His motto was "stick to simplicity," and he disliked the "childish ornaments," "baby house appendages," and "painted gimcrackery" which were almost as common in suburban England as in the United States. Even though he believed that the "grand effect of architecture must be form and proportion," he did not reject the

popular idea that architecture should be evocative of certain
moods and associated ideas. From his comments upon English
buildings it is clear that his aesthetic system demanded that a
building produce in the observer a deeply felt emotion. At
Salisbury Cathedral, for example, he was disappointed because
only once or twice was there awakened in him "anything like
a sense of sublimity." When this did happen, the rationalist
in Olmsted forced him "to analyze what had occasioned it."
His conclusion was: "My face was turned towards two great,
dark windows, a considerable space of unbroken wall about
them, and a square, massive buttress, all in the deep shade
between two transepts. From the simple, solitary grandeur and
solemnity of the dark recess there had come a sermon on
humility and endurance, to me more eloquent than all else of
the great Cathedral."

His experience with English architecture also intensified
his sense of the importance of a proper relationship between
a building and its site. The *"stuck up* and easy pretentious air"
of suburban villas in Liverpool and Birkenhead, he found
due to "some disunity in the design—often, perhaps to a want
of keeping between the mansion and its grounds or situation."
Similarly, when outside a church he was moved by a feeling
of sublimity, it was "due less to the architectural style than to
the connection and harmony of the mass with the ground
upon which it was placed."

It is clear from the *Walks and Talks* that Frederick Law
Olmsted was beginning to develop a philosophy of man's relationship with his surroundings. In the transcendentalist milieu
of the 1850's he was being increasingly impressed by the pro-
found influence of the visual environment on man's well
being. That it eventually became his life's work to shape that
environment is not surprising.

PREFACE

I do not deem it necessary to apologize for this memoir of a farmer's visit to England. Every man in traveling will be directed in peculiar paths of observation by his peculiar tastes, habits, and personal interests, and there will always be a greater or less class who will like to hear of just what he liked to see. With a hearty country appetite for narrative, I have spent, previous to my own journey, a great many long winter evenings in reading the books, so frequently written by our literary tourists, upon England; and although I do not recollect one of them, the author of which was a farmer, or whose habits of life, professional interests, associations in society, and ordinary standards of comparison were not altogether different from my own, I remember none from which I did not derive entertainment and instruction.

Notwithstanding, therefore, the triteness of the field, I may presume to think, that there will be a great many who will yet enjoy to follow me over it, and this although my gait and carriage should not be very elegant, but so only as one farmer's leg and one sailor's leg, with the help of a short, crooked, half-grown academic sapling for a walking stick, might be expected to carry a man along with a head and a heart of his own.

And as it is especially for farmers and farmers' families that I have written, I expect that all who try to read the book, will be willing to come into a warm, good-natured, broad country kitchen fireside relation with me, and permit me to speak my mind freely, and in such language as I can readily command, on all sorts of subjects that come in my way, forming their own views from the facts that I give them, and taking my opinions for only just what they shall seem to be worth.

Some explanation of a few of the intentions that gave direction to my movements in traveling may be of service to the reader.

The wages, and the cost and manner of living of the laboring men, and the customs with regard to labor of those countries and districts, from which foreign writers on economical subjects are in the habit of deriving their data, had been made a subject of more than ordinary and other than merely philanthropical interest to me, from an experience of the difficulty of applying their calculations to the different circumstances under which work must be executed in the United States. My vocation as a farmer, too, had led me for a long time to desire to know more of the prevailing, ordinary, and generally-accepted practices of agriculture than I could learn from Mr. Coleman's book, or from the observations of most of the European correspondents of our agricultural periodicals; the attention of these gentlemen having been usually directed to the exceptional, improved modes of cultivation which prevail only among the amateur agriculturists and the bolder and more enterprising farmers.

The tour was made in company with two friends, whose purposes somewhat influence the character of the narrative. One of them—my brother—hoped by a course of invigorating exercise, simple diet, and restraint from books and other in-door and sedentary luxuries, to reëstablish his weakened health, and especially to strengthen his eyes, frequent failures of which often seriously annoyed and interrupted him in the study of his profession. The other, our intimate friend from boyhood, desired to add somewhat to the qualifications usually inquired after in a professed teacher and adviser of mankind, by such a term and method of study as he could afford to make of the varying developments of human nature, under different biases and institutions from those of his own land.

We all thought that it should be among those classes which form the majority of the people of a country that the truest exhibition of national character should be looked for, and that in their condition should be found the best evidence of the wisdom of national institutions.

In forming the details of a plan by which we could, within certain limits of time and money, best accomplish such purposes as I have indicated, we were much indebted to the information and advice given by Bayard Taylor, in his "Views a-Foot."

This volume contains a narrative of the earlier, and to us most interesting, though not the most practically valuable, part of our journey. I was in the habit of writing my diary in the form of a letter, to be sent as occasion offered to friends at home. It is from this desultory letter-diary, with such revision and extension and filling up of gaps as my memory and pocket-book notes afford, that this book has been now made.

FRED. LAW OLMSTED

Tosomock Farm, Southside,
Staten Island, 1859

CONTENTS

CHAPTER I

Emigrant Passenger Agents—Second Cabin—Mutiny—
Delay—Departure   1

CHAPTER II

At Sea—Incidents—Sea Sociability—A Yarn—Sea Life—
Characters—English Radicals   5

CHAPTER III

Sailors—"Sogers"—Books—Anecdotes   19

CHAPTER IV

On Soundings—English Small Craft—Harbor of Liverpool   22

CHAPTER V

The First of England—The Streets—A Railway Station—The Docks at Night—Prostitutes—Temperance—
The Still Life of Liverpool—A Market   29

CHAPTER VI

The People at Liverpool—Poverty—Merchants—Shopkeepers—Women—Soldiers—Children—Donkeys and
Dray-Horses   37

CHAPTER VII

Liverpool Continued—Irish Beggars—Condition of
Laborers—Cost of Living—Prices—Bath House—Quar-

antine—The Docks—Street Scene—"Coming Yankee"
        Over Nonsense—Artistic Begging   41

CHAPTER VIII
Birkenhead—Ferry-Boats—Gruff Englishmen—The Abbey—Flour—Market—The Park—A Democratic Institu-
        tion—Suburban Villas, etc.   48

CHAPTER IX
A Railway Ride—Second Class—Inconvenient Arrange-
ments—First Walk in the Country—England Itself—A
Rural Landscape—Hedges—Approach to a Hamlet—
The Old Ale-House and the Old John Bull—A Talk
with Country People—Notions of America—Free
Trade—The Yew Tree—The Old Rural Church and
Graveyard—A Park Gate—A Model Farmer—The Old
Village Inn—A Model Kitchen—A Model Landlady   57

CHAPTER X
Talk with a Farmer; with a Tender-hearted Wheel-
wright—An Amusing Story—Notions of America—
Supper—Speech of the English—Pleasant Tones—
Quaint Expressions—The Twenty-ninth of May—Zac-
cheus in the Oak Tree—Education—Bed-chamber—A
        Nightcap, and—a Nightcap   63

CHAPTER XI
The Break of Day—A Full Heart—Familiar Things—
The Village at Sunrise—Flowers—Birds—Dog Kennels
—"The Squire" and "The Hall"—Rooks—Visit to a
Small Farm—The Cows—The Milking—The Dairy-
Maids—The Stables—Manure—Bones—Pasture—White
Clover—Implements—Carts—The English Plow and
        Harrow   69

CHAPTER XII
Breakfast at the Inn—A Tale of High Life—The Garden
of the Inn—An Old Farm-House—Timber Houses—
Laborers' Cottages—Wattles and Noggin Walls—A
"Ferme Ornee"—A Lawn Pasture—Copper-leaved
Beeches—Tame Black Cattle—Approach to Chester   73

CHAPTER XIII

Chester Without—A Walk on the Walls—Antiquities—
Striking Contrasts 78

CHAPTER XIV

Chester Within—Peculiarities of Building—The Rows
—A Sea Captain—Romancing—An Old Inn—Old English Town Houses—Timber Houses—Claiming an Inheritance—A Cook Shop—One of the Alleys—Breaking
into the Cathedral—Expulsion—The Curfew 85

CHAPTER XV

Chester Market—The Town Common—Race-Course—
The Yeomanry Cavalry, and the Militia of England—
Public Wash-House 92

CHAPTER XVI

Visit to Eaton Hall—The Largest Arch in the World—
The Outer Park—Backwoods Farming—The Deer Park
—The Hall—The Parterre—The Lawn—The Fruit
Garden—Stables 95

CHAPTER XVII

Gamekeeper—Game Preserves—Eccleston, a Pretty Vil-
lage—The School-House—Draining—Children Playing
—The Riverside Walk—Pleasure Parties—A Contrast-
ing Glimpse of a Sad Heart—Saturday Night—Ballad
Singer—Mendicants—Row in the Tap-Room—Woman's
Feebleness—Chester Beer, and Beer-Drinking 101

CHAPTER XVIII

Character of the Welsh—The Cathedral; the Clergy,
Service, Intoning, the Ludicrous and the Sublime—A
Reverie—A Revelation—The Sermon—Communions—
Other Churches—Sunday Evening—Character of the
Townspeople 109

CHAPTER XIX

Clandestine Architectural Studies—A Visit to the Marquis of Westminster's Stud—Stable Matters 119

CHAPTER XX

The Cheshire Cheese District and English Husbandry
upon Heavy Soils—Pastures; Their Permanence—The
Use of Bones as a Manure in Cheshire—A Valuable
Remark to Owners of Improved Neat Stock—Breeds of
Dairy Stock—Horses   125

CHAPTER XXI

Tillage—Size of Farms—Condition of Laborers—Fences
—Hedges—Surface Drainage—Under Drainage—Valu-
able Implements for Stiff Soils, Not Used in the United
States   132

CHAPTER XXII

The General Condition of Agriculture—Rotation of
Crops—Productiveness—Seeding Down to Grass—Com-
parison of English and American Practice—Practical
Remarks—Rye-Grass, Clover—Biennial Grasses—Guano
—Lime—The Condition of Laborers, Wages, etc.—
Dairy-Maids—Allowance of Beer   137

CHAPTER XXIII

Remarks on the Cultivation of Beet and Mangel-Wurzel   144

CHAPTER XXIV

Delightful Walk by the Dee Banks, and Through Eaton
Park—Wrexham—A Fair—Maids by a Fountain—The
Church—Jackdaws—The Tap-Room and Tap-Room
Talk—Political Deadness of the Laboring Class—A
Methodist Bagman   147

CHAPTER XXV

Morning Walk Through a Coal District—Ruabon—An
Optimist with a Welsh Wife—Graveyard Notes—A
Stage-Wagon—Taxes—Wynstay Park—Thorough Drain-
ing—A Glimpse of Cottage Life—"Sir Watkins Williams
Wyn"   151

CHAPTER XXVI

Stone Houses—Ivy—Virginia Creeper—A Visit to a
Welsh Horse-Fair—English Vehicles—Agricultural Notes
—Horses—Breeds of Cattle; Herefords, Welsh, and

Smutty Pates—Character of the People—Dress—Powis
Park 156

CHAPTER XXVII

English Vehicles—A Feudal Castle and Modern Aristocratic Mansion—Aristocracy in 1850—Primogeniture—
Democratic Tendency of Political Sentiments—Disposition Towards the United States—Combativeness—Slavery 161

CHAPTER XXVIII

Paintings—Cromwell—Pastoral Ships—Family Portraits
and Distant Relations—Family Apartments—Personal
Cleanliness—The Wrekin 169

CHAPTER XXIX

Visit to a Farm—Farm-House and Farmery—Fatting
Cattle—Sheep—Vetches—Stack Yard—Steam Threshing
—Turnip Sowing—Excellent Work—Tram Road—
Wages 172

CHAPTER XXX

Visit to Two English Common Schools 176

CHAPTER XXXI

Shrewsbury—Angling in Curricles—Sheep-walks—Effect
of Thorough Draining on Dry Soils—Gorse—Church
Stretton—Churchyard Literature—Encounter with an
Enthusiastic Free-Trader 178

CHAPTER XXXII

Country Carrier's Cart—Independent Breakfast—Beauty
—Old Inn—Jack up the Chimney—Bacon and Bread;
Beer and Rum—Ludlow—An Apostolic Church—The
Poor-House—*Case* of a Broken Heart—Refreshment 183

CHAPTER XXXIII

Physical Education—A Rustic Village—Farm-House
Kitchen—An Orchard—Stables—Leominster—A Trout
Brook—Fruit Culture 188

CHAPTER XXXIV

English Orchard Districts—The Most Favorable Soils

and   Climate—Lime—Practical   Deduction—Diseases—
      Prevention and Remedies—Suggestions   192

CHAPTER XXXV

Decay of Varieties—Two Theories: Knight's, Downing's
—English Theory and Practice—Practical Deductions—
Causes of Decay—Remedies—Hints to Orchardists—
Special   Manures—Pruning—Thorough   Drainage—A
      Satirical Sketch—Shooting the Apple-Tree   198

CHAPTER XXXVI

Roofs; Shingles; Tile; Thatch: The Advantages and Dis-
advantages of Each—The Use of Thatch in America—
Hereford—Christian Hospitality—A Milk Farm—The
Herefords—A Dangerous Man—Primitive Christianity   208

CHAPTER XXXVII

The County Jail—English Prison Discipline—The Perfection of the Present—Education and Taxation—What
Next?—Captain Machonochie—The Mark System—The
      Christian Idea of Punishment   214

CHAPTER XXXVIII

A Hit—The Debtor's Prison—Utter Cleanliness—"City"
and "Town"—"Down" and "Up"—Hereford Cathedral
      —Church and State—The Public Promenade   222

CHAPTER XXXIX

Shady Lanes—Rural Sketches—Herefordshire and Mon-
mouthshire Scenery—Points of Difference in English and
American Landscapes—Visit to a Farm-House—The Mis-
tress—The Farm-House Garden—A Stout Old English
Farmer—The   Stables   and   Stock—Turnip   Culture—
Sheep—Wheat—Hay—Rents—Prices—A Parting—Cider 226

CHAPTER XL

Walk with a Rustic—Family Meeting—A Recollection
of the Rhine—Ignorance and Degraded Condition of the
English Agricultural Laborer—How He Is Regarded by
His Superiors—The Principles of Government—Duties
of the Governing—Education—Slavery—The Diet of
      Laborers—Drink—Bread—Bacon—Fresh Meat   235

CHAPTER XLI

Tintern Abbey and the Wye—English Screw Steamers— Tide Deluge—St. Vincent's Rocks—Bristol-built Vessels —The Vale of Gloucester—Whitfield "Example Farm" —Hedge-row Timber—Drainage—Buildings—Stock— Soiling—Manure—Wheat—Beets and Turnips—Disgraceful Agriculture—The Landed Gentry—Wages of Laborers   245

CHAPTER XLII

Bath—Warminster—Surly Postmaster—A Doubtful Character—Polite Innkeeper and Pretty Chambermaid —The Tap-Room Fireside—Rustic Civility—Rainy Morning in a Country Inn—Coming to Market—The Road in a Storm—Scudding   251

CHAPTER XLIII

The South-Downs—Wiltshire Landscape—Chalk and Flint—Irrigation—The Cost and Profit of Water-Meadows—Sewerage Water—Irrigation in Old Times   257

CHAPTER XLIV

Flocks, Dogs, and Shepherds of Salisbury Plain—Village Almshouses—Ostentation in Alms-Giving—A Forced March—At Home in Salisbury—The Street Brooks— The Cathedral—Architectural Remarks and Advice— Village Churches   266

CHAPTER XLV

Salisbury Plain—Strange Desert Character of the Scenery —The Agriculture—Sainfoin and Lucerne—Large Farms—Effect on Laborers—Paring and Burning—When Expedient—Expense—Sheep-Folding—Moveable Railways and Sheds   272

CHAPTER XLVI

An Arcadian Hamlet—Out of the World, but not Beyond the Reach of the Yankee Peddler—The Cottages of the Downs—Grout and Cobble-stones—Character of the Laboring Class of the Downs—Want of Curiosity—Old Stockbridge, Winchester, William of Wykeham—His

Legacy to Wayfarers—The Cathedral—Some Remarks
on Architectural Situation—Search for Lodgings—
Motherly Kindness—Railroad Mismanagement—Waterloo Day at Portsmouth   278

CHAPTER XLVII

The Deceit of Descriptions of Scenery—The Soul of a
Landscape—The Isle of Wight; Its Characteristics—Ap-
propriate Domestic Architecture—Genial Climate—
Tropical Verdure—The Cliffs of Albion—Osborne—
The Royal Villa—Country Life of the Royal Family
—Agricultural Inclination and Rural Tastes—The
Royal Tenantry   285

CHAPTER XLVIII

The Queen's Yacht—Yachts of the R. Y. Club; their
Build and Rig—Comparison with American Yachts and
Pilot-Boats—Seamanship—Cut of Sails—The Navy-Yard
at Portsmouth—Gun-Boats—Steamers—Evening at Portsea—Curiosity—About Boasting and Some English Characteristics—Conversation with a Shopkeeper on the
"Glory of England"   289

CHAPTER XLIX

Rural Police—The "Anchor" Inn—The Garden—"Old
Coaching Times"—Heath Land—A Dreary Landscape
—Murder and a Highway Adventure—Human Vanity   295

CHAPTER L

London Lads—Railway Ride—Observations in Natural
History   299

CHAPTER LI

Rural Laborers near London—Our Mother Tongue—
Cockneys—Provincialists—On the Naturalization of
Foreign Words—Authorities—Suburban London—Lon-
don—The Thames—"Saint Paul's from Blackfriar's
Bridge"   302

CHAPTER LII

A Pilgrimage   308

APPENDIX A Information and Advice for those wishing
                to make a Pedestrian Tour in England, at
                        the least practicable expense   311
APPENDIX B Principles of the Mark System, framed to
                mix Persuasion with Punishment, and
                make their effect improving, yet their
                            operation severe   318

CHAPTER I

Emigrant   Passenger   Agents—Second   Cabin—Mutiny—
Delay—Departure

WE INTENDED, if we could be suited, to take a second cabin
state-room for our party of three, and to accommodate me, my
friends had agreed to wait till after "planting." While I therefore hurried on the spring work upon my farm, they in the city
were examining ships and consulting passenger agents. The
confidence in imposition those acquire who are in the habit of
dealing with emigrant passengers, was amusingly shown in the
assurance with which they would attempt to lie down the most
obvious objections to what they had to offer; declaring that a
cabin disgusting with filth and the stench of bilge-water was
sweet and clean; that darkness in which they would be grop-
ing was very light (a trick, certainly, not confined to their
trade); that a space in which one could not stand erect, or a
berth like a coffin, was very roomy, and so forth.

Finally we were taken in by the perfect impudence and
utter simplicity in falsehood of one of them, an underling of
"a respectable house"—advertised passenger agents of the ship
—which, on the lie being represented to it, thought proper to
express its "regret" at the young man's error, but could not be
made to see that it was proper for it to do any thing more—
the error not having been discovered in time for us to con-
veniently make other arrangements.

We had engaged a "family room" exclusively for ourselves, in the large and neatly-fitted cabin of a new, clean, first-class packet. We thought the price asked for it very low, and to secure it beyond a doubt, had paid half the money down at the agent's desk, and taken a receipt, put some of our baggage in it, locked the door, and taken the key. The ship was hauling out from her pier when we went on board with our trunks, and found that the spacious second cabin had been stowed half full of cotton, and the remaining space lumbered up with ship stores, spare sails, etc. The adjoining rooms were evidently occupied by steerage passengers, and the steward was trying keys to let them into ours. The mate cursed us for taking the key, and the captain declared that no one had been authorized to make such arrangements as had been entered into with us, and that he should put whom he pleased into the room.

We held on to the key, and appealed first to the agents and then to the owners. Finally we agreed to take a single roommate, a young man whom they introduced to us, and whose appearance promised agreeably, and with this compromise were allowed to retain possession. The distinction between second cabin and steerage proved to be an imagination of the agents—those who had asked for a steerage passage were asked a little less, and had berths given them in the second-cabin state-rooms, the proper steerage being filled up with freight. The captain, however, directed the cook to serve us, allowed us a light at night in our room, and some other special conveniences and privileges, and generally treated us, after we got to sea, as if he considered us rather more of the "gentleman" class than the rest;—say about two dollars apiece more.

After the ship had hauled out in the stream, and while she lay in charge of the first mate, the captain having gone ashore, there was a bit of mutiny among the seamen. Nearly the whole crew refused to do duty, and pledged each other never to take the ship to sea. Seeing that the officers, though prepared with loaded pistols, were not disposed to act rashly, we offered to assist them, for the men had brought up their chests and were collecting handspikes and weapons, and

threatened to take a boat from the davits if they were not sent
on shore. It was curious to see how the steerage passengers,
before they had any idea of the grounds of the quarrel, but as
if by instinct, almost to a man, took sides against the lawful
authority.

Having had some experience with the ways of seamen, I
also went forward to try to pacify them. (Like most Connecticut boys, I knocked about the world a few years before I
settled down, and one of these I spent in a ship's forecastle.)
The only thing that the soberest of them could say was, that a
man had been killed on the ship, and they knew she was going
to be unlucky; and that they had been shipped in her when
too drunk to know what they were about. Perceiving all that
the most of them wanted was to get ashore to have their spree
out, and as there was no reasoning with them, I advised the
mate to send them a fiddle and let them get to dancing. He
liked the idea, but had no fiddle, so as the next best pacifying
expedient, ordered the cook to give them supper. They took to
this kindly, and after using it up fell to playing *monkey-
shines,* and with singing, dancing and shouting, kept themselves in good humor until late in the evening, when they, one
by one, dropped off, and turned in. The next morning they
were all drunk or sulky, and contented themselves with refusing to come on deck when ordered.

When the captain came on board and learned the state of
things, he took a hatchet, and with the officers and carpenter,
jumped into the forecastle, and with a general knocking down
and kicking out, got them all on deck. He then broke open
their chests and took from them six jugs of grog which they
had concealed, and threw them overboard. As they floated
astern, a Whitehall boatmen picked them up, and after securing the last, took a drink and loudly wished us luck.

Two or three of the most violent were sent on shore (not
punished, but so rewarded), and their places supplied by others. The rest looked a little sour, and contrived to meet with a
good many accidents as long as the shore-boats kept about us;
but when we were fairly getting clear of the land, and the
wind hauled a bit more aft, and the passengers began to wish
she would stop for just one moment, and there came a whirr-

rushing noise from under the bows—the hearty *yo-ho—heave-o-hoii*—with which they roused out the stu'n-sails, was such as nobody the least bit sulky could have begun to find voice for.

A handsome Napoleonic performance it was of the captain's: the more need that I should say that in my mind he disgraced himself by it; because, while we lay almost within hail of the properly constituted officers of the law, and under the guns of a United States fortress, such dashing violence was unnecessary and lawless;—only at sea had he the right, or could he be justified in using it.

I suppose that some such difficulties occur at the sailing of half the ships that leave New York. I have been on board a number as they were getting under way, and in every one of them there has been more or less trouble arising from the intoxicated condition of the crew. Twice I have seen men fall overboard, when first ordered aloft, in going down the harbor.

The ship did not go to sea until three days after she was advertised to sail, though she had her crew, stores, and steerage passengers on board all that time. I do not know the cause of her detention; it seemed unnecessary, as other large ships sailed while we lay idle; and if unnecessary, it was not honest. The loss of three days' board, and diminution by so much of the stores, calculated to last out the passage, and all the other expenses and inconveniences occasioned by it to the poor steerage passengers, may seem hardly worthy of notice; and I should not mention it, if such delays, often much more protracted, were not frequent—sometimes adding materially to the suffering always attending a long passage.

At noon on the 3d of May we passed out by the light-ship of the outer bar, and soon after eight o'clock that evening the last gleam of Fire-Island light disappeared behind the dark line of unbroken horizon.

CHAPTER II

At Sea—Incidents—Sea Sociability—A Yarn—Sea Life—
Characters—English Radicals

At Sea, May 23

WE ARE RECKONED today to be about one hundred and fifty
miles to the westward of Cape Clear; ship close-hauled, head-
ing north, with a very dim prospect of the termination of our
voyage. It has been thus far rather dull and uneventful. We
three have never been obliged to own ourselves actually sea-
sick, but at any time during the first week we could hardly
have declared that we felt perfectly well, and our appetites
seemed influenced at every meal as if by a gloomy apprehension of what an hour might bring forth. Most of the other
passengers have been very miserable indeed. I notice they
recover more rapidly in the steerage than in the cabin. This I
suppose to be owing to their situation in the middle of the
ship, where there is the least motion, to their simple diet, and
probably to their having less temptation to eat freely, and
greater necessity to "make an effort," and move about in fresh
air.

We have met one school of small whales. There might
have been fifty of them, tumbling ponderously over the waves,
in sight at once. Occasionally one would rise lazily up so near,
that, as he caught sight of us, we could seem to see an expres-

5

sion of surprise and alarm in his stolid, black face, and then he would hastily throw himself under again, with an energetic slap of his flukes.

One dark, foggy night, while we were "on the Banks," we witnessed a rather remarkable exhibition of marine pyrotechny. The whole water, as far as we could see, was lustrous white, while near the eye it was full of spangles, and every disturbance, as that caused by the movement of the ship, or the ripples from the wind, or the surging of the sea, was marked by fire flashes. Very singular spots, from the size of one's hand to minute sparks, frequently floated by, looking like stars in the milky-way. We noticed also several schools, numbering hundreds, of what seemed little fishes (perhaps an inch long), that darted here and there, comet-like, with great velocity. I tried, without success, to catch some of these. It was evident that, besides the ordinary phosphorescent animalculæ, there were various and distinct varities of animated nature around us, such as are not often to be observed.

Some kind of sea-bird we have seen, I think, every day, and when at the greatest distance from land. Where is their home? is an oft-repeated question, and, What do they eat? They are mysteries, these feathered Bedouins. Today, land and long-legged shore birds are coming on board of us. They fly tremulously about the ship, sometimes going off out of sight and back again, then lighting for a few moments on a spar or line of rigging. Some have fallen asleep so; or suffered themselves, though panting with apprehension, to be taken. One of these is a swallow, and another a wheat-ear. Some kind of a lark, but not recognizable by the English on board, was taken several days since. It had probably been lost from the Western Islands.

We have seen but very few vessels; but the meeting with one of them was quite an event in sea life. She was coming from the eastward, wind north, and running free, when we first saw her, but soon after took in her studding-sails and hauled up so as to come near us. When abeam, and about three miles distant, she showed Bremen colors, laid aback her mainsail and lowered a quarter-boat, which we immediately squared away to meet, and ran up our bunting: every body on deck, and great excitement. With a glass we could see her decks loaded with emigrants; and as her masts and sails appeared entirely uninjured, it could only be conjectured that she was distressed for provisions or water. The carpenter was sent to sound the water tanks, and the mate to make an estimate of what stores might be safely spared, while we hastened to our room, to scribble notes to send home. We finished them soon enough to see a neat boat, rowed by four men, come alongside, and a gentlemanly young officer mount nimbly up the side-ladder. He was received on deck by our second mate, and conducted aft by him to the cabin companion, where the captain, having put on his best dress-coat and new Broadway stove-pipe hat, stood, like a small king, dignifiedly waiting. After the ceremony of presentation, the captain inquired, "Well, sir, what can I have the pleasure of doing for you?" The young man replied that he came from the ship so-and-so, Captain——, who sent his compliments, and desired *"Vaat is te news?"* This cool motive for stopping two ships in mid-ocean, with a fresh and favorable wind blowing for each, took the captain plainly aback; but he directly recovered, and taking him into the cabin, gave him a glass of wine and a few minutes' conversation with a most creditable politeness; a chunk of ice and a piece of fresh meat were passed into the boat, and the steerage passengers threw some tobacco to the men in her. The young officer took our letters, with some cigars and newspapers, and went over the side again, without probably having perceived that we were any less gregarious beings than himself. The curbed energy and suppressed vexation of our officers, however, showed itself before he was well seated in his boat, by the violent language of command, and the rapidity with which the yards were sharpened and the ship again brought to her course.

This occurrence brought to the mind of our "second dickey" that night, a boarding affair of his own, of which he told us in the drollest manner possible. I wish you could hear his drawl, and see his immovably sober face, but twinkling eye, that made it all seem natural and just like him, as he spun us the yarn.

He was once, he said, round in the Pacific, in a Sag-Harbor whaler, "rayther smart, we accounted her," when they tried to speak an English frigate, and did not get quite near enough. So, as they had nothing else to do, they "up't and chased her," and kept after her without ever getting any nearer for nearly three days. Finally, the wind hauled round ahead and began to blow a little fresh, and they overhauled her very rapidly, so that along about sunset they found themselves coming well to windward of her, as they ran upon opposite tacks. They then hove-to, and he was sent in a boat to board her, and she promptly came-to also, and waited for him.

Dressed in a dungaree jumper, yellow oil-skin hat, and canvass trowsers, he climbed on board the frigate and was addressed by the officer of the deck.

"Now then, sir, what is it?"

"Are you the cap'en of this ere frigate, sir?"

"What's your business, sir?"

"Why, our cap'en sent his compliments to yourn, sir, and —if you are a going home—he wished you'd report the bark Lucreetshy Ann, of Sag-Harbor, Cap'en J. Coffin Starbuck, thirty-seven days from [Wahoo] Oahu, seven hundred and fifty barrels of sperm, and two hundred and fifty o' right; guess we shall to in to Tuckeywarner [Talcahuano]."

"Is that all, sir?"

"Well, no; the old man said, if you was a mind to, he'd like to have me see if I could make a trade with yer for some 'backy. We hain't had none now a going on two week, and he's a most sick. How is't—yer mind to?"

"Is that all your business, sir?"

"Well—yes; guess 'tis—about all."

"I think you had better go into your boat, sir."

He thought so too, when he saw the main-yard immediately afterwards begin to swing round. As the officer stepped below, he went over the side. When he called out to have the painter let go though, he was told to wait a bit, and directly a small parcel of tobacco was handed down, and the same officer, looking over the rail, asked,

"Did you say the *Lucretia Ann?*"

"Ay, ay, sir; Lucreetshy Ann, of Sag-Harbor."

"Mr. Starrboard, I believe."

"'Buck' sir, 'buck.' How about this 'backey?"

The lieutenant, raising his head, his cap, striking the mainsheet as it was being hauled down, was knocked off and fell into the water, when one of the whalers immediately lanced it and held it up dripping.

"Hallo mister; I say, what shall we do with this cap? Did you mean ter throw it in?"

The officer once more looked over the side, with half a dozen grinning middies, and imperturbably dignified, replied,

"You will do me the favor to present it to captain Buck, and say to him, if you please, that when he wishes to communicate with one of Her Majesty's ships again, it will be proper for him to do so in person."

"Oh, certainly—oh, yes; good night to yer. Here, let's have that cap. Give way, now, boys," so saying he clapped it on the top of his old souwester, and as the frigate forged ahead, the boat dropped astern, and was pulled back to the Lucretia Ann.

We had only three days of bad "weather," and those we enjoyed, I think, quite as much as any. The storm was preceded by some twenty-four hours of a clear, fresh north-wester, driving us along on our course with foaming, sparkling and most exhilarating speed. It gives a fine sensation to be so borne along, like that of riding a great, powerful and spirited horse, or of dashing yourself through the crashing surf, and in your own body breasting away the billows as they sweep down upon you. Gradually it grew more and more ahead, and blew harder and harder. When we came on deck early in the morning, the horizon seemed within a stone's throw, and there was a grand sight of dark marbled swelling waves, rushing on tumultuously, crowding away and trampling under each other, as if panic-struck by the grey, lowering, misty clouds that were sweeping down with an appearance of intense mysterious purpose over them. The expression was of vehement energy blindly directed. The ship, lying-to under the smallest storm-stay-sail, seemed to have composed herself for a trial, and, neither advancing nor shrinking, rose and fell with more than habitual ease and dignity. Having been previously accustomed only to the fidgety movements of a smaller class of vessels, I was greatly surprised and impressed by her deliberate movements; the quietness and simplicity with which she answered the threats of the turbulent elements.

"If only that north-wester had continued"—every body is saying—"we might have been in Liverpool by this." It's not unfashionable yet at sea to talk about the weather. I am to write about what is most interesting us? Well, the wind and weather. Bad time when it comes to that? Well, now, here I am, sitting on a trunk, bracing myself between two berths, with my portfolio on my knees—imagine the motion of the vessel, the flickering, inconstant half-light that comes through a narrow piece of inch-thick glass, which the people on deck are constantly crossing; exclamations from them, dash of waves and creaking of timber, and various noises both distracting and stupefying, and if you can't understand the difficulty of thinking connectedly, you may begin to that of writing.

John's eyes have been bad, and we have read aloud with him a good deal; but it is hard work even to read on board ship. We have listened to a good deal of music, and to a bad deal, and had a few staggering hops with the ladies on the quarter deck. We contrived a set of chess-men, cutting them out of cardboard, fitting them with cork pedestals, and a pinpoint to attach them to the board so they would not slip off or blow away. Charley has had some capital games, and I believe found his match with Dr. M., one of the cabin passengers returning home from the East Indies by way of California, who proposes to introduce him at the London chess club.

I told you in my letter by the pilot-boat, how we had been humbugged about the second cabin. While this has reduced the cost of our passage to a very small sum, we have had almost every comfort that we should have asked. Our room is considerably more spacious, having been intended for a family apartment, and has the advantage of much less motion than those of the first cabin. For a ship's accommodations it has, too, a quite luxurious degree of ventilation and light. There is a large port in it that we can open at pleasure, having only been obliged to close it during two nights of the gale. Our stores have held out well, and the cook has served us excellently.

We have hardly tasted our cured meat, and with this and our hard bread we are now helping out some of our more unfortunate neighbors. Split peas and portable soup (*bouillon*), with fresh and dried fruit, have been valuable stores.

As the captain desired us to use the quarter-deck privileges, we have associated as we pleased with the first-cabin passengers, and found several valuable acquaintances among them.

Our roommate, a young Irish surgeon, is a very good fellow, apparently of high professional attainments, and possessed of a power of so concentrating his attention on a book or whatever he is engaged with, as not to be easily disturbed, and a general politeness in yielding to the tastes of the majority that we are greatly beholden to. He is a devoted admirer of Smith O'Brien, and thinks the Irish rising of '48 would have been successful, if he [O'B.] had not been too strictly honest and honorable a man to lead a popular revolt.

Of his last winter's passage, in an emigrant ship, across the Atlantic, he gives us a thrilling account.

He had been appointed surgeon of a vessel about to sail from a small port in Ireland. She was nearly ready for sea, the passengers collecting and stores taken on board, when some discovery was made that involved the necessity of withdrawing her. Another ship was procured from Liverpool, and the stores, passengers, doctor and all, hastily transferred to her in the night, as soon as she arrived. They got to sea, and he found there was hardly a particle of any thing in the medicine chest. He begged the captain to put back, but the captain was a stubborn, reckless, devil-may-care fellow, and only laughed at him. That very night the cholera broke out. He went again to the captain, he beseeched him, he threatened him; he told him that on his head must be the consequences; the captain didn't care a——rope yarn for the consequences, he would do anything else to oblige the doctor, but go back? not he! The doctor turned the pigs out of the long-boat, and made a temporary hospital of it. It was a cold place, but anything was better than that horrible steerage. Nevertheless, down into the steerage the doctor would himself go every morning, nor leave it till every soul had gone or been carried on deck before him. He searched the ship for something he could make medicine of. The carpenter's chalk was the only thing that turned up. This he calcined and saved, to be used sparingly. He forced those who were the least sea-sick to become nurses; convalescents, and those with less dangerous illness, he placed beds for on the galley and the hen-coops, and made the captain give up his fowls and other delicacies to them. Fortunately fair weather continued, and with sleepless vigilance and strength, as it seemed to him almost miraculously sustained, he continued to examine and send on deck for some hours each day, every one of the three hundred passengers. On the first cholera symptoms appearing, he gave the patient chalk, and continued administering it in small but frequent doses until the spasmodic crisis commenced; thence he troubled him only with hot fomentations. The third day out a man died and was buried. The captain read the funeral service, and after the body had disappeared beneath the blue water, the doctor took advantage of the solemn moment again to appeal to him.

"Captain, there are three hundreds souls in this ship—"

"Belay that, doctor; I'll see every soul of 'em in Davy's locker, sir, before I'll put my ship back."

The doctor said no more, but turned away with a heavy heart to do his duty as best he could.

I cannot describe the horrors of that passage as he would. Nevertheless, as far as simple numbers can give it, you shall have the result.

Out of those three hundred souls, before the ship reached New York, there died—one; and he, the doctor declared most soberly, was a very old man, and half dead with a chronic [something] when he came on board. So much for burnt chalk and—fresh air!

But seriously, this story, (which, as I have repeated it, I believe is essentially true,) though not in itself a painful one, not the less strikingly shows with what villainous barbarity, by disregard or evasion of the laws of England, and the neglect or connivance of the port officers, the emigrant traffic is carried on. Some of the accounts of the three other medical men on board, who are also returning from passages in emigrant ships, would disgust a slave-trader. They say that many of the passengers will never go on deck unless they are driven or carried, and frequently the number of these is so great, that it is impossible to force them out of their berths, and they sometimes lie in them in the most filthy manner possible, without ever stepping out from the first heave of the sickening sea till the American pilot is received on board. Then their wives, husbands, children, as the case may be, who have served them with food during their prostration, get them up, and, if they can afford it, change their garments, throwing the old ones, with the bed and its accumulations, overboard. So, as any one may see, from a dozen ships a day often in New York, they come ashore with no disease but want of energy, but emaciated, enfeebled, infected, and covered with vermin. When we observe the listlessness, even cheerfulness, with which they accept the precarious and dog-like subsistence which, while in this condition, the already crowded city affords them, we see the misery and degradation to which they must have been habituated in their native land. When in a year afterwards we find that the same poor fellows are plainly growing active, hopeful, enterprising, prudent, and, if they have been favorably situated, cleanly, tidy, and actually changing to their very bones as it seems—tight, elastic, well-knit muscles taking the place of flabby flesh, as ambition and blessed discontent take the place of stupid indifference—we can infer with some confidence what was at the bottom of their previous debasement.

Dr. M. gives much happier accounts of the English governmental emigrant ships to Australia, in which he has made two voyages. Some few of their arrangements are so entirely commendable, and so obviously demanded by every consideration of decency, humanity, and virtue, that I can only wonder that the law does not require all emigrant vessels to adopt them. Among these, that which is most plainly required, is the division of the steerage into three compartments: married parties with their children in the central one, and unmarried men and women having separate sleeping accommodations in the other two.

The others of our midship passengers are mostly English

artisans, or manufacturing workmen. There are two or three farmers, a number of Irish servants, male and female, and several nondescript adventurers; two Scotchmen only, brothers, both returning from Cuba sugar plantations, where they have been employed as engineers. They tell us the people there are all for annexation to the United States; but as they cannot speak Spanish, their information on this point cannot be very extensive. Besides ourselves, there is but one American-born person among them. She is a young woman of quite superior mind, fair and engaging, rather ill in health, going to England in hopes to improve it, and to visit some family friends there. The young men are all hoping the ship will be wrecked, so they can have the pleasure of saving her, or dying in the attempt. One goes into the main-chains and sits there for several hours, all alone, every fine day, for no other reason that we can conceive, but to drop himself easily into the water after her, in case she should fall overboard. There are three or four other women, and as many babies and little boys and girls. They do not cry very often, but are generally in high spirits, always in the way, frolicking or eating, much fondled and scolded, and very dirty.

The most notable character in our part of the ship, is one Dr. T., another returning emigrant physician. He appears to have been well educated, and is of a wealthy Irish family. His diploma is signed by Sir Astley Cooper, whose autograph we have thus seen. Though a young man, he is all broken down in spirit and body from hard drinking. He makes himself a buffoon for the amusement of the passengers; and some of the young men of the first cabin are wicked enough to reward him sometimes with liquor, which makes him downright crazy. Even the pale-faced student, who kept his neighbors awake with his midnight prayers while he was sea-sick, has participated in this cruel fun. Dr. T. has been "smutten," as the second mate says, by a young lady of the first cabin, who does not altogether discourage his gallant attentions. He keeps up the habits of a gentleman in the reduction of his circumstances, eating his dinner at four o'clock, (being thus enabled to cook it while the first-cabin people are below eating theirs, which is served at half-past three). He declares it was only to oblige the owners that he took a berth in the second cabin, and he certainly should not have done so, if he had suspected the promiscuous character of the company he should be associated with there. The forenoon he spends in combing his hair and whiskers, cleaning his threadbare coat, smoothing his crushed hat, and polishing his shoes. Now, indeed, since he has become conscious of the tender passion, and can feed on love, he has traded off a part of his stock of bread for a pair of boots, which enables him to dispense with stockings and straps, much to his relief in dances and fencing bouts. Towards noon he comes on deck with his coat buttoned to the neck; he wears a stock and no collar; his hat is set on rakishly; he has a yellow kid glove for his right hand, the thumb only is missing—his thumb, therefore, is stuck under the breast of his coat, allowing the rest to be advantageously displayed; his other hand is carried habitually in the mode of Mr. Pickwick, under the skirt of his coat. He has in his mouth the stump of a cigar that he found last night upon the deck, and has saved for the occasion. After walking until it is smoked out with the gentlemen—to whom he manages to give the impression that he has just finished his breakfast—he approaches, with a really elegant air, to the ladies, and, gracefully bowing, inquires after their health. Then, after gazing upwards at the sun a moment he takes the attitude, "Napoleon at St. Helena," his left hand hidden under his right arm, and, in a deep, tremulous voice, says "Ourre nooble barruck still cleaves the breeny ailiment, and bears us on with velucitay 'twarrd th' expectant shoorres of Albeeon's eel. Ah! what a grrand expanse it is of weeld-washing waterrers! Deleeghtful waytherr, 'pon my worrud." He is a good fencer, boxer, card player, and trickster; a safe waltzer, even in a rolling ship; and when half-seas over, dances a jig, hornpipe, or *pas seul*, and turns a *pirouette* on the top of the capstan; plays a cracked clarionet, and can get something out of every sort of muscial instrument; he spouts theatrically, gives imitations of living actors, sings every thing, *improvises*, and on Sunday chants from the prayer-book, so that even then the religiously inclined may conscientiously enjoy his entertainment. A most rare treasure for a long passage! Some of our passengers declare they would have died of dullness if it had not been for him.

There is another Irishman (from the North), who has

written a poem as long as Paradise Lost, the manuscript of
which he keeps under lock and key, in a small trunk, at the
head of his bed, and, as they say, fastened to a life-preserver. It
is never out of his head, however, and he manages to find
something to quote from it appropriate to every occasion. You
might suppose he would be made use of as a butt, but some-
how he is only regarded as a bore. I incline to think him a true
poet, for he is a strange fellow, often blundering, stupidly as it
seems, upon "good hits," and, however inconsistently, always
speaking with the confidence of true inspiration. We have a
godless set around us, and he is very impatient of their card-
playing and profanity—particularly if the weather is at all
bad—declaring that he is not superstitious, but that he thinks,
if a man is ever to stand by his faith, it should be when he is
in the midst of the awful ocean, and in an unlucky ship.
"Nay," he asserts again, "he is *not* superstitious, and no one
must accuse him of it, but if he were not principled against it,
he would lay a large wager that this ship never does arrive at
her destined port." His poem runs somewhat upon socialism,
whether approvingly or condemnatory, I have not yet been
able quite to understand. I rather think he has a scheme of his
own for remodeling society. He uses a good deal of religious
phraseology; he is liberal on doctrinal points, does not enlist
under any particular church banner, and says himself, that he
can bear "any sort of religion [or irreligion] in a man, so he is
not a papist." Towards all persons of the Roman church, he
entertains the most orthodox contempt and undisguised
hatred, as becomes, in his opinion, an Irish Protestant-born
man.

There is a good-natured fellow, who has been a flat-boat-
man on the Mississippi, and more lately a squatter somewhere
in the wilds of the West. His "painter" and cat-fish stories,
with all his reckless airs and cant river phrases, have much
entertained us; of course he has no baggage, but a "heap of
plunder." He has a rough, rowdy, blustering, half barbarous
way with him, and you would judge from his talk sometimes,
that he was a perfectly lawless, heartless savage; yet, again,
there is often evident in his behavior to individuals a singularly delicate sense of propriety and fitness, and there is not a

man in the ship with whom I would sooner trust the safety of a woman or child in a time of peril. The great fault of the man is his terrific and uncontrollable indignation at any thing which seems to him mean or unjust, and his judgment or insight of narrow-mindedness is not trustworthy.

He has formed a strong friendship, or cronyship, for an Englishman on board, who is a man of about the same native intelligence, but a strange contrast to him in manner, appearance, and opinions, being short, thick-set, slow of speech, and husky-voiced. He is a stone-cutter by trade, and returns to England because, as he says, there is no demand for so fine work as he is able to do, in America, and he will be better paid in London. These two men are always together, and always quarreling. Indeed, the Englishman has, with his slowness and obstinate deafness to reason on any matter that he has once stated his views of, an endless battery of logic and banterings to reply to, for he is the only defender of an aristocratic form of government amongst us; every other man, Irish, Scotch, or English, being a thoroughgoing, violent, radical democrat. Most of them, indeed, claim the name of red republican, and carry their ideas of "liberty" far beyond any native American I have known. What is more remarkable and painful, nearly all of them, except the Irish, are professedly Deists or Atheists, or something of the sort, for all their ideas are evidently most crude and confused upon the subject, and amount to nothing but pity, hatred, or contempt for all religious people, as either fools or hypocrites, impostors or imposed upon. There is only one of them who seems to have ever thought upon the matter at all carefully, or to be able to argue upon it, and he is so self-satisfied (precisely what he says, by the way, of every one who argues against him), that he never stops arguing, while a hearer remains.

A remark of one of the farmers, an Englishman, and a very sensible fellow, upon these sentiments so generally held among our company, seemed to me true and well expressed. I think my observation of the lower class of Englishmen in the United States generally confirms it. "I have often noticed of my countrymen," said he, "that when they cease to honor the king, they no longer fear God." That is, as I understand it, when they are led to change the political theory in which they have been instructed, they must lose confidence in a religious creed which they owe about equally to the circumstances of their birth, neither having been adopted from a rational process in their own minds. Seeing the childish absurdity of many forms which they have been trained to consider necessary, natural, and ordered of God, they lose confidence in all their previous ideas that have resulted from a merely receptive education, and religion and royalty are classed together as old-fashioned notions, nursery bugbears, and romances. It is partly the result of the abominable masquerade of words which is still constantly played off in England on all public occasions, clothing government with antiquated false forms of sacredness. The simple majesty and holy authority that depends on the exercise of justice, love, and good judgment, so far from being made more imposing by this mummery, is lost sight of; while all the folly, indiscretion, and injustice of the administration of the law by fallible and unsanctified agents, is inevitably associated in the minds of the ignorant with all that is holy and true.

The only idea now, these, our shipmates, entertain of Christianity, seems to be, that it is the particular humbug by which the clergy make the people think that they must support them in purple and fine linen, just as royalty is the humbug on which the Queen is borne, and government the humbug by which the aristocracy are carried on their shoulders: all, of course, in combination. And nothing would convince them of the sincerity of the clergy short of their martyrdom—even that, I fear, should the time come for them to act as judges, they would rather attribute to pride, or, at best, to an exceptional deluded mind. With these ideas, nothing but thorough contempt for him, or fear of punishment, would prevent them from putting a bishop to the test of the stake, if he should fall into their hands.

CHAPTER III

Sailors—"Sogers"—Books—Anecdotes

IF THE PURPORT of my title would permit it, I should like to
write a long chapter on our ship's crew, and the general subject of American officers and seamen. I will, however, but give,
in this one word, my testimony, as one having had some experience, to the tyranny, barbarity, and lawlessness with which in
most of our merchant ships the common seamen are treated;
and the vice, misery, and hopelessness to which, as a body,
they are left on our shores, by the neglect or ill-judged and
parsimonious assistance of those who compass sea and land to
make proselytes of the foreign heathen.

Our ship's crew, as is usual in a Liverpool packet, are
nearly all foreigners—English, Scotch, Irish, Danes, French,
and Portuguese. One boasts of being "half-Welsh and half-
Heelander." Judging from this specimen, I have not a very
high opinion of the cross. The mate is a Dane, the second and
third mates Connecticut men. The captain, also, is from
somewhere "down east." He is a good and careful seaman,
courteous in his manners, and a religious man; much more
consistently so than pious captains whom I have known before
proved to be, after getting on blue water. He never speaks to
the seamen, or directly has any thing to do with them. In fact,
except when he is taking observations, or in bad weather, or

an emergency, you would never see in him any thing but a floating-hotel keeper. It is plain, nevertheless, that his eye is every where, and a single incident will show that the savage custom of the sea has not been without the usual influence upon him. He went to the kitchen the other day and told the cook he must burn less wood. The cook, who is a peculiarly mild, polite, peaceable little Frenchman, replied that he had been careful not to use more than was necessary. The captain immediately knocked him down, and then quietly remarking, "You'll take care how you answer me the next time," walked back to join the ladies. The cook fell on the stove, and was badly burned and bruised.

The men complain that their food is stinted and poor, and they are worked hard, at least they are kept constantly at work; men never exert themselves much when that is the case. It has been evident to me that they all *soger* systematically. (*Sogering* is pretending to work, and accomplishing as little as possible.) It is usually considered an insult to accuse one of it, but one day I saw a man so evidently trying to be as long as he could at some work he had to do in the rigging, that I said to him:

"Do you think you'll make eight bells of that job?"

He looked up with a twirl of his tongue, but said nothing.

"Have you been at it all the watch?"

"Ay, sir, I have."

"A smart man would have done it in an hour, I should think."

"Perhaps he might."

"Do you call yourself a soger?"

"Why, sir, we all soger, reg'lar, in this here craft. D'ye see, sir, the capten's a mean man, and 'ould like to get two days work in one out on us. If he'd give us watch-and-watch, sir, there'd be more work done, you mote be sure, sir."

Sunday is observed by sparing the crew from all labor not necessary to the sailing of the ship, but as it is the only day in which they have watch-and-watch, or time enough to attend to such matters, they are mostly engaged in washing and mending their clothes. We had selected a number of books at the Tract-house, which we gave away among them. They were received with gratitude, and the pictures at least read with interest. The printed matter was read somewhat also; I noticed three men sitting close together, all spelling out the words from three different books, and speaking them aloud, in a low, monotonous tone. If they had come to a paragraph in Latin, I doubt if they would have understood what they read any less. The truth is, as I have often noticed with most sailors, *a book is a book,* and they read it for the sake of reading, not for the ideas the words are intended to convey, just as some people like to work out mathematical problems for the enjoyment of the work, not because they wish to make use of the result. I saw a sailor once bargaining with a shipmate for his allowance of grog, offering him for it a little book, which he said was "first-rate reading." After the bargain was closed, I looked at the book. It was a volume of Temperance tales. The man had no idea of making a practical joke, and assured me, with a grave face, that he had read it all through. One Sunday, in the latter part of a passage from the East Indies, one of my watchmates, an old sea-dog, closed a little carefully preserved Testament, and slapping it on his knee, said, with a triumphant air, as if henceforth there was laid up for him a crown of glory and no mistake: "There! I've read that book through, every word on't, this v'yage; and, damn me, if I han't got more good out on't than I should 'a got going aft long with the rest on ye, to hear that old Pharisee (the captain) make his long prayers." Then after gazing at it a few moments, he added, musingly, as if reflecting on the mutability of human affairs, "I hook't that book from a feller named Abe Williams, to the Home, down to Providence, 'bout five years ago. His name was in't, but I tore it out. I wonder what's become on him now; dead—as like as not," (puts it up and takes out his pipe;) "well, God'll have mercy on his soul, I hope."

CHAPTER IV

On Soundings—English Small Craft—Harbor of Liverpool

AT SUNSET YESTERDAY the mate went to the royal yard to look for land, but could not see it. By our reckoning, we were off Mizzen Head, a point to the westward of Cape Clear, steering east by south, fresh wind and rising, going nine knots, thick weather and rain. Several gannets (a kind of goose with white body and black wings) were about us. Some one said they would probably go to land to spend the night, and there was pleasure in being so made to realize our vicinity to it. Several vessels were in sight, all running inside us, and steering northeast. We thought our captain over anxious to give Cape Clear a wide berth, and were sorry not to make the land before dark. After sunset it grew thicker, and the wind, which had been increasing all day, by midnight was a gale. We got in all sail but the reefed topsails; then hove-to, and found bottom in fifty-five fathoms. I was quite satisfied now with the captain's prudence; the sea was running high, and the crags of Ireland could not be many miles distant. As it was, I felt perfectly safe, and turned in, sleeping soundly till nine o'clock this morning. About an hour later, they made the light on the old Head of Kinsale, where the Albion was lost some thirty years since. The captain says we passed within ten miles of Cape Clear light without seeing it. He was just right in his reckoning, and the vessels that went inside of us were all wrong, and he thinks must have got into trouble. We are now nearly up to Waterford, and off a harbor where, many years ago, a frigate was lost, with fifteen hundred men. It is foggy yet, and we can only see the *loom* of the land.

Monday, May 27th

The Channel yesterday was thick with vessels, and I was much interested in watching them. A collier brig, beating down Channel, passed close under our stern. We were going along so steadily before it that I had not before thought of the violence of the wind. It was surprising to see how she was tossed about. Plunging from the height of the sea, her white figure-head would divide the water and entirely disappear, and for a moment it would seem as if some monster below had seized her bowsprit, and was taking her down head foremost; then her stern would drop, and a white sheet of spray dash up, wetting her foresail almost to the foretop; then she would swing up again, and on the crest of the billow seem to stop and shake herself, as a dog does on coming out of the surf; then, as the wind acted on her, she would fall suddenly over to the leeward, and a long curtain of white foam from the scuppers would be dropped over her glistening black sides. It was very beautiful, and from our quiet though rapid progress, showed the superior comfort of a large ship very strikingly. We have not rolled or pitched enough during all the passage to make it necessary to lash the furniture in our room. Afterwards, we saw a Welsh schooner, then a French lugger, with three masts, then a cutter with one, all quite different in rig and cut of sail from any thing we ever see on our coast.

About four o'clock, we sighted Tuscar light, and could see beyond it, through the fog, a dark, broken streak on which we imagined (as the dull-eyed said) darker spots of wood and lighter spots of houses, and which we called Ireland. We saw also, at some distance, the steamer which left Liverpool the day before, for Cork. She was very long and low, and more clipper-like in her appearance than our sea-going steamers of the same class. At sunset we were out of sight of land again and driving on at a glorious rate, passing rapidly by several large British ships going the same course.

I was up two or three times during the night, and found the captain all the while on deck in his India-rubber clothes, the mate on the forecastle, look-outs aloft, every thing drawing finely, and nothing to be seen around us but fog, foam and fire-flashing surges. At three o'clock this morning, John called me, and I again came on deck. It was still misty, but there was LAND—dark and distinct against the eastern glow—no more "imagination." It was only a dark ledge of rocks, with a white light-house, and a streak of white foam between it and the dark blue of the sea; but it seemed thrillingly beautiful. In a few minutes the fog opened on our quarter, and disclosed, a few miles off, a great, sublime mountain, its base in the water, its head in the clouds. The rock was the Skerrys; the mountain, Holyhead. Very soon, high, dark hills, piled together confusedly, dimly appeared on our right—dimly and confused, but real, substantial, unmistakable, solid ground—none of your fog-banks. These were on the island of Anglesea. Then, as the ship moved slowly on, for the wind was lulling, past the Skerrys, the fog closed down and hid it all again, and we went below. When again we came up it was much lighter, and the brown hills of Anglesea were backed up by the blue mountains of Wales, distinct against the gray cloud behind them. Soon a white dot or two came out, and the brown hill-sides became green, with only patches of dark brown— ploughed ground—real old mother earth. As it grew still lighter, the white spots took dark roofs, and coming to Point Linos, a telegraph station was pointed out; our signal was hoisted, and in five minutes we had spoken our name to a man in Liverpool. We had just begun to distinguish the *hedge-rows,* when there was a sudden flash of light, disclosing the cottage windows, and Charley, looking east, exclaimed, "THE SUN OF THE OLD WORLD."

A long, narrow awkward, ugly thing, some thought—a cross of a canal boat with a Mystic fishing-smack—with a single short mast, a high-peaked mainsail, a narrow staysail, coming to the stem-head, and without any bowsprit; so, out from the last fogbank, like an apparition, comes the pilot-boat. Directly she makes more sail, and runs rapidly towards us. Our yatchman-passenger, coming on deck, calls her by name, and says that she is considered a model, and that a portrait of her has been published. To say the right thing of her, she does look staunch and weatherly now, the sort of craft altogether, if he were confined to her tonnage, and more mindful of comfort than of time, that one might choose to make a winter's cruise in off Hatteras, or to bang through the ice after Sir John Franklin. The pilot she has this moment sent aboard of us, does not, in his appearance, contrast unfavorably with our own pilots. He is an intelligent, burly, harsh-voiced Englishman—a trustworthy looking sort of a man, only rather too dressy for his work. He brings no news; pilots never do. When we took on board the New York pilot, in my passage from the East Indies, we had had no intelligence from home for more than six months. The greatest news the pilot had for us, turned out to be that another edition of Blunt's Coast Pilot was out. I contrived to keep myself within earshot of him and the captain, as they conversed for half an hour after he came on our deck, and this was all I could learn, and except the late arrivals and departures and losses of vessels; this was all we got from him in two days. Our Liverpool pilot, however, brings us a Price Current and Shipping List, in which we find allusion to "the unfavorable news from France," as affecting the state of trade, but whether it is of floods, famine, or revolution, who knows? In the same way, we understand that the loyal English nation are blessed with another prince, and are stopping their mills to give God thanks for it. There is a slight fall in cotton, too, reported, and since he read of it, our Louisianian has been very busy figuring and writing letters.

After the pilot came the first English shower, ("It's a fine day," says the boatman, just now coming on board—we have had three showers since then,) and then it fell calm, and the ship loitered as if fatigued with her long journey. It is now noon, and while I am writing, a low, black, business-like steam-tug has taken hold of the ship, and means to get her up to the docks before night. On her paddle-boxes are the words in letters once white, and the only thing pretending to be white about her, "The Steam-Tug Company's Boat, No. 5, the LIVER of Liverpool." Long life to her then, for she is as a friendly hand stretched out from the shore to welcome us. A good-looking little scullion, too, she is, much better fitted for her business than our New York tow-boats.

May 28th

We were several hours in getting up to town yesterday, after I had written you. Long before anything else could be seen of it but a thick black cloud—black as a thunder cloud, and waving and darkening one way and the other, as if from a volcano—our approach to a focus of commerce was evident in the number of elegant, graceful, well-equipped and ship-shape looking steamers, scores of ships—graceful, spider-rigged New York liners, and sturdy quarter-galleried, carved and gilt, pot-sided, Bristol built, stump-to'-gallant-masted old English East-Indiamen, (both alive with cheering emigrants, hopeful of Australian and Michiganian riches, and yet defiant of sea-sickness,) dropping down with the tide, or jerked along by brave little steam-tugs, each belching from her chimney, long, dense, swelling volumes of smoke; with hosts of small craft lounging lazily along, under all sorts of sooty canvass.

These small craft are all painted dead black, and you cannot imagine how clumsy they are. The greater part of them are single masted, as I described the pilot-boat to be. In addition to the mainsail and fore-staysail (an in-board jib), they set a very large gaff topsail, hoisting as a flying sail, with a gaff crossing the topmast (like our men-of-war's boat sails): their bowsprit is a spar rigging out, like a studding-sail boom, and with this they stretch forth before them an enormous jib, nearly as long in the foot as in the hoist, and of this, too, before the wind, some of them make a beam-sail. If it blows fresh, they can shorten in their bowsprit, and set a smaller jib; and about the time our sloops would be knotting their second reef and taking their bonnets off, they have their bowsprit all in board, their long topmast struck, and make themselves comfortable under the staysail and a two-reefed mainsail. If it comes on to blow still harder, when ours must trust to a scud, they will still be jumping through it with a little storm stay-sail, and the mainsail reefed to a triangle.

These single-masted vessels are called cutters, not sloops, (a proper sloop I did not see in England;) and our word cutter, wrongly applied to the revenue schooners, is derived from the English term revenue cutter, the armed vessels of the British preventive service, being properly cutters. Cutters frequently carry yards and square sails. We saw one to-day with square sail, topsail, top-gallant and royal set. I have heard old men say, that when they were boys, our coasting sloops used to have these sails, and before the revolution, our small craft were, not uncommonly, cutter-rigged. Instead of being of whitewashed cotton, the sails of the coasters here are tanned hemp, having the appearance, at a little distance, of old brown velvet. In sailing qualities, the advantage is every way with us; in the build, the rig, and in the cut, as well the material of the sails; for our cotton duck will hold the wind much the best. Ninety-nine in a hundred of our single-masted market-boats, in a light wind, would run around the faster coaster in the Mersey with the greatest ease. They are not calculated for working to windward rapidly, but are stiff and weatherly, and do very well for boxing through the Channel, I suppose; but for such business we should rig schooner fashion, and save the expense of an extra hand, which must be wanted to handle their heavy mainsail and boom. Further up, we saw, on the beach, several cutter-rigged yachts. They were wide of beam, broad sterned, sharp built, and deep, like our sea-going clippers.

The immediate shores grew low as we entered the Mersey. It was nearly calm; but though the surface of the water was glassy smooth, it was still heaving with the long muscular swell of the sea until we reached the town. We approached nearer the land, where, on the right hand, there was a bluff point, bare of trees, with large rocks cropping out at its base; beneath the rocks, a broad, hard, sand beach, and low on the water's edge, a castle of dark brown stone, the only artificial defense, that I noticed, of the harbor. The high ground was occupied by villas belonging to merchants of Liverpool, and the place is called New Brighton, and bears a resemblance to our New Brighton. There is the same barrenness of foliage, and some similarity in the style of the houses, though there are none so out of taste as some of those that obtrude upon the scenery of

Staten Island, and none so pretty as some of the less prominent there.

As we entered the cloud that had hitherto interrupted
our view in front, we could see, on the left, many tall chimneys and steeples, and soon discerned forests of masts. On the
right, the bank continued rural and charming, with all the
fresh, light verdure of spring. Below it we could distinctly
see—and quite amusing it was—many people, mostly women
and children, riding donkeys and driving pony-carriages on
the beach. It seemed strange, in our pleasure at seeing them,
that they did not stop to look at us. There were bathing-
wagons, too, drawn by a horse out into three or four feet
water, and women floundering into it out of them, and getting
back again very hastily, as if they found it colder than they
had expected. We approached incomplete structures of stone
work along the water's edge, in which men and horses were
clustering like bees. Soon we passed them, and were looking
up at immense walls, each with its city of enclosed shipping
securely afloat fifteen or twenty feet higher than the water on
which we were, it being now low ebb. At five, in the rumble
and roar of the town, our anchor dropped. The ship could not
haul into the docks until midnight tide, and the steam-tug
took us, who wished it, to the shore, landing us across the
Dublin steamer at the Prince's Dock quay.

CHAPTER V

The First of England—The Streets—A Railway Station—
The Docks at Night—Prostitutes—Temperance—
The Still Life of Liverpool—A Market

AT THE HEAD of the gang-plank stood a policeman, easily recognized and familiar, thanks to Punch, who politely helped us
to land, thus giving us immediate occasion to thank the government for its hospitality, and its regard for our safety and
convenience. It was a real pleasure to stamp upon the neat,
firm, solid mason-work of the dock, and we could not but be
mindful of the shabby log wharves we had stumbled over as
we left New York. We were immediately beset by porters, not
rudely, but with serious, anxious deference and care to keep a
way open before us. I was assisting a lady, and carried her bag;
a man followed me pertinaciously. "I have no baggage," said
I. "But, sir, this bag?" "Oh, I can carry that." "Excuse me, sir;
you must not, indeed; *gentlemen* never does so in *this country*." After handing the lady into a hackney-coach, we walked
on. The landing-place was spacious, not encumbered with
shanties or piles of freight, and though there was a little rain
falling, there was a smooth, clean stone pavement, free from
mud, to walk upon. There was a slight smell of bituminous
smoke in the air, not disagreeable, but, to me, highly pleasant.
I snuffed it as if passing a field of new mown hay—snuffed and

pondered, and at last was brought to my mind the happy fireside of my friend, in the indistinct memory of which this peculiar odor of English coal had been gratefully associated.

Coming on shore with no luggage or any particular business to engage our attention, we plunged adventurously into the confused tide of life with which the busy streets were thronged, careless whither it floated us. Emerging from the crowd of porters, hackmen, policemen, and ragged Irish men and women, on the dock, we entered the first street that opened before us. On the corner stood a church—not un-American in its appearance—and we passed, without stopping, to the next corner, where we paused to look at the dray-horses, exceedingly heavy and in elegant condition, fat and glossy, and docile, but animated in their expression. They were harnessed, generally, in couples, one before another, to great, strong, low-hung carts, heavy enough alone to be a load for one of our cartmen's light horses. Catching the bustling spirit of the crowd, we walked on at a quick pace, looking at the faces of the men we met more than anything else, until we came to a wall of hewn drab stone, some fifteen feet high, with a handsomely cut balustrade at the top. There was a large gateway in it, from which a policeman was driving away some children. People were going in and out, and we followed in to see what it was. Upstairs, we found ourselves on a broad terrace, with a handsome building fronting upon it. Another policeman here informed us that it was a railway station. The door was opened as we approached it by a man in a simple uniform, who asked us where we were going. We answered that we merely wished to look at the building. "Walk in gentlemen; you will best take the right-hand platform, and return by the other." A train was backing in; a man in the same uniform stood on the rear car, and moved his hand round as if turning an imaginary driving-wheel, the engine at the other end being governed by his motions—forward—slower—slower —faster—slower—stop—back. The train stopped, the doors were unlocked by men in uniform, and there was a rush of passengers to secure good seats. Women with bundles and band-boxes were shoved this way and that, as they struggled to hoist themselves into the doors; their parcels were knocked out of their hands, porters picked them up and threw them in, reckless where.

Going into the street again, we wandered on till it was quite dark, with no other object but to get a general impression of the character of the town. We looked into a few houses where we saw a sign of "Clean and well-aired beds," and found that we should have no difficulty in getting comfortable lodgings at a very moderate price. From nine until twelve we were waiting at the dock for the ship to haul in, or trying in vain to get a boat to go on board of her. There were many vessels lying near the great gates, all standing by, when they should be opened at high-water, to be hauled in.

The broad promenade outside the dock walls was occupied by the police, stevedores, watermen, boarding-house keepers, and a crowd of women, waiting to help in the ships or to receive their crews when the tide should have risen enough to admit them. I was surprised at the quietness and decency of these "sailors' wives," as they called themselves; they were plainly and generally neatly dressed, and talked quietly and in kind tones to each other, and I heard no loud profanity or ribaldry at all. Whether this was owing to the presence of the police, I cannot say, but I am sure it would be impossible to find, in America, vice, shame, and misery, so entirely unassociated with drunkenness or excitement and riot. They were not as young as girls of the same sort in the streets of New York, and in the strong gas light their faces seemed expressive of a quite different character; generally they were sad, but not ill-natured or stupid. It occurred to me that their degradation must have been reached in a different way, and had not brought with it such banishment from all good as they would suffer with us. As they stood, companioned together with each other, but friendless, some with not even hats to protect them from the rain, others, with their gowns drawn up over their head, and others, two together, under a scanty shawl, it would have been difficult, I thought, for any one not to have been softened towards those abandoned thus to seek support of life that night. We could not but think the cheerful words with which the sailors recognized and greeted them, as the ships hauled near, were as much dictated by pity and sympathy as by any worse impulses. They said, "If nobody else is waiting to welcome us, we know that you will be glad that we are coming to the land once more; so cheer up, and we will help each other again to enjoy a short space of jollity, excitement, and forgetfulness."

Tired of waiting for the ship, and a good deal fatigued with our tramp on the pavements, about half-past twelve we went back into the town, and by the very obliging assistance of the policemen found lodgings in a "Temperance Hotel," still open at that late hour. We were a little surprised to find a number of men in the coffee-room drinking beer and smoking. The subject of their conversation was some project of an association of working-men to combine their savings, and make more profitable investment of them than could be made of the small amounts of each separately. There were late newspapers on the table, and we sat up some time longer to read them, but they were still at it, puffing and drinking, and earnestly discussing how they could best use their money, when we went up to bed. We had good beds, in pleasant rooms, for which we paid but twenty-five cents each.

The next morning we got our trunks from the ship, the customhouse officers searching them before they left the dockyard. Books, letters, and daguerreotypes were examined minutely, but the officers were very civil and accommodating; so also were the cartmen that took them to the inn for us. The expense of getting our luggage through the searching office, and carting it a mile, was only twenty-five cents for each trunk, and "tuppence for beer."

We went to a small lodging-house that we had examined last night, and found it neat and comfortable, and kept by an agreeable woman. We have a large front room, comfortably furnished, and down stairs is a quiet parlor and dining room. We breakfast in the house, and dine and sup at an eating-house. The whole cost of living so, with care, need be but about seventy-five cents each a day. As good entertainment would cost more in New York. We have made a few purchases of clothing, and find every thing we want cheaper than in New York.

The common building material is a light, greyish-red brick. Stone of different colors is used in about the same proportion that it is in New York. The warehouses are generally higher than the same class of buildings there, but the dwelling houses lower, seldom over three stories. The old houses, in narrow streets, are generally small, and often picturesque from the incongruous additions and improvements that have been made to them at intervals. At the railway station, we noticed such differences in the windows of a two story house near us, as these: There were two below, one of these, being a shop front, was entirely modern, with large panes of glass in light wooden sashes. The other was of small panes, set in heavy wood work, such as you see in our oldest houses. One of the upper windows had small square panes set in lead; those of the other were lozenge-shaped, and in neither were they more than three inches wide. The frames were much wider than they were high, and they opened sideways. In the newer part of the city, the fashionable quarter, there are a good many brick-walled houses faced with stucco. Others are of Bath stone, and these are not unfrequently painted over of the original color of the stone. Bath stone, which is the most common material of mason work, is a fine-grained freestone, very easy to the chisel. It is furnished much cheaper than our brown stone, so much so that there would be a chance of exporting it to America with profit. There is a finer sort, called by the masons Caen stone, which is brought from Normandy. The color of both is at first buff, but rapidly changes to a dark brown.* There are some buildings of red sandstone, of a little lighter color than that now so much used in New York. In buildings mainly of brick, stone is used more than with us; and there are none of those equivocating, sanded-wood parapets, porticos, steps, etc.; all is the *real grit*. The bricks are mottled, half red and half greyish yellow; the effect, at a little distance, being, as I said, a yellow or greyish-red, much pleasanter than the bright red color of our Eastern

* Caen stone does not darken much unless from soot. It is now frequently imported, and several fine buildings have been made of it in New York.

brick. Every thing out of doors here soon gets toned down, as the artists say, by the smoke. Perhaps it is partly on this account that pure white paint is never used; but the prevailing taste is evidently for darker colors than with us. The common hues of the furniture and fitting up of shops, for instance, is nearly as dark as old mahogany. This gives even the dram-shops such a rich, substantial look, that we can hardly recognize them as of the same species as our tawdry "saloons," painted, gilded, and bedizened to catch flies with their flare. There are no "oyster cellars," but oysters "in the shell," are exposed in stands about the street, like those of our "hot corn," and apple women. Liquor shops, always with the ominous sign of *"Vaults,"* are very frequent, and often splendid. The tea and coffee shops are among the richest in the streets. The bakers' fronts are also generally showy, and there are a great many of them. It seems to be the general custom, for poor families at least, to make their own bread, and send it in to them to be baked. The first night we were ashore, we got some bread and butter, and American cheese, at a baker's, and saw in ten minutes a dozen loaves called for. They had sheet-iron checks, with numbers on them, which were given up on the presentation of a corresponding check, and, for a loaf of ten or twelve pounds, a penny for baking—in the same way that passengers' baggage is checked on our railroads.

Wood is used in the interior of houses more than I had imagined it would be. Its cost is high. I inquired the price of what looked like a common "Albany board," such as I buy in New York for sixteen cents; it was of the value of about thirty-five cents. The kitchens, as far as we have observed, are on the street floor, level with the living apartments. Coarse pottery and wicker-work utensils are more common than with us. Few of the houses in the town have trees about them. Occasionally an old mansion is set a little back, and has a little scrubby foliage in front of it—most commonly of elms dwarfed [by smoke] to the size and natural shape of a green-gage plum tree. There are, though, in the better part of the town, some charming public grounds. I have seen nothing in America so fine.

The surface of the ground on which the town is built is

irregular, and the streets crooked and running at every angle with each other. Generally they are short, and, if long, at every few blocks the names are changed. The names are often singular; many, far apart, have the same with different prefixes, as Great and Little, North and South, etc. We are in "Great Cross Hall street;" after a slight turn it is called "Tythe Barn street;" and further on Chapel street. *Tythe Barn,* I understand, is derived from the name of the building in which the tithes were deposited when they were taken in kind—a tenth of the hay, wheat, poultry, etc. There is a steep ascent near us called "Shaw's Brow;" it is fitted with smooth stone tracks for cart-wheels, with narrow stones between them set *on end* for the horses' feet—double teams here generally going *tandem.* The best streets are paved only one-quarter the distance across them, the intermediate space being macadamized. This makes a very pleasant road. There is generally a wide sidewalk, which is flagged as in our cities; but in the commercial streets it is oftener paved like the carriage way, and in the narrowest, there is none at all. The streets are very clean, and all the sidewalks, gutters, and untraveled spaces, appear to be swept every day.

I have been through two markets. One of them is an immensely large building, covering about two acres, right in the center of the town; it is clean, light, and well ventilated. What a wonder it is that the people of New York will put up with such miserable, filthy, crowded hovels as their markets are! In this building there are over five hundred stalls and tables. It has its own superintendent of weights and measures, and a thorough and constant police. There are twelve men whose employment is to keep it clean. The garbage is passed readily through traps into vaults below, from which it is removed at night. The rules for those who use it, are excellent to secure healthy condition of food, neatness, order, and fair play, and they are strictly enforced. To my mind, this structure and the arrangements connected with it are an honor to Liverpool, not second to her docks. And she has three other large public markets, besides small ones for particular purposes. The meat stalls are frequently owned by women, and, except a better supply of birds and rabbits, did not offer any thing different

from those of our butchers. A part of the market seemed to be
occupied by country women for the sale of miscellaneous
wares.

The fish market was in another building, which was entirely occupied by women, nice and neat, though skinning eels
and cleaning fish. The milk market also seemed to be altogether in the hands of women. Milk is not peddled about as in
New York, but sold from cellar shops. If one wants a cup of
tea, our landlady runs across the street for a penny-worth of
milk. "From hand to mouth" so, seems to be common with
many things. The material for our breakfast is mostly bought
after we have ordered it. As we did not mention what we
would have till after the shops were closed last night, we had
to wait till nine o'clock for it this morning. Business hours
begin later than in America. I think the market is not open
till eight, which they speak of as "early."

CHAPTER VI

The People at Liverpool—Poverty—Merchants—Shopkeepers—Women—Soldiers—Children—Donkeys and Dray
Horses

I HAVE MENTIONED the most general features of the town,
which, at first sight, on landing in Europe from New York,
strike me as peculiar. Having given you its still life, you will
wish me to people it.

After we had wandered for about an hour through the
streets the first afternoon we were ashore, I remarked that we
had not yet seen a single nicely dressed man, hardly one that
in America would have been described as "of respectable appearance." We were astonished to observe with what an un-
mingled stream of poverty the streets were swollen, and J.
remarked that if what we had seen was a fair indication of the
general condition of the masses here, he should hardly feel
justified in dissuading them from using violent and anarchical
means to bring down to themselves a share of the opportuni-
ties and comforts of those "higher classes" that seem to be so
utterly separated from them. There are a great many Irish in
Liverpool, but the most that we had thus far seen evidently
were English, yet not English as we have known them. Instead
of the stout, full-faced John Bulls, we had noticed but few
who were not thin, meagre, and pale. There was somewhat

rarely an appearance of actual misery, but a stupid, hopeless, state-prison-for-life sort of expression. There were not unfrequently some exceptions to this, but these were mostly men in some uniform or livery, as railroad hands, servants, and soldiers.

The next morning, in the court-yard of the Exchange (the regular 'Change assemblage seemed to meet out of doors), we saw a large collection of the merchants. There was nothing to distinguish them from a company of a similar kind with us, beyond a general Englishness of feature and an entire absence of all oddities—with astonishing beards and singularities of costume. One young man only wore small clothes and leggins, which would perhaps have disagreeably subjected him to be noticed with us. They were stouter than our merchants, and more chubby-faced, yet not looking in vigorous health. They were, on the whole, judging by a glance at their outsides, to be more respected than any lot of men of the same number that I ever saw together in Wall street. Many of them, and most of the well-dressed men that we have seen in the streets, have a green leaf and simple *posy* in a button-hole of their coats.

The shopkeepers of the better class, or retail merchants, are exactly the same men, to all appearance, who stand behind the counters with us. *Merchant,* means only a wholesale dealer in England; retailers are *shopkeepers.* The word *store* is never applied to a building; but the building in which goods are stored is a *warehouse.*

Women are more employed in trade than with us; I have no doubt with advantage. The women in the streets are more noticeably different from ours than the men. In general, they seem cheaply and coarsely clad. Many of the lower class have their outer garments ordinarily drawn up behind, in the scrubbing-floor fashion. Caps are universally worn, and being generally nice and white, they have a pleasant effect upon the face. The very poorest women look miserably. We see bruised eyes not unfrequently, and there is evidently a good deal of hard drinking among them. They are larger and stouter, and have coarser features than any women we are accustomed to see. There are neither as many pretty nor as many ugly faces as with us; indeed, there are very few remarkably ill-favored in that respect, and almost none strikingly handsome. The best faces we have seen were among the fish-stalls in market. With scarcely an exception, the fish-women were very large and tall, and though many of them were in the neighborhood of fifty, they had full, bright, unwrinkled faces, very ruddy cheeks, and a cheerful expression. English women, generally, appear more bold and self-reliant than ours; their *action* is more energetic, and their carriage less graceful and drooping. Those well dressed, whom we have seen, are no exceptions. Those we have met to converse with are as modest and complaisant as could be desired, yet speak with a marked promptness, straightforwardness and confidence which is animating and attractive. We met a small company last night at the residence of a gentleman to whom we had a letter, and spent the evening precisely as we should at a small tea-party at home; we might easily have imagined ourselves in New England. The gentlemen were no way different, that we noticed, from cultivated men with us, and the ladies only seemed rather more frank, hearty and sincere, than we should expect ours to be to strangers.* There was nothing in their dresses, that I can think of, as peculiar, yet a general air, not American—a heavier look and more *crinkles,* and darker and more mixed-up colors. We see many rather nice looking women probably coming in from the country, driving themselves about town as if they understood it, in jaunty-looking chaises and spring-carts.

There are a good many soldiers moving about in fine undress uniforms: one regiment is in blue, which I did not suppose the British used. The men look well—more intelligent than you would suppose. Many are quite old, greyheaded, and all are very neat and orderly in the streets.

The children look *Punchy*. It strikes me the young ones are dressed much older, while the young men are clothed much more boyishly than in America.

There are lots of the queerest little donkeys in the streets; some of them would not weigh more than Nep [my Newfoundland], and most of them are not as large as our two-year-

---

* These ladies were Irish. The remark hardly applies to English ladies, certainly not unless you meet them domestically. The English in their *homes*, and the English *"in company,"* are singularly opposite characters.

old steers. They are made to draw enormous loads. I saw one
tugging a load of coal, on the top of which two stout Irishmen
sat, and stopped them to ask the weight. It was 1200 [besides
themselves], and the top of the donkey's back was just even
with my waist. The driver said he bought her five years ago for
two pounds [$10], and she was then called an old one. Here is
one now coming up the hill with a great load of furniture, a
man on behind it, and a boy on the shafts—a poor little rat of
a thing, with the meekest expression you can conceive of. It is
just as much as he can stagger along with, and the boy jumps
off to relieve—no! the young satan has gone to his head and is
cudgeling him. The poor little donkey winces and turns his
head, and drops his ears, and nearly falls down. The boy stops
[probably a policeman heaves in sight] and takes his seat on
the shaft again, and the donkey reels on. The man aft has
continued his smoking all the while, without taking any notice of the delay. As I write, there goes by another—a very
handsome, large fat one, drawing a market cart, with a pretty
county girl among the hampers driving.

CHAPTER VII

Liverpool Continued—Irish Beggars—Condition of Laborers—Cost of Living—Prices—Bath House—Quarantine—
The Docks—Street Scene—"Coming Yankee" Over Nonsense—Artistic Begging

I HAVE LEARNED nothing reliable about the price of labor here;
the Irish emigration keeps it lower in Liverpool than elsewhere. This reminds me of beggars, and of a placard posted
everywhere about the streets today. The beggars are not very
frequent, and are mostly poor, pitiable, sickly women, carrying half-naked babies. The placard is as follows: "The SELECT
VESTRY inform their fellow-citizens, that in consequence of the
extremely low price of passage from Ireland—4d. (8 cts.)
—great numbers are coming here apparently with no other
object than to beg. They earnestly desire that nothing should
be given them. As a specimen, they mention the following: An
Irish woman, pretending to be a widow, was taken up, who
had obtained 3s. 2d. (80 cts.) in an hour and a half after her
arrival. Her husband was found already in custody."

The people all seem to be enjoying life more, or else to be
much more miserable, than in America.* The laborers seem

* I was surprised to find this remark in my first letter from Liverpool, for it is the precise counterpart of my impression on landing again
in the United States, after six months absence in Europe. I observe

haggard and stupid, and all with whom I have talked, say a poor man can hardly live here. There is a strong anti-free-trade growling among them, and they complain much of the repeal of the Navigation Laws, asserting that American ships are now getting business that was formerly in the hands of the English alone, and so American sailors do the labor in the docks which was formerly given to the stevedores and working men of the town.

Clothing, shoes, etc., and rents, are a good deal cheaper than in New York, and common articles of food but little higher. I have obtained the following as specimens of prices for a few ordinary necessaries of life (1st of June):

Beef, mutton, and *pork,* fine, 12½ cts. a pound; *lamb,* 16 cts.; *veal,* 10 cts.

Salmon, 33 cts. a pound; *fresh butter,* 27 cts.; *potatoes,* 31 cts. a peck.

Fowls, 75 cts. a pair; *rabbits,* 50 cts. a pair; *pigeons,* 37 cts. each.

Best Ohio flour, ("superfine,") $6.25 a barrel.

Bread, 2½ cts. a pound, or a loaf of twelve pounds, 30 cts.

Bread of best quality, 3 cts. per lb., or loaf of twelve pounds, 35 cts.

Sugar is higher, and tropical fruits, pine-apples, oranges, etc., are sold by the hucksters for more money than in New York.

Gas.—The town is well lighted by gas, and it is much used in private houses—much more generally than in New York. Price $1.12 per 1000 feet.

Water.—Water is conveyed through the town and to the shipping in tubes, through which I believe it is forced by steam-engines by several companies. The manner in which they are remunerated I did not learn.

---

lately, that the Earl of Carlisle has said something of similar import. I do believe the people of the United States have less of pleasure and less of actual suffering than any other in the world. Hopefulness, but hope ever unsatisfied, is marked in every American's face. In contrast with Germany, it is particularly evident that most of us know but little of the virtuous pleasure God has fitted us to enjoy in this world.

Bathing.—There is a very large and elegant bath-house (covering half an acre), built of stone, by the corporation, at an expense of $177,000. It is fitted with suitable accommodations for all classes of bathers, at various prices. There is a public bath (45 by 27 feet) for gentlemen, and another for ladies. The water is all filtered, and the cold baths have a constant fresh supply and outflow. A steam engine is employed for pumping, etc. There are also floating baths in the river, as at New York; and beach-bathing and sea-swimming can be enjoyed at a few minutes distance, by ferry, from the town.

Quarantine.—There are no buildings or ground employed for quarantine, but a number of large hulks are moored in the bay for this purpose. Quarantine vessels are anchored near them, and keep a yellow flag flying. It is a great many years since a vessel has been quarantined here, however, the medical men being generally agreed that such precaution is useless, or effective of more harm than good.

We have not made a business of sight-seeing, and I want to give you the general aspect of the first English town to us, rather than show up the lions. The Liverpool docks, however, are so extensive, and so different from any thing we have of the kind in America, that you will wish me to give a few particulars of them.

The Docks are immense basins, enclosed from the river, or dug out from the bank, walled up on all sides by masonry, and protected on the outside, from the sea, by solid stone piers or quays. In these quays are gates or locks, through which, at high water, vessels enter or leave. When the water has slightly fallen they are closed, and the water being retained, the ships are left securely floating at a height convenient for removing their cargoes. The docks are all enclosed by high brick walls, but between these and the water there is room enough for passing of carts, and for the temporary protection of goods under wooden sheds, as they are hoisted out, and before they can be removed. The streets about the docks are mostly lined with very large and strong fire-proof warehouses. The quay outside the docks is broad enough to afford a wide terrace upon the river, which is called the Marine Parade, and is much resorted to as a promenade. Stone stairs at intervals descend to the bottom of the river, and there are similar ones within the docks to give access to small boats. There are buoys and life-preservers lashed to the rails of the bridges, and small houses occasionally, furnished with instruments and remedies, for the resuscitation of drowning persons.

There are graving docks in which the depth of water can be regulated at pleasure, for the inspection and repair of the bottoms of vessels; and there are large basins for coasters, to which there are no gates, and in which the tide rises and falls, leaving them in the mud at the ebb. The large docks are connected with each other, and with the graving docks, by canals, so a vessel can go from one to another at any time of tide, and without going into the river.

But you have yet no idea of the spaciousness and grandeur of the docks. Some of them enclose within their walls ten or twelve acres, half of which, or more, is occupied by vessels. The twelve now completed (there are more building) extend along in front of the town uninterrupted by buildings for more than two miles, or further than from Whitehall Stairs to Corlear's Hook, in New York. On the other side of the river, a considerably larger extent of docks is laid out and constructing. A basin for coasters, which covers over sixteen acres, and in which there is twelve feet at low water, is just completed there.

Each dock has its own dock-master, customhouse superintendent, and police force. The police seems to us perfect. It is composed of well-instructed young men, most courteous and obliging, at the same time prompt and efficient. It quite surprised me to see our fierce ship masters submit like lambs to have their orders countermanded by them.

There are three docks for the convenience of steamers alone. The American steamers, I suppose, are too large to go into them, for they are lying in the stream.

The docks were built by the town, and besides the wonderful increase of its commerce which they have effected, the direct revenue from them gives a large interest on their cost. The charges are more moderate than at other British ports, and this has, no doubt, greatly helped to draw their commerce here. This is the principal ground, for instance, of the selection of Liverpool in preference to Bristol as the port of departure for transatlantic steamers.* The foreign commerce of Liverpool is the most valuable of any town in the world. Its immense business is probably owing to its being the best port in the vicinity of the densest manufacturing district of England. It is not naturally a good harbor, but a very exposed and inconvenient one. The amount paid by vessels for dockage has in some years been $1,000,000, and the whole is expended by the corporation in improvements of the town and for public purposes.

The small steam-craft do not usually go into the docks, but land passengers on the quays outside. The ferry-boats, of which there are half a dozen lines crossing the Mersey, all come to one large floating wharf, from which the ascent to the quays is made easy at all times of tide, by a sufficiently long, hinged bridge.

There is a Sailor's Home now building here, which will certainly be a noble record of the justice and liberality of the merchants of the port to their humble associates on the sea. It is situated in an open public place, not far from the Custom House and City Hall. It is built of stone, in the Elizabethan style, and was considered a design worthy of giving Prince Albert honor in the laying of its cornerstone. It is already a stately edifice.

There are chapels for seamen in several (possibly in all) of the docks.†

Later. We have left Liverpool, and while breathing this

---

* The port charges at Bristol have been lately greatly reduced, and are now lower than those of Liverpool, or any other port in the kingdom.

† The laws of the port require: That for three hours at high water, there shall be an efficient person on the deck of every vessel in the docks or basins; That the anchor shall be in-board, jib-boom run in, etc.; That no article of freight shall be allowed to remain on the dock-quays for more than forty-eight hours [penalty, $1.25 an hour]; That no light or fire shall be allowed [without special permission] on any vessel in the docks or basins at any time. This last regulation prevents cooking on board, and makes it necessary for the crews to live on shore. The consequent customs are very inconvenient, expensive, and demoralizing to the seaman.

delicious fragrance of hawthorn and clover, it is hard to think back to the stirring dusty town, but I will try for a few minutes to do so, and then bring you with me (I wish I could!) out into the country.

A great deal that interested us at Liverpool I must omit to tell you of. I should like to introduce you to some of the agreeable acquaintances we met there, but in what we saw of social life there was hardly any thing to distinguish it from America. We were much pleased with some of the public gardens and pleasure grounds that we visited, and when we return here I may give you some account of them. I meant to have said a little more about the style of building in the newer and extending parts of the city; it did not differ much, however, from what you might see at home, in some of the suburbs of Boston for instance.

It would be more strange to you to see long, narrow streets, full from one end to the other, of the poorest-looking people you ever saw, women and children only, the men being off at work, I suppose, sitting, lounging, leaning on the door-steps and sidewalks, smoking, knitting, and chatting; the boys playing ball in the street, or marbles on the flagging; no break in the line of tall, dreary houses, but strings of clothes hung across from opposite second-story windows, to dry; all dwellings, except a few beer, or junk shops, in the cellars. You can see nothing like such a dead mass of pure poverty in the worst quarter of our worst city. In New York, such a street would be ten times as filthy and stinking, and ten times as lively; in the middle of it there would be a large fair building, set a little back (would that I could say with a few roods of green turf and shrubbery between it and the gutter, in which the children are playing), with the inscription upon it, "Public Free School;" across from the windows would be a banner with the "Democratic Republican Nominations;" hand organs would be playing, hogs squealing, perhaps a stampede of firemen; boys would be crying newspapers, and the walls would be posted with placards, appealing, with whatever motive, to patriotism and duty, showing that statesmen and demagogues could calculate on the people's reading and thinking a little there. There would be gay grog-shops, too, with liberty poles before them, and churches and Sunday school rooms (with lying faces of granite-painted pine) by their side. The countenances of the people here exhibited much less either of virtuous or vicious character, than you would discern among an equally poor multitude in America, yet among the most miserable of them (they were Irish) I was struck with some singularly intelligent, and even beautiful faces, so strangely out of place, that if they had been cleaned and put in frames, so the surroundings would not appear, you would have taken them for those of delicate, refined, and intellectual ladies.

Thursday Morning, May 30th

We packed all our traveling matter, except a few necessaries, in two trunks and a carpet-bag, and I took them in a hackney carriage to the freight station, to be sent to London. The trunks were received, but the bag the clerks refused, and said it must be sent from the passenger station. I had engaged to meet my friends in a few minutes at the opposite side of the town from the passenger station, and the delay of going there would vexatiously disarrange our plans. I therefore urged them to take it, offering to pay extra freight, etc. They would be happy to accommodate me, but their rules did not admit of it. A *carpet-bag* could not be sent from that station at any price. I jumped on to the box, and drove quickly to the nearest street of shops, where, at a grocers, I bought for a twopence a coffee-sack, and enclosing the bag, brought it in a few minutes back to the station. There was a good laugh, and they gave me a receipt at once for *a sack*—to be kept in London until called for.

On the quay, I noticed a bareheaded man drawing with colored crayons on a broad, smooth flagstone. He had represented, in a very skillful and beautiful manner, a salmon laid on a china platter, opposite a broken plate of coarse crockery; between these were some lines about a "rich man's dish" and a "poor man's dinner." He was making an ornamental border about it, and over all was written, *"Friends! I can get* NO WORK; *I must do this or starve."*

His hat, with a few pence in it, stood by the side of this.

CHAPTER VIII

Birkenhead—Ferry-Boats—Gruff Englishmen—The Abbey
—Flour—Market—The Park—A Democratic Institution—
Suburban Villas, etc.

THE FERRY-BOAT by which we crossed to Birkenhead was very small and dingy. There was no protection from the weather on board of her, except a narrow, dark cabin under deck. There were uncushioned seats all around the outside, against the rail, and the rest of the deck was mostly filled up with freight, spars, etc. She had a bowsprit, and a beautiful light, rakish mast and topmast fitted to carry a gaff sail. She was steered with a wheel in the stern. The pilot or master (a gentleman with a gold band on his hat and naval buttons) stood on the paddle-boxes to direct, and a boy stood over the engine to pass orders below. The engine was under deck, the tops of the cylinders only appearing above it. It was, however, entirely exposed to observation, and showed excellent workmanship, and was kept perfectly clean and highly polished. It was of entirely different construction from any American engine, having three oscillating cylinders. The "hands" looked like regular tars, wearing tarpaulins, with the name of the boat in gilt letters on the ribbon, blue baize shirts, and broad-bottomed trowsers hung tight on the hips. The boat came alongside the wharf, ran out her hawsers, and took in her passengers by a narrow gangplank; and yet she makes her trip once in ten minutes. There would not be room enough on her decks for one of our Rockaways to stand, and she seemed to have no idea of ferrying any thing but foot-passengers. What would the good people of Birkenhead think of a Fulton ferry-boat, with its long, light, and airy rooms, their floors level with the street, and broad carriage-roads from stem to stern, crossing and recrossing without turning round, or ever a word of command, or a rope lifted from morning till evening and from evening till morning? The length of the ferry is about the same as the South Ferry of Brooklyn, and the fare one penny.

Birkenhead is the most important suburb of Liverpool, having the same relation to it that Charlestown has to Boston, or Brooklyn to New York. When the first line of Liverpool packets was established, there were not half a dozen houses here; it now has a population of many thousands, and is increasing with a rapidity hardly paralleled in the New World. This is greatly owing to the very liberal and enterprising policy of the land-owners, which affords an example that might be profitably followed in the vicinity of many of our own large towns. There are several public squares, and the streets and places are broad, and well paved and lighted. A considerable part of the town has been built with reference to general effect, from the plans and under the direction of a talented architect, GILESPIE GRAHAM.

We received this information while crossing in the ferry-boat, from a fellow-passenger, who, though a stranger, entered into conversation, and answered our inquiries with a frankness and courtesy that we have thus far received from every one in England. By his direction, we found near the landing a square of eight or ten acres, about half of it enclosed by an iron fence, and laid out with tasteful masses of shrubbery (not trees) and gravel walks. The houses about it stood detached, and though of the same general style, were sufficiently varied in details not to appear monotonous. These were all of stone.

We left this, and were walking up a long, broad street, when the gentleman who had crossed at the ferry with us joined us again, and said that as we were strangers we might like to look at the ruins of an Abbey which were in the vicinity, and he had come after us that if we pleased he might conduct us to it.

Right in the midst of the town, at the corner of a new brick house, we came upon an old pile of stone work. Old, indeed!—under the broken arch of a Gothic window, the rain-water had been so long trickling as to wear deep channels; cracking, crumbling, bending over with age, it seemed in many places as if the threatening mass had only been till now withheld from falling prostrate by the faithful ivy that clung to it, and clasped it tight with every fibre.

You cannot imagine the contrast to the hot, hurrying, noisy world without, that we found on entering the little enclosure of the old churchyard and abbey walls. It was all over-shadowed with dense foliage, and only here and there through the leaves, or a shattered arch round which the ivy curled with enchanting grace, would there be a glimpse of the blue sky above. By listening, we could still hear the roar of wheels, rumbling of rail-cars, clanging of steamboat bells, and the shouts of jovial sea-captains, drinking gin and water in a neighboring tea-garden, over which the American flag was flying. But within the walls there was no sound but the chirps of a wren, looking for her nest in a dark cranny; the hum of bees about an old hawthorn bush; the piping of a cricket under a gravestone, and our own footsteps echoed from mysterious crypts.

Our guide having pointed out to us the form of the ancient structure, and been requited for his trouble by seeing the pleasure he had given us, took his leave. We remained a long time, and enjoyed it, as you may think.

Did you ever hear of Birkenhead Abbey? I never had before. It has no celebrity; but coming upon it so fresh from the land of youth, as we did, so unexpectant of any thing of the kind—though I have seen far older ruins, and more renowned, I have found none so impressive.

A ruined end of the old prior's house had been repaired and roofed over many years ago, and was used as a school-house—many years ago, for the ivy on it was very strong and gnarled, and bushes and grass were growing all over the roof. I send you a hasty sketch of it;—wouldn't you like the memory of such a school?

At the market-place we went into a baker's shop, and, while eating buns, learned that the poorest flour in market was American and the best French. Upon examination of his stock, we thought he had hardly a fair sample of American flour; but his French flour was certainly remarkably fine, and would be so considered at Rochester. He said it made much whiter bread than either American or English, and he used but little of it unmixed, except for the most delicate pastry. French and English flour is sold in sacks, American in barrels. He thought American flour was not generally *kiln-dried,* as it should be for exportation,* and was much injured in consequence. When we left he obligingly directed us to several objects of interest in the vicinity, and showed us through the market. It is but little less in size, and really appears finer and more convenient, than the one I described in Liverpool. The roof, which is mostly of glass, is high and airy, and is supported by two rows of slender iron columns, giving to the interior the appearance of three light and elegant arcades. The contrivances to effect ventilation and cleanliness are very complete. It was built by the town, upon land given to it for the purpose, and cost $175,000.

The baker had begged of us not to leave Birkenhead without seeing their New Park, and at his suggestion we left our knap-sacks with him, and proceeded to it. As we approached the entrance, we were met by women and girls, who, holding out a cup of milk; asked us—*"Will you take a cup of milk, sirs?—good, cool, sweet cow's milk, gentlemen, or right warm from the ass!"* And at the gate was a herd of donkeys,

---

* The great bulk of the flour we are now (1851) exporting to England is of inferior quality, worth about $3.50, when common superfine is $4.50. It is used extensively by the *millers* in England to mix with a superior quality of their own grinding, of English wheat. By the way, the custom of taking a toll in kind, as a compensation for grinding at grist-mills, which our fathers brought from England, and which we retain, is now obsolete there. The millers make their charges in money, and are paid as in any other business.

some with cans of milk strapped to them, others saddled and bridled, to be let for ladies and children to ride.

The gateway, which is about a mile and a half from the ferry, and quite back of the town, is a great, massive block of handsome Ionic architecture, standing alone, and unsupported by any thing else in the vicinity, and looking, as I think, heavy and awkward. There is a sort of grandeur about it that the English are fond of, but which, when it is entirely separate from all other architectural constructions, always strikes me unpleasantly. It seems intended as an impressive preface to a great display of art within; but here, as well as at Eaton Park, and other places I have since seen, it is not followed up with great things, the grounds immediately within the grand entrance being simple, and apparently rather overlooked by the gardener. There is a large archway for carriages, and two smaller ones for people on foot, and, on either side, and over these, are rooms which probably serve as inconvenient lodges for the laborers. No porter appears, and the gates are freely opened to the public.

Walking a short distance up an avenue, we passed through another light iron gate into a thick, luxuriant, and diversified garden. Five minutes of admiration, and a few more spent in studying the manner in which art had been employed to obtain from nature so much beauty, and I was ready to admit that in democratic America there was nothing to be thought of as comparable with this People's Garden. Indeed, gardening had here reached a perfection that I had never before dreamed of. I cannot undertake to describe the effect of so much taste and skill as had evidently been employed; I will only tell you, that we passed by winding paths, over acres and acres, with a constant varying surface, where on all sides were growing every variety of shrubs and flowers, with more than natural grace, all set in borders of greenest, closest turf, and all kept with most consummate neatness. At a distance of a quarter of a mile from the gate, we came to an open field of clean, bright, green-sward, closely mown, on which a large tent was pitched, and a party of boys in on one part, and a party of gentlemen in another, were playing cricket. Beyond this was a large meadow with groups of young trees, under which a flock of sheep were reposing, and girls and women with children, were playing. While watching the cricketers, we were threatened with a shower, and hastened to look for shelter, which we found in a pagoda, on an island approached by a Chinese bridge. It was soon filled, as were the other ornamental buildings, by a crowd of those who, like ourselves, had been overtaken in the grounds by the rain; and I was glad to observe that the privileges of the garden were enjoyed about equally by all classes. There were some who were attended by servants, and sent at once for their carriages, but a large proportion were of the common ranks, and a few women with children, or suffering from ill health, were evidently the wives of very humble laborers. There were a number of strangers, and some we observed with note-books and portfolios, who seemed to have come from a distance to study in the garden. The summer-houses, lodges, bridges, etc., were all well constructed, and of undecaying materials. One of the bridges which we crossed was of our countryman REMINGTON's patent, an extremely light and graceful erection.

I obtained most of the following information from the head working-gardener.

The site of the park and garden was, ten years ago, a flat, clay farm. It was placed in the hands of MR. PAXTON, in June, 1844, by whom it was roughly laid out in its present form by June of the following year.* Carriage roads, thirty-four feet wide, with borders of ten feet, and walks varying in width, were first drawn and made. The excavation for a pond was also immediately undertaken, and the earth obtained from these sources used for making mounds and to vary the surface, which has been done with much naturalness. The whole ground was thoroughly under-drained, the minor drains of stone, the main of tile. By these sufficient water is obtained to fully supply the pond, or lake, as they call it, which is from twenty to forty feet wide, and about three feet deep, and meanders for a long distance through the garden. It is stocked with aquatic plants, gold fish, and swans.

---

* Mr. Kemp has the credit of the design with the public. I suppose that he was employed by Paxton to perfect his plan and superintend the construction.

The roads are macadamized. On each side of the carriage way, and of all the walks, pipes for drainage are laid, which communicate with deep main drains that run under the edge of all the mounds or flower beds. The walks are laid first with six inches of fine broken stone, then three inches cinders, and the surface with six inches of fine rolled gravel. All the stones on the ground which were not used for these purposes, were laid in masses of rock-work, and mosses and rock-plants attached to them. The mounds were finally planted with shrubs, and heaths and ferns, and the beds with flowering plants. Between these and the walks and drives, is everywhere a belt of turf (which, by the way, is kept close cut with short, broad scythes, and shears, and swept with *hair-brooms,* as we saw). Then the rural lodges, temples, pavillion, bridges, orchestra for a band of instrumental music, etc., were built. And so, in one year, the skeleton of this delightful garden was complete.

But this is but a small part. Besides the cricket and an archery ground, large valleys were made verdant, extensive drives arranged—plantations, clumps, and avenues of trees formed, and a large park laid out. And all this magnificent pleasure ground is entirely, unreservedly, and for ever, the people's own. The poorest British peasant is as free to enjoy it in all its parts as the British queen. More than that, the baker of Birkenhead has the pride of an OWNER in it.

Is it not a grand, good thing? But you are inquiring who *paid* for it. The honest owners—the most wise and worthy townspeople of Birkenhead—in the same way that the New Yorkers pay for "the Tombs," and the Hospital, and the *cleaning* (as they say) of their streets.

Of the farm which was purchased, one hundred and twenty acres have been disposed of in the way I have described. The remaining sixty acres, encircling the park and garden, were reserved to be sold or rented, after being well graded, streeted, and planted, for private building lots. Several fine mansions are already built on these (having private entrances to the park), and the rest now sell at $1.25 a square yard. The whole concern cost the town between five and six hundred thousand dollars. It gives employment at present to ten gardeners and laborers in summer, and to five in winter.

The generous spirit and fearless enterprise that has accomplished this, has not been otherwise forgetful of the health and comfort of the poor.* Among other things, I remember, a public washing and bathing house for the town is provided. I should have mentioned also, in connection with the market, that in the outskirts of the town there is a range of stone slaughter-houses, with stables, yards, pens, supplies of hot and cold water, and other arrangements and conveniences, that enlightened regard for health and decency would suggest.

The consequence of all these sorts of things is that all about the town, lands, which a few years ago were almost worthless wastes, have become of priceless value; where no sound was heard but the bleating of goats and braying of asses complaining of their pasturage, there is now the hasty click and clatter of many hundred busy trowels and hammers. You may drive through wide and thronged streets of stately edifices, where were only a few scattered huts, surrounded by quagmires. Docks of unequaled size and grandeur are building, and a forest of masts grows along the shore; and there is no doubt that this young town is to be not only remarkable as a most agreeable and healthy place of residence, but that it will soon be distinguished for extensive and profitable commerce. It seems to me to be the only town I ever saw that has been really built at all in accordance with the advanced science, taste, and enterprising spirit that are supposed to distinguish the nineteenth century. I do not doubt it might be found to have plenty of exceptions to its general character, but I did not inquire for these, nor did I happen to observe them. Certainly, in what I have noticed, it is a model town, and may be held up as an example, not only to philanthropists and men of taste, but to speculators and men of business.

After leaving the park, we ascended a hill, from the top of which we had a fine view of Liverpool and Birkenhead. Its sides were covered with villas, with little gardens about them. The architecture was generally less fantastic, and the style and

* "Few towns, in modern times, have been built with such regard to sanitary regulations as Birkenhead; and in no instance has so much been done for the health, comfort, and enjoyment of a people, as by those energetic individuals with whose names the rise and progress of Birkenhead are so intimately connected."—*Dr. J. H. Robertson.*

materials of building more substantial, than is usually employed in the same class of residences with us. Yet there was a good deal of the same *stuck-up* and uneasy pretentious air about them that the suburban houses of our own city people so commonly have. Possibly this is the effect of association, in my mind, of steady, reliable worth and friendship with plain or old-fashioned dwellings, for I often find it difficult to discover in the buildings themselves the elements of such expression. I am inclined to think it is more generally owing to some disunity in the design—often, perhaps, to a want of keeping between the mansion and its grounds, or its situation. The architect and the gardener do not understand each other, and commonly the owner or resident is totally at variance in his tastes and intentions from both; or the man whose ideas the plan is made to serve, or who pays for it, has no true, independent taste, but had fancies to be accommodated, which only follow confusedly after custom or fashion. I think, with Ruskin, it is a pity that every man's house cannot be really his own, and that he cannot make all that is true, beautiful, and good in his own character, tastes, pursuits, and history, manifest in it.

But however fanciful and uncomfortable many of the villa houses about Liverpool and Birkenhead appear at first sight, the substantial and thorough manner in which most of them are built will atone for many faults. The friendship of nature has been secured for such. Dampness, heat, cold, will be welcome to do their best; every day they will improve. In fifty or a hundred years fashions may change, and they will appear, perhaps, quaint, possibly grotesque; but still strong, home-like, and hospitable. They have no shingles to rot, no glued and puttied and painted gimcrackery, to warp and crack and moulder; and can never look so shabby, and desolate, and dreary, as will nine-tenths of the buildings of the same denomination now erecting about New York, almost as soon as they lose the raw, cheerless, impostorlike airs which seem inseparable from their newness.

CHAPTER IX

A Railway Ride—Second Class—Inconvenient Arrange-
ments—First Walk in the Country—England itself—A
Rural Landscape—Hedges—Approach to a Hamlet—The
Old Ale-house and the Old John Bull—A Talk with
Country People—Notions of America—Free Trade—The
Yew Tree—The Old Rural Church and Graveyard—A
Park Gate—A Model Farmer—The Old Village Inn—A
Model Kitchen—A Model Landlady

WE WERE VERY TIRED when we again reached the baker's. After
passenger-life at sea, a man's legs need to be brought into
active service somewhat gradually. As we had spent more time
than we had meant to at Birkenhead, we determined to rest
ourselves for a few minutes, and get a start of a few miles into
the country by the railroad. A seat, however, on the hard
board benches of an English second-class rail-carriage,
crowded, and your feet cramped under you, does not remove
fatigue very rapidly.

A heavy cloud darkened the landscape, and as we
emerged in a few moments from the dark tunnel, whirling out
of town, big drops of rain came slanting in upon us. A lady
coughed, and we closed the window. Soon the road ran
through a deep cutting, with only occasionally such depres-
sions of its green-sodded bank, that we could, through the

dusty glass, get glimpses of the country. In successive gleams:

A market-garden, with rows of early cabbages, and lettuce, and peas;—

Over a hedge, a nice, new stone villa, with the gardener shoving up the sashes of the conservatory, and the maids tearing clothes from the drying-lines;—

A bridge, with children shouting and waving hats;—

A field of wheat, in drills as precisely straight, and in earth as clean and finely tilled, as if it were a garden-plant;—

A bit of broad pasture, with colts and cows turning tail to the squall; long hills in the back, with some trees and a steeple rising beyond them;—

Another few minutes of green bank;—

A jerk—a stop. A gruff shout:

"BROMBRO!"

A great fuss to get the window on the other side from us open; calling the conductor; having the door unlocked; squeezing through the ladies' knees, and dragging our packs over their laps—all borne with a composure that shows them to be used to it, and that they take it as a necessary evil of railroad traveling. The preparations for rain are just completed as we emerge upon a platform, and now—down it comes in a torrent. We rush, with a quantity of floating muslin, white ankles, and thin shoes, under an arch. With a sharp whistle and hoarse puffing the train rumbles onward; grooms pick up the lap-dog and baskets; flaunting white skirts are moved again across the track; another rush, in which a diminutive French sun-shade is assisted by a New York umbrella to protect a new English bonnet; a graceful bow in return, with lifting eyebrows, as if in inquiry; and we are altogether crowded in the station-house.

In a few minutes they go off in carriages, and room is left us in the little waiting-room to strap on our knapsacks. The rain slackens—ceases, and we mount, by stone steps up a bank of roses and closely-shaven turf, to the top of the bridge over the cutting.

There we were right in the midst of it! The country—and such a country!—green, dripping, glistening, gorgeous! We stood dumb-stricken by its loveliness, as, from the bleak April and bare boughs we had left at home, broke upon us that English May—sunny, leafy, blooming May—in an English lane; with hedges, English hedges, hawthorn hedges, all in blossom; homely old farm-houses, quaint stables, and hay-stacks; the old church spire over the distant trees; the mild sun beaming through the watery atmosphere, and all so quiet—the only sounds the hum of bees, and the crisp grass-tearing of a silken-skinned, real (unimported) Hereford cow, over the hedge.

No longer excited by daring to think we should see it, as we discussed the scheme round the old home-fire; no longer cheering ourselves with it in the stupid, tedious ship; no more forgetful of it in the bewilderment of the busy town—but there we were, right in the midst of it; long time silent, and then speaking softly, as if it were enchantment indeed, we gazed upon it and breathed it—never to be forgotten. Ah, me!

At length we walked on—rapidly—but frequently stop-ping, one side and the other, like children in a garden; hedges still, with delicious fragrance, on each side of us, and on, as far as we can see, true farm-fencing hedges; nothing trim, stiff, nice, and amateur-like, but the verdure broken, tufty, low, and natural. They are set on a ridge of earth, thrown out from a ditch beside them, which raises and strengthens them as a fence. They are nearly all hawthorn, which is now covered in patches, as if after a slight fall of snow, with clusters of white or pink blossoms over its light green foliage. Here and there a holly bush, with bunches of scarlet berries, and a few other shrubs, mingle with it. A cart meets us—a real heavy, big-wheeled English cart; and English horses—real big, shaggy-hoofed, sleek, heavy English cart-horses; and a carter—a real apple-faced, smock-frocked, red-headed, wool-hatted carter—breeches, stockings, hob-nailed shoes, and *"Gee-up Dobbin"* English carter.

Little birds hop along in the road before us, and we guess at their names, first of all electing one to be Robin-Redbreast. We study the flowers under the hedge, and determine them nothing else than primroses and buttercups. Through the gates we admire the great, fat, clean-licked, contented-faced cows, and large, white, long-wooled sheep.

What else was there? I cannot remember; but there was that altogether that made us forget our fatigue, disregard the rain, thoughtless of the way we were going—serious, happy, and grateful. And this excitement continued for many days.

At length, as it becomes drenching again, we approach a stone spire. A stone house interrupts our view in front; the road winds round it, between it and another; turns again, and there on our left is the church—the old ivy-covered, brown stone village church, with the yew-tree—we knew it at once, and the heaped-up, green, old English churchyard. We turn to the right; there is the old ale-house, long, low, thatched-roofed. We run in at the open door; there he sits, the bluff and hearty old fellow, with the long-stemmed pipe and the foaming pewter mug on the little table before him. At the same moment with us comes in another man. He drops in a seat—raps with his whip. *Enter* a young woman, neat and trim, with exactly the white cap, smooth hair, shiny face, bright eyes and red cheeks we are looking for.

"*Muggoyail, lass!*"

Mug of ale—ay, that's it! Mug of ale!—Fill up! fill up! and the toast shall be—"MERRIE ENGLAND! HURRAH!"

We sit with them for some time, and between puffs of smoke, the talk is of "the weather and the crops." The maid leaves the door open, so we can look into the kitchen, where a smart old woman is ironing by a bright coal fire. Two little children venture before us. I have just succeeded in coaxing the girl on to my knee, as C. mentions that we are Americans. The old woman lays down her iron and puts on her spectacles to look at us. The stout man who had risen to take an observation of the weather, seats himself again and calls for another mug and *twist*. The landlord (a tall thin man, unfortunately) looks in and asks how times go where we come from. Plenty of questions follow, that show alike the interest and the ignorance of our companions about America, it being confused apparently in their minds with Ireland, Guinea, and the poetical Indies. After a little straightening out, and explanation of the distance to it, its climate and civilized condition, they ask about the present crops, the price of wheat, about rents, tithes, and taxes. In return, we get only grumbling. "The country is ruined;" "things weren't so when they were young as they be now;" and so on, just as a company of our tavern-lounging farmers would talk, except that every complaint ends with blaming Free Trade. "Vree-trade—hoye, sirs—Vree-trade be killing the varmers."

We left them as soon as the shower slackened, but stopped again immediately to look at the yew through the churchyard gate. It was a very old and decrepit tree—with dark and funereal foliage—the stiff trunk and branches of our red-cedar, with the leaf of the hemlock, but more dark and glossy than either. The walls of the church are low, but higher in one part than another. The roof, which is slated, is high and steep. The tower is square, with buttresses on the corners, on the tops of which are quaint lions rampant. It is surmounted by a tall, symmetrical spire—solid stone to the ball, over which, as I am the son of a Puritan, is a weather-cock, and not a cross. There are little, narrow windows in the steeple, and swallows are flying in and out of them. Old weather-beaten stone and mortar, glass, lead, iron, and matted ivy, but not a splinter of wood or a daub of paint. Old England for ever! —Amen.

A mile or two more of such walking as before the shower, and we came to a park gate. It was, with the lodges by its side, neat, simple, and substantial. The park was a handsome piece of old woods, but, as seen from the road, not remarkable. We were told, however, that there was a grand old hall and fine grounds a long way within. Near the park there were signs of an improving farmer: fields of mangel-wurzel in drills; large fields, partly divided by wire fences, within which were flocks of sheep; marks of recent under-draining; hedges trimmed squarely, and every thing neat, straight, and business-like.

As it grows dark we approach another village. The first house on the left is an inn—a low, two-story house of light drab-colored stone. A bunch of grapes (cast in iron) and a lantern are hung out from it over the foot-path, and over the front door is a square sign—"THE RED LION—*licensed to sell foreign spirits and beer, to be drunk on the premises.*" We

turn into a dark hall, and opening a door to the left, enter—
the kitchen? Such a kitchen! You would not believe me if I
could describe how bright every thing is. You would think the
fireplace a show-model, for the very bars of the grate are
glistening. It is all a-glow with red-hot coals; a bright brass teakettle swings and sings from a polished steel crane—hook,
jack, and all like silver; the brass coal-scuttle, tongs, shovel,
and warming-pan are blazingly radiant, and the walls and
mantel-piece are covered with bright plate-covers, and I know
not what other metallic furniture, all burnished to the highest
degree.

The landlady rises and begs to take our wet hats—a
model landlady, too. What a fine eye!—a kind and welcoming
black eye. Fair and stout; elderly—a little silver in her hair,
just showing its otherwise thick blackness to be no lie; a broad-
frilled, clean, white cap and collar, and a black dress. Ah ha!
one of the widows that we have read of. We hesitate to cross
the clean-scoured, buff, tile floor with our muddy shoes; but
she draws arm-chairs about the grate, and lays slippers before
them, stirs up the fire, though it is far from needing it, and
turns to take our knapsacks. "We must be fatigued—it's not
easy walking in the rain; she hopes we can make ourselves
comfortable."

There is every prospect of it.

CHAPTER X

Talk with a Farmer; with a Tender-hearted Wheelwright—
An Amusing Story—Notions of America—Supper—
Speech of the English—Pleasant Tones—Quaint Expres-
sions—The Twenty-ninth of May—Zaccheus in the Oak
Tree—Education—Bed-chamber—A Nightcap, and . . .
a Nightcap

ON ONE SIDE near the fire there was a recess in the wall, in
which was a *settle,* (a long, high-backed, wooden seat.) Two
men with pipes and beer sat in it, with whom we fell to
talking. One of them proved to be a farmer, the other a jack-of-
all-trades, but more distinctly of the wheelwright's, and a wor-
shiper of and searcher after ideal women, as he more than
once intimated to us. We were again told by the farmer that
free trade was ruining the country—no farmer could live long
in it. He spoke with a bitter jocoseness of the regularity of his
taxes, and said that though they played the devil with every
thing else, he always knew how tithes would be. He paid, I
think he said, about a dollar an acre every year to the church,
though he never went to it in his life; always went to chapel,
as his father did before him. He was an Independent; but
there were so few of them thereabouts that they could not
afford to keep a minister, and only occasionally had preaching.
When he learned that we were from America, he was anxious

to know how church matters were there. Though a rather
intelligent man, he was utterly ignorant that we had no State
Church; and though a dissenter, the idea of a government
giving free trade to all sorts of religious doctrine seemed to be
startling and fearful to him. But when I told him what the
rent (or the interest on the value) of my farm was, and what
were its taxes, he wished that he was young that he might go
to America himself; he really did not see how he should be
able to live here much longer. He rented a farm of about fifty
acres, and was a man of about the same degree of intelligence
and information that you would expect of the majority of
those owning a similar farm with us. Except that he was somewhat stouter than most Yankees, he did not differ much in
appearance or dress from many of our rather old-fashioned
farmers.

The tender-hearted wheelwright could hardly believe
that we were really born and brought up in America. He
never thought any foreigners could learn to speak the language so well. He too was rather favorably struck with the
idea of going to America, when we answered his inquiries with
regard to mechanics' wages. He was very cautious, however,
and cross-questioned us a long time about the cost of every
thing there—the passage, the great heat of the climate, the
price of beer; and at length, touching his particular weakness,
he desired to be told candidly how it would be if he should
marry before he went. If he should get a wife, a real handsome
one, would it be safe for him to take her there? He had heard
a story—perhaps we knew whether it was true or not—of a
man who took a handsome wife out with him, and a black man,
who was a great rich lord in our country, took a great liking to
her, and offered the man ten thousand pounds for her, which
he refused; and so the great black lord went away very wroth
and vexed. When he was gone, the woman upbraided her
husband: "Thou fool, why didst thee not take it and let me go
with him? I would have returned to thee tomorrow." Then
the man followed after the black lord, and sold his wife to him
for ten thousand pounds. But the next day she did not return,
nor the next, neither the next; and so the man went to look

for her; and lo! he found her all dressed up in silk and satin, 'lighting from a coach, and footmen waiting upon her. So he says to her, "Why didst thee not return the next day?" *"Dost take me for a fool, goodman?"* quoth she, and stepped back into her fine coach and drove off; and so he lost his handsome wife.

Besides the kitchen, there were, on the lower floor of the inn, two or three small dining or tea rooms, a little office or accounting closet for the mistress, and a *tap-room,* which is a small apartment for smoking and drinking. These are all plainly but neatly furnished. There is a large parlor above stairs, somewhat elegantly furnished. The kitchen, tap-room, and office are low rooms, and over these is the parlor. The dining-rooms are higher, and over them are the bed-chambers. Thus the parlor is allowed a high ceiling, level with the eaves of the roof, and you enter it from a landing some steps lower than the bed-chambers. The latter are carried up under the roof, with dormer windows, and are very pleasant rooms. It will be seen that all the traveler's apartments are thus made spacious at the expense of height in the others, and that yet there is a convenient arrangement and connection of the whole.

We had supper in a little back room, as neat as care and scouring could make and keep it. The table was much such a one as Mrs. Marcombe, in Hanover, would have set for a couple of tired White Mountain pedestrians, except the absence of any kind of cakes or pies. The ham had a peculiar taste, and was very good—C. says the least unpleasant of any he was ever tempted to eat. It had been dried by hanging from the ceiling of the kitchen, instead of being regularly *smoked,* as is our practice. The milk and butter (which was not in the least salted) were very sweet and high-flavored.

In the evening we had a long talk with the old woman and her daughter. The latter was a handsome person, with much such a good, beaming face as her mother, but with youth, and more refinement from education and intelligence. She also was a widow, with two sweet, shy little girls.

There are peculiarities in the speech of these women that

would distinguish them anywhere from native Americans. Perhaps the novelty of them is pleasing, but it has seemed to us that the speech of most of the people, above the lowest class of laborers whom we have met, is more agreeable and better than we often hear at home. Perhaps the climate may have effect in making the people more steadily animated—the utterance more distinct and varied. Sentences are more generally finished with a rising inflection, syllables are more forcibly accented, and quite often, as with our landlady, there is a rich musical tone in the conversational voice, to which we are not yet so much accustomed but that it compels us to listen deferentially. I wonder that beauty of speech is not more thought of as accomplishment. It is surely capable of great cultivation, and should not be forgotten in education.

Except in the lower class, the choice of words seems often elegant, and we hear few idiomatic phrases or provincialisms. Where we do notice them, in the class I am now speaking of, it would not seem an affectation of singular language in an educated person with us, but rather a fortunate command of vigorous Saxon words. We have never any difficulty in understanding them, while we do sometimes have to reconstruct our sentences, and find substitutes for some of our words, before we are plainly understood. The "H" difficulty is an exception to all this, with nearly all the people, except the most polished, that we have met. Is it not singular? Among the lowest classes, however, there are many words used that puzzle us; others are pronounced curiously, and many of our common words are used in new combinations. There is an old-fashioned, quaint set of words in common use that we only understand from having met with them in old books—in the Bible, for instance. The words *Master* and *Mistress* (instead of Mister and Misses, as we have got to pronounce them), and *lad* and *lass,* are usual. *"Here, lad!" "Wull, Maister?"* I first heard in the Liverpool market. I passed a man, there, too, leading a dray-horse, with a heavy load, up one of the steep streets. He was encouraging him in this way: "Coom on, my lad! coom on, my good lad!" When he had reached the brow, he stopped and went before the noble beast, who, with glistening eyes, and ears playing beautifully, bowed his head to be patted: *"Good lad! good lad! Well, thee's done it!"**

We had noticed yesterday, in Liverpool, that the omnibuses were decorated with branches of trees, ribbons, and flags; the union-jack (British ensign) was hoisted in several places, the children seemed to be enjoying a half-holiday in the afternoon, and once we saw them going together in an irregular procession, carrying a little one dressed with leaves and crowned with a gilt paper cap, and singing together in shrill chorus some verses, of which we only understood the frequent repetition of the words: "The twenty-ninth of May! the twenty-ninth of May!" It occurred to C. to ask whether all this was intended to celebrate any thing. "Oh, surely," our hostess said, "it was the twenty-ninth of May—King Charles-and-the-Oak day." In her husband's time, they used always to keep it in good style, ornamenting their house all over with oak boughs; and all the stagecoaches and the horses used to be decked with oak boughs too. "How beautifully," says C. aside, "do such pretty simple customs keep alive the remembrance of old historic facts!" "But why do they carry about the *child?*" She did not recollect clearly, but she had the impression that King Charles was a baby when it occurred. She had forgotten exactly how it was, she said, "but it told all about it in the Bible." "In the Bible! mother; you mean in the History of England, do you not?" said her daughter, smiling. "Was it?" replied the old lady; "I never had time to read much in the large History of England. Let me see—why, no; now I am sure it was in the Bible. Don't you remember—what's his name—Zack—Zack—Zacheriah? yes, Zacheriah; how he climbed up into an oak tree to see King Charles go by!"

A large and most powerful class, including many even of the more conservative of the Dissenters in England, are terribly afraid of a national system of education that shall be free from Church influence. The people had better be left to grow

* A gentleman, riding towards Chowbet, and seeing a boy in the road, shouted out to him, "My lad, am I half-way to Chowbet?" Young Lancashire looked up at the querist, and said, "Hah con aw tell, tha' foo', when I doon't know wheear ta' coom fra?"—*Liverpool Paper.*

up in ignorance, rather than that they should not be instructed in theological dogmas. I have actually heard a refined and educated gentleman, occupying an influential position, advocate the idea that all the education the common people needed was so much as would enable them to read their Bible, prayer-book, and catechism. Except for this he would never let them have a teacher, but would leave them to the parson. He would break up every Dissenter's school—have no school in the land that was not a part of the Church. The godless system of education which was now favored in high quarters (on the plan of our New England common schools!) he verily believed, if adopted, would be a national sin that God would arise in his anger to punish.

Our landlady had lived almost to old age under the shadow of the Church, in which the story of Zaccheus is every year read aloud, and in which a religious celebration of the Restoration of King Charles is by law performed every 29th of May. But a person of sound faculties, native-born, could not probably be found in New England, whose godless education would not have made impossible such a confusion of religious instruction as had been given her.

I am writing now in my bedroom. Though the ceiling is low, it is large and well furnished. There are large pitchers of water, foot-bath, and half-a-dozen towels. The bed is very large, clean, and deeply curtained. The landlady has sent me up a glass of her home-brewed beer, with a nightcap, which I noticed she hung by the fire when I left the kitchen. The chambermaid has drawn down the bedclothes, and says, "The bed has been well aired, sir." Good night.

CHAPTER XI

The Break of Day—A Full Heart—Familiar Things—
The Village at Sunrise—Flowers—Birds—Dog Kennels—
"The Squire" and "The Hall"—Rooks—Visit to a Small
Farm—The Cows—The Milking—The Dairy-Maids—The
Stables—Manure—Bones—Pasture—White Clover—Imple-
ments—Carts—The English Plow and Harrow

31st May

IT WAS VERY EARLY this morning when I became gradually
aware of the twittering of house-sparrows, and was soon after
brought to more distinct consciousness of time and place by
the long, clear note of some other stranger bird. I stepped
from bed and kneeled at a little, low, latticed window, curtained without by a woodbine. Parting the foliage with my
hands, I looked out upon a cluster of low-thatched cottages,
half overgrown with ivy; a blooming hawthorn hedge, enclosing a field of heavy grass and clover glistening with dew; a few
haystacks; another field beyond, spotted with sheep; a group
of trees; and then some low hills, over which the dawn was
kindling, with a faint blush, the quiet, smoky clouds in a gray
sky. It may seem an uninteresting landscape, but I gazed upon
it with great emotion, so great that I wondered at it. Such a
scene I had never looked upon before, and yet it was in all its
parts as familiar to me as my native valley. Land of our poets!

Home of our fathers! Dear old mother England! It would be strange if I were not affected at meeting thee at last face to face.

I dressed, and worked my way through the dark, crooked stairs to the kitchen, where, on the bright steel fender, I found my shoes dry and polished. I walked through the single short street of the hamlet. The houses were set closely together, with neat little gardens about them. They were of every age; one I noticed marked with the date 1630—about the time of the first settlement in Connecticut. It was of stone, narrow, with a steep roof covered with very small slates. The windows were much wider than high, and filled with little panes of glass set in strips of lead. Except in this and the materials of which it was built, it was not unlike some of the oldest houses that we yet see in our first Puritan villages, as Hadley and Wethersfield. At the other end of the hamlet was another inn—"The Blue Lion," I believe, and a tall hostler opening the stable doors was dressed just as I wanted to see him—jockey-cap, long striped waistcoat, breeches, and boots.

As I returned, I saw the farmer who had been at the inn the night before, and asked him to let me see his cows. He said they were coming down the lane, and if I went with him I should meet them. Passing a group of well-built, neat, low buildings, he said they were the Squire's kennels. They were intended for greyhounds, but he had his pointers in them now.

"The Squire's! But where's the Squire's house?"

"Yon's the Hall," pointing to a distant group of trees, above which a light smoke was rising straight up in the calm air, and a number of large black birds were rapidly rising and falling. "Yon's the Hall; ye see the rooks."

"The rooks! Then those are rooks, are they?"

"Ay, be they; rooks—do ye not know what rooks be?"

"Yes, but we don't have them in America."

"No! not have rooks? They be main good in a pie, sir."

We met the cows, of which there were about a dozen, driven by a boy towards the farm-house. They were large and in good order; with soft, sleek skin, and, like every cow I have seen in England, look as if they had just been polished up for exhibition. He could tell nothing of their breed except of one, a handsome heifer, which he said came partly of Welsh stock. He took me across a field or two to look at a few cows of the Squire's. They were finer than any of his, and seemed to be grade short-horns.

The cows were driven into hovels, which he called *shippens,* and fastened at their mangers by a chain and ring, sliding on an upright post (the latest fashion with us), eight of them in an apartment, standing back to back. Three or four of his daughters came out to milk—very good looking, modest young women, dressed in long, loose, grey, homespun gowns. They had those high wooden tubs to milk in that we see in the old pictures of sentimental milk-maids. It seems constantly like dreaming to see so many of these things that we have only known before in poetry or painting.

The dairy-house and all the farm buildings were of brick, interworked with beams of wood and thatched. They were very small, the farm being only of fifty acres, and the hay and grain always kept in stacks. The arrangements for saving manure were poor—much the same as on any tolerably good farm with us—a hollowed yard with a pool of liquid on one side. He bought some dung and bones in Liverpool, but not much. He esteemed bones most highly, and said they did immense good hereabout. They made a sweeter, stronger, and more permanent pasture. Where he had applied them twelve years ago, at the rate of a ton to an acre, he could see their effect yet. He took me into an adjoining field which, he said, was one of the best pastures in the village. It had been plowed in narrow lands, and the ridges left high, when it was laid down. The sward was thicker, better *bottomed,* than any I ever saw in America. He sowed about a bushel of grass seeds to the acre, seeding down with oats. For cheese pasture, he valued white clover more than any thing else, and had judged, from the taste of American cheese, that we did not have it. For meadows to be mowed for hay, he preferred sainfoin and ray-grass. He had lately underdrained some of his lowest land with good effect. His soil is mostly a stiff clay, resting on a ledge of rocks.

The farm-carts were clumsy and heavy (for horses), with

very large wheels, with broad tires and huge hubs, as you have seen the English carts pictured. The plow was a very long, sharp, narrow one, calculated to plow about seven inches deep, and turn a slice ten inches wide, with a single pair of horses. The stilts, of iron, were long and low, and the beam, also of iron, very high, with a goose-neck curve. It is a very beautiful instrument, graceful and strong; but its appearance of lightness is deceptive, the whole being of iron; and this, with its great length, though adding to its efficiency for nice, accurate work, in perfectly smooth and clear, long fields, would entirely unfit it for most of our purposes. On the rocky, irregular, hillside farms of New England, or the stump lands of the West, it would be perfectly useless; but I should think it might be an admirable plow for our New York wheat lands, or perhaps for the prairies, after they had been once broken.

The harrow used on the farm was also of iron, frame and all, in three oblong sections, hinged together. These were about all the tools I saw, and they were left in a slovenly way, lying about the farm-yard and in the road.

CHAPTER XII

Breakfast at the Inn—A Tale of High Life—The Garden
of the Inn—An Old Farm-House—Timber Houses—Laborers' Cottages—Wattles and Noggin Walls—A "Ferme
Ornee"—A Lawn Pasture—Copper-leaved Beeches—Tame
Black Cattle—Approach to Chester

I RETURNED to my room in the inn, and had written a page or
two of this before any one was stirring. Then I heard the
mistress waking the servants, and soon after "John the Boots"
came to my door to call me, as I had requested.

After prevailing with difficulty upon the landlady and her
daughter to breakfast with us, we had a very sociable time
with them over the tea and eggs which they had prepared for
us. They were interested to hear of the *hard* coal we burned
(anthracite), that made no smoke, and of *wood* fires, and of
our peculiar breakfast dishes, griddle-cakes, and Indian bread.
They told of other members of their family—two or three in
Australia—and of the clergy and gentry of the neighborhood.
They spoke kindly and respectfully of the vicar—"a sporting
man, sir, and fond of good living," the old lady added, after
mentioning his charity and benevolence. In speaking of the
gentry, it was difficult for her to believe that we did not know
the general history of all the families. We asked about a park
we had passed. It was —— Park, and had a remarkable story

to be told of it; but so constantly did she anticipate our knowledge, taking for granted that we knew all that had occurred until within a short time, that it was long before we could at all understand the news about it. As you are probably equally ignorant, I will tell you the tale connectedly, as we finally got it.

It had been the property of Sir T——, who occupied the Hall in it until his death, a year or two ago, and had been in his family many hundred years. The estate included several villages—the whole of them, every house and shop, even the churches—and was valued at £800,000 ($4,000,000). On the death of Sir T., Sir W., his son, inherited his title and estate. But Sir W. was a sporting man, and had previously gambled himself in debt to Jews in London £600,000. He came to the Hall, however, and remained there some time, keeping two packs of hounds. He was a good landlord, and the family were beloved. Lady M. had established and maintained a National (church) School; and in the winter was in the habit of serving out a large quantity of soup every day to the poor of the estate. But at length the bailiffs came, and Sir W. went to France, and his family dispersed among their relatives all over the kingdom. Lady M. last winter had been very ill, and nothing ailed her, the physicians said, but sorrow.

And now they were going to sell it—they did not know how they could—but they showed us a considerable volume, illlustrated with maps and lithographs, of "plans and particulars" of the estate, on the first page of which "Messrs. —— had the honor to announce that they had been instructed by the honorable proprietor, to sell at auction, on a certain six days, upwards of fifteen hundred acres of very fine rich land, let to an old and respectable tenantry, including the whole of the town of——, together with several manors and manorial rights, which have been commuted at £500 per annum." They showed us also another volume, containing in one hundred and twelve quarto pages, descriptions of the furniture, plate, library, paintings, wines, etc., with many engravings—a curious exposure of noble housekeeping to our republican eyes. Seeing that we were interested in the book, the landlady offered it to us; it was of no use to her, she said, and we were quite welcome to it. It was really of some value, and we offered to pay for it, but she would not sell it.

Before we left, they showed us through the little garden of the inn; it was beautifully kept, and every thing growing strongly. Then, after buckling on our knapsacks, and bringing us another mug of *home-brewed,* our kind entertainers took leave of us with as much good feeling and cordiality as if we were old friends, who had been making them a short visit, following us out into the road, with parting advice about the roads and the inns, and at last a warm shaking of hands.

The country we walked over for a few miles after leaving the village, was similar to that we saw yesterday—flattish, with long, low undulations—the greater part in pasture, and that which was not, less highly cultivated than I had expected to find much land in England, the stock upon it almost altogether cows, and these always looking admirably well; the fields universally divided by hedges, which, though they add much to the beauty of the landscape, when you are in a position to look over it, greatly interrupt the view, and always are ill-trimmed, irregular, and apparently insecure. We met no one on the road, saw very few habitations, and only two men at work, plowing, for several miles; then a cluster of cottages, an inn, and a large old *timber-house.* As I had been informed (very wrongly) that these were getting rare in England, and it was very peculiar and striking, I stopped to sketch it.

Imagine a very large, old-fashioned New England farmhouse, with the weather-boarding stripped off and all the timber exposed. Fill up the intervals with brick, and plaster them over even with the outer surface of the beams; then whitewash this plastered surface and blacken the timber, and you have the walls of the house. A New England house, however, would have three times as many windows. The roof is mostly of very small old slates, set with mortar, and capped (ridged) with thick quarried stones. It is repaired with large new slates in several places, and an addition that has been made since the main part was erected, which is entirely of brick in the walls, with no timber, is heavily thatched with straw, as are also all the out-buildings.

The rear of the farm-house probably contains the dairy,

and is covered with thatch to secure a more equable temperature.

All the other buildings in the hamlet were similarly built
—timber and whitewashed walls, and thatch roofs. While I
was sketching, the farmer, a stout old man, and the first we
have seen in top-boots, came out and entered into conversation with us. He was much amused that I should think his
house worth sketching, and told us it had been long [rented]
in his family. He had no idea how old it was. He described the
cottages, which were certainly very pretty to look at, as exceedingly uncomfortable and unhealthy—the floors, which were of
clay, being generally lower than the road and the surrounding
land, and often wet, and always damp, while the roofs and
walls were old and leaky, and full of vermin. The walls of
these cottages are all made by interlacing twigs (called *wattles*) between the timbers, and then *plashing* these with mud
(*noggin*), inside and out, one layer over another as they dried,
until it is as thick as is desired; then the surface is made
smooth with a trowel, and whitewashed.

A few miles further on we came to a large, park-like pasture, bounded by a neatly trimmed hedge, and entered by a
simple gate, from which a private road ran curving among a
few clumps of trees to a mansion about a furlong distant. We
entered, and rested ourselves awhile at the foot of some large
oaks. The house was nearly hidden among trees, and these,
seen across the clear grass land, formed, we thought, the finest
mass of foliage we had ever seen. A peculiar character was
given it by one or two purple-leaved beeches—tall trees,
thickly branched from the very ground. The cattle in this
pasture-lawn were small and black, brisk and wild-looking,
but so tame in reality that, as we lay under the tree, they came
up and licked our hands like dogs. The whole picture completely realized Willis's ideal-sketch, "The Cottage *Insou-
cieuse.*"

After this the country was more elevated and broken, and
the walk delightful. We saw many beautiful things, but have
seen so many, more interesting, since, that I hardly remember
them. The road was more traveled. We met a stage-coach, with
no inside passengers, but the top overloaded, and a stylish

carriage-and-four, the near wheeler and leader ridden by postillions in bright livery, and within an old gentleman, wearing a velvet cap, and a young lady under a blue hood. The fields, too, were more tilled; and one of fifty acres, which was ridged for some root crop, was the most thoroughly cultivated piece of merely farming ground I ever saw.

About the middle of the forenoon, we came to the top of a higher hill than we had before crossed, from which we looked down upon a beautiful rich valley, bounded on the side opposite us by blue billowy hills. In the midst of it was the smoke and chimneys and steeples of a town. One square, heavy brown tower was conspicuous over the rest, and we recognized our first cathedral.

As we approached the town, the road became a crooked paved street, lined with curious small houses, between which we passed, stopping often to admire some singular gable, or porch, or grotesque carving, until it was spanned by a handsome brown stone arch, not the viaduct of a railroad, as at first seemed likely, but one of the four gateways of the city. Passing under it, we found on the inner side a flight of broad stairs leading on to the city wall, which we ascended. At the top, on the inside of the wall, was a printer's shop, in which guidebooks were offered for sale. Entering this we were received by an obliging young man, who left the press to give us chairs, and with whom we had an interesting conversation about the town and about his trade. Printers' wages, if I recollect rightly, were about one quarter more in New York than in Chester. After purchasing a guide-book and a few prints of him, we accepted his invitation to leave our knapsacks in his shop, and take a walk on the walls before entering the town.

CHAPTER XIII

Chester without—A Walk on the Walls—Antiquities—
Striking Contrasts

MY JOURNAL IS BEHINDHAND several days. Meantime, I have
seen so much, that if I had a week of leisure I should despair
of giving you a good idea of this strange place. But that you
may understand a little how greatly we are interested, I will
mention some of the objects that we have seen, and are seeing.
Use your imagination well to fill up the hints, rather than
descriptions, of these that I shall give you. You need not fear
that, when you come here, the reality will disappoint you.

We are on the top of the wall, a few feet from the archway
through which we entered the town. Look down now on the
outside. The road, just before it enters the gate, crosses, by a
bridge, a deep ravine. In it, some seventy feet below us, you
see the dark water, perhaps of old the *fosse*, but now a modern
commercial canal. A long, narrow boat, much narrower than
our canal-boats, laden with coals, is coming from under the
bridge; a woman is steering it; and on the cabin, in large red
letters, you see her name, "Margaret Francis," and the name of
the boat—"Telegraph." The arch was turned by a man now
living, but that course of stones—the dark ones between the

ivy and the abutment—was laid by a Roman mason, when Rome was mistress of the world.

Walk on. The wall is five feet wide on the top, with a parapet of stone on the outside, and an iron rail within. Don't fear, though it is so far and deep to the canal, and the stone looks so time-worn and crumbling; it is firm with true Roman cement, the blood of brave men. Here it is strengthened by a heavy tower, now somewhat dilapidated. Look up, and you see upon it the rude carving of a Phœnix; under it, on an old tablet, these words:

"ON THIS TOWER STOOD CHARLES THE FIRST, AND SAW
HIS ARMY DEFEATED."

Within the tower is the stall of a newsman. Buy the Times, which has come some hundred miles since morning, with the information that yesterday the president of a French Peace Society was shot in a duel. (A fact.)

Pass on. On one side of us are tall chimneys, built last year, through which, from fierce forge-fires, ascend black smoke and incense of bitumen to the glory of mammon. Close on the other side stands a venerable cathedral, built by pious labor of devout men, centuries dead, to the laud and service of their God. We look into the burying-ground, and on the old gravestones observe many familiar New England names.

Again, narrow brick houses are built close up to the wall, and, now, on both sides; the wall, which you can stride across, being their only street or way of access. Here, again, it crosses another broad road, and we are over another entrance to the city—the "New Gate;" it is not quite a century old. We look from it into a market-place. Narrow, steep-gabled houses, with their second story threatening the sidewalks, surround it. But the market-building is modern. See! the sparrow lighting on the iron roof burns her feet and flies hastily over to the heavy, old brown thatch, where the little dormers stick out so clumsily cosy.

Odd-looking vehicles and oddly-dressed people are passing in the street below us: a woman with a jacket, driving two stout horses in one of those heavy farm-carts; an omnibus, with the sign of "The Green Dragon," very broad, and carrying many passengers on the top; the driver, smartly-dressed, tips his whip with a knowing nod to a pretty Welsh girl, who is carrying a tub upon her head. There are scores of such damsels, neat as possible, with dark eyes, and glossy hair half covered by white caps, and fine, plump forms, in short striped petticoats and hob-nailed shoes. There goes one, straight as a gun-barrel, with a great jar of milk upon her head. And here is a little donkey, with cans of milk slung on each side of him, and behind them, so you cannot see why he does not slip off over his tail, is a great brute, with two legs in knee-breeches and blue stockings, bent up so as to be clear of the ground, striking him with a stout stick across his long, expressive ears. A sooty-faced boy, with a Kilmarnock bonnet on his head, carrying pewter pots, coming towards us, jumps suddenly one side, and, ha! out from under us, at a rattling pace, comes a beautiful sorrel mare, with a handsome, tall, slightly-made young man in undress military uniform; close behind, and not badly mounted either, follow two others—one also in uniform, with a scarlet cap and a bright bugle swinging at his side; the other a groom in livery, neat as a pin; odd again, to American eyes, those leather breeches and bright top-boots. Lord Grosvenor, going to review the Yeomanry, says the printer. His grandfather built this gate and presented it to the corporation; you may see his arms on the key-stone. But we must go on.

On the left an old tower, and under it the ragged outline and darker color of still older masonry. A swallow has just found a cranny big enough wherein to build her nest, that Father Time has been chiseling at eight hundred years. Eight hundred? Yes; for it was rebuilt then. You can see some of the real old wall at the other end—no, not that round Saxon arch, but beyond the trees—a low wall with a heavy clothing of ivy. The steamboat is just coming out from behind it now. In the year 973, King Edgar landed at this church from a boat, in which he had been rowed by eight conquered kings. A smoky old tub is that steamboat, but doubtless a faster and more commodious craft than Edgar's eight king-power packet.

We cross another gateway, and pass a big mill. The dam

was built—I don't know when. But they say it had a bad name with the Puritans, who undertook to expunge it, but failed, because, like a duck, it kept under a high flood of water until the Cavaliers, making a dash to save it, spiked their guns.

Our path turns suddenly, and runs along the face of a stone wall, supported by brackets high above the water of the river, but some distance below the parapets—parapets of a Castle. Soon we pass a red-coated sentry, and now you see a tower that looks older than the rest. The battle-axes of William the Conqueror once clanged where that fellow now lounges with a cigar. Beyond, on the esplanade, were wont to assemble the feudal armies of the Earls of Chester, whose title is now borne by the German Prince's eldest son. Quite a different appearance they must have made from this regiment of Irishmen in cloth jackets and leather helmets.

Stop one moment to look at the bridge; step back to the angle—there you see it—half-a-dozen arches of different forms and shades of color, not particularly handsome, but worth noticing. The blackest of the arches was turned half a century before Jamestown was founded—that is, it was then rebuilt. The original bridge, from which the stones for it were taken, was built by Ethefleda. Who was she? She was "the queen" here a thousand years ago, I believe; you'll be shown her great-grandmother's cradle somewhere about town probably.

Just above is another bridge. What a fine arch. Yes; the widest in the world, it is said. That was not built by a queen; but a little girl was the first to cross it, who afterwards "developed" into "her most gracious Majesty, Victoria, whom God long preserve," as the loyal guide-book hath it.

". . . . Poor fellow! he is very lame."

"Probably an imposter, sir; don't encourage him."

"He asks a penny to keep him from starving; his son has not been able to get work lately, or he would not let him beg."

"There's enough work for him if he really wants it; it's what they all say. Give a ha'penny, then, and be rid of him. Now, look over there, between the trees, and see the entrance to the Marquis of Westminster's Park."—A great, fresh pile of bombastic towers and battlements to flank a gate and protect the woman who opens it from—rain and frost. It is but recently finished, and costs, says the printer, £10,000.

What says the beggar? Free trade and the Irish have cut down wages, since he used to work on the farms, from five shillings to eighteen pence.

He reasserts it. He has stood himself at Chester Cross on the market day, and refused to work for four-and-sixpence, and all the beer he could drink. It may be true—the printer tells us; in the old Bonaparte years, in harvest time, it was not unlikely to have been so. With wheat at a guinea a bushel, the farmers did not have the worst of it. Soldiers can't reap, but they must eat. The government borrowed money to give the farmers for supporting the war, and now the farmers are paying the debt.

Hark! horns and kettle-drums! It is the band of the Yeomanry; we shall see them directly. . . . There! Five squadrons of mounted men trotting over a broad green meadow below us. Well mounted they seem to be, and well seated too. Fox hunting makes good cavalry. Doubtless many of those fellows have been after the hounds.

Possibly. But never one of them charged a buffalo herd, I'll be bound.

This green plain—a sort of public lawn in front of the town—is about twice as large as Boston Common, and is called "The Roodee." It is free from trees, nothing but a handsome meadow, and the Chester race-course runs round it. On this course, by the way, the greatest number of horses ever engaged in a single match have been run. In 1848, the entries were one hundred and fifty-six, of which one hundred and six accepted.

Right below us, on the meadow, there is pitched a *marquée*. It belongs to a cricket club. I only want you to notice the beautiful green sward of their playing ground. It is shaven so clean and close. You see men sweeping it with hairbrooms.

In this garden, on the other side of the wall, there was

once a nunnery. A subterranean passage exists, by which, if
you could keep a candle burning, you might pass from it
under the city back to the cathedral.

. . . . Are you tired of ruins? Here is one more that may
rouse your Puritan blood: a heavy tower built into the wall,
connected with a larger one at some distance outside. How old
they look! No paintings and no descriptions had ever conveyed to me the effect of age upon the stone itself of these very
old structures. How stern! how venerable! how silent—yet telling what long stories! We will not ask for the oldest of them,
but—you see there, where the battlements are broken down in
one place—that breach was made by a ball thrown from the
hill yonder; and the cannon that sent it was aimed by OLIVER
CROMWELL himself.

How beautiful, how indescribably beautiful, are those
glossy tresses of ivy, falling over the blackened ramparts, like
the curls of a child asleep on its grandfather's shoulder—
Whew! They have pierced the wall right under us, and here
goes an express train fifty miles an hour, from Ireland to
London, by way of Holyhead. The Roman masonry, that re-
sisted the Roundhead batteries, has surrendered to the engines
of peace.

But, as we move on, higher marks of civilization are
pointed out to us. Here, close to the wall, and in the shadow
of the old tower, is a public bath and wash-house. A little back
is a hospital, and near it a house of refuge. Across the valley is
a gloomy looking workhouse, and in another direction a much
more cheering institution, beautifully placed on a hill, among
fine, dark, evergreen trees, through which you can see the
bright sunshine and smile of God falling upon it. It is the
Training College—a normal school, for preparing teachers for
the church schools of the diocese. And here, on the left, as we
approach the north gate again, is an old charity school-house,
the Blue-coat Hospital. The boys at play are all young George
Washingtons, dressed in long-skirted blue coats, and breeches,
and stockings.

. . . . So here we are, back at the good-natured printer's

office, having been a circuit of three miles on the walls of the
city. Its population is twenty-five thousand, and as you have
observed that nearly all the houses are low, you cannot suppose that much room is taken up by streets and unoccupied
grounds, where that number is accommodated in such limited
space, you will be ready to explore the interior with curiosity.
If your taste for the quaint and picturesque is at all like mine,
you will be in no danger of disappointment.

CHAPTER XIV

Chester Within—Peculiarities of Building—The Rows—A
Sea Captain—Romancing—An Old Inn—Old English
Town Houses—Timber Houses—Claiming an Inheritance
—A Cook Shop—One of the Alleys—Breaking into the
Cathedral—Expulsion—The Curfew

THE FOUR GATES of the city are opposite, and about equally
distant from each other. Four streets run from them, meeting
in the centre and dividing it into four quarters. These principal streets vary in width from one to three rods, and besides
them there are only a few narrow alleys, through which carts
can pass. But the whole city is honeycombed with by-ways,
varying from two to five feet in width; sometimes open above,
and sometimes built over; crooked and intricate, and, if he
cares where they lead him to, most puzzling to a stranger.
Besides these courts, alleys, and foot-paths, there is another
highway peculiarity in Chester, which it will be difficult to
describe; but—

Imagine you have entered the gate with us, after the walk
on the wall. The second story of most the old houses is thrown
forward, as you have seen it in the "old settlers' " houses at
home. Sometimes it projects several feet, and is supported by
posts in the sidewalk. Soon this becomes a frequent, and then
a continuous arrangement; the posts are generally of stone,

forming an arcade, and you walk behind them in the shade.
Sometimes, instead of posts, a solid wall supports the upper
house. You observe, as would be likely in an old city, that the
surface is irregular; we are ascending a slight elevation. Notwithstanding the old structure overhead, and the well-worn,
thick, old flagging under foot, we notice that the shop fronts
are finished with plate-glass, and all the brilliancy of the latest
commercial taste and art. Turning, to make the contrast more
striking, by looking at the little windows and rude carvings of
the houses opposite, we see a banister or hand-rail separates
the sidewalk from the carriageway, and are surprised, on stepping out to it, to find that the street is some ten feet below us.
We are evidently in the second story of the houses. Finding
steps leading downwards, we descend into the street and discover another tier of shops, on the roofs of which we have been
walking.

Going on, we shortly come to where the two streets meet
in the centre of the town. Passing over the ground where the
"cross" and the pillory, and other institutions of religion and
justice and merry-making formerly stood, we ascend steps, and
are again in one of those singular walks called by the inhabitants "The Rows." There are no more stylish shop fronts; but
dark doorways and old windows again, and on almost every
door-post little black and red checkers, which hieroglyphics, if
you are not sufficiently versed in Falstaffian lore to understand, you can find rendered in plain black and white queen's
English on the beam overhead—"Licensed to sell beer," etc.
Generally there will be an additional sign, naming the inn or
tavern, always in letters, and almost never in portraiture. I
remember "The Crown and Castle," "The Crown and Anchor," "The Castle and Falcon," "The King's Head," "The
Black Bear," "The Blue Boar," "The Pied Bull," "The Green
Dragon," "The White Lion," "The Sun and Apple Tree,"
"The Colliers' Arms," "The Arms of Man," "The Malt
Shovel," etc., etc.

Instead of columns and a hand-rail, or a dead wall on the
street side of the row, it is now and then contracted by a room,
which is sometimes occupied by a shop, and sometimes seems
to be used as a vestibule and staircase to apartments overhead,

for we see a brass plate with the resident's name, and a bell-pull, at the door.

On the inner side there are frequent entrances to the narrow passages that I mentioned, which may be long substitutes for streets, communicating, after a deal of turning and splitting into branches, with some distant alley or churchyard, with the front doors of wealthy citizens' houses opening upon them; or they may be merely alleys between two tenements leading to a common yard in the rear; or again, if you turn into one, it may turn out to be a private hall, and after one or two short turns, end in a kitchen. Never mind—don't retreat; put on a bold face, take a seat by the fire as if you were at home, and call for a mug of beer. Ten to one it will be all right. Almost every other housekeeper seems to be a licensed taverner.

We had great sport while nominally engaged in finding lodgings to suit us. Many of the places at which we applied were merely houses of refreshment, and had no spare bedrooms. In one of these, "The Boot Inn," we found an old sea-captain, who, some twenty years ago, had traded to New York, and enjoyed talking and making inquiries about persons he had met and places he had visited. Fortunately we knew some of them, and so were constrained to sit down to bread and cheese and beer, and listen to some tough yarns of Yellow Jack and Barbary pirates. At one end of the kitchen was a table with benches on three sides of it, and a great arm-chair on the other. Over the chair hung a union-jack, and before it on the table was a strongly bound book, which proved to be "The Record of the Boot Inn Birthday Club." The bond entered into by each member on entering this association was, that he should treat the club to plenty of good malt liquor on his every future birthday. There was a constitution and many by-laws, the penalty for breaking which was always to be paid in "beer for the club."

At other inns we would be shown, by delightfully steep, narrow, crooked, and every way possible inconvenient stairways, up through low dark spaces of inclined plane, into long, steep-roofed, pigeon-house like rooms having an air as gloomy and mysterious as it was hot and close. Then, upon our declin-

ing to avail ourselves of such romantic and typhous accommodations, instead of being reconducted down by the tortuous
path of our ascent, we would be shown, through a back door
in the third story, out upon a passage that seemed to be also
used as a public street (footway), doors opening from it, which
were evidently entrances to residences in the rear.

Finally we were suited; and now I am writing on an old
oak table, with spiral legs, sitting in an old oak chair, with an
Elizabethan carved back, my feet on an old oak floor (rather
wavy), stout old oak beams over my head, and low walls of old
oak wainscot all around me. Resting on an old oak bench by
the window, is a young man with a broad-brimmed felt hat,
slouched half over his face. Across the street, so near we might
jump into it if we were attacked from the rear, is a house with
the most grotesquely-carved and acutely-pointed gable possible
to be believed real, and not a bit of scene painting, with the
date, "1539," cut in awkward figures over the cockloft window,
high in the apex. For fifteen minutes there has been a regular
"clink, clink," deadening all other sounds but the clash of
sabres against spurs, and distant bugle-calls, as a body of
horsemen are passing in compact columns through the narrow
street, from the castle, out by the north gate, towards *Rowton
Moor.*

To be sure, it is a California and not a Cavalier sombrero
that shades my friend, and the men of war outside are gentle
yeomen, carrying percussion-lock carbines indeed, but who
have fought for nothing so valiantly as for the corn laws. But
when shall I again get as near as this to *Prince* Charlie or the
Ironsides? At least, there will be no prompter's bell summon-
ing carpenters to slide off the picture. That 1539 over the way
is TRUE; I can see the sun shine into the figures. Away with
1850! *What, ho! a cup of sack!*

The house is full of most unexplainable passages and
unaccountable recesses, of great low rooms and little high
rooms, with ceilings in various angles to the walls, and the
floor of every one at a different elevation from every other, so
that from the same landing you step up into one and down
into another, and so on. Back of a little kitchen and big
pantry, down stairs, we have another parlor. In it is a grand

old chimney, and opposite the fireplace a window, the only one in the room. It is but three feet high, but, except the room occupied by a glass *buffet* in one corner and a turned-up round-table in the other, reaches from wall to wall. To look out of it, you step on to a platform, about four feet broad, in front of it, and on this is an old, long, highbacked *settee.*

As I lay in bed last night, I counted against the moon seventy-five panes of glass in the single window of our sleeping apartment. The largest of them was four by three, and the smallest three by one inches. They are set in lead sashes, and the outer frame is of iron, opening on hinges.

There are none but timber houses all about us; the walls white or yellow, and the timbers black. The roofs are often as steep as forty-five degrees with the horizon, and the gables always front on the street. If the house is large there will be several gables, and each successive story juts out, overhanging the face of that below. There is no finical vergeboard, or flimsy "drapery" in the gable, but the outermost rafter (a stout beam that you cannot fear will warp off or blow away) is boldly projected, and your attention perhaps invited to it by carving. Porches, bow-windows, dormers, galleries (in the rows), and all the prominent features of the building, are generally more or less rudely carved. One house near us is completely covered with figures. C. says they represent Bible scenes. There is one compartment which he understands to be a tableau of the sacrifice of Isaac, Abraham being represented, according to his exegesis, by a bearded figure, dressed in a long flapped waistcoat and kneebreeches.

Another house has these words cut in the principal horizontal beam: *"God's Providence is mine Inheritance—1652."* It is said the family residing in it was the only one in the city that entirely escaped the great plague of that year.

We cannot keep still, but run about with boyish excitement. We feel indeed like children that have come back to visit the paternal house, and who are rummaging about in the garret among their father's playthings, ever and anon shouting, "See what I've found! see what I've found!" If we had been brought here blindfolded from America, and were now, after two days' visit, sent back again, we should feel well repaid for the long sea passage. If we were to stay here a month, we should scarcely enjoy less than we now do, rambling about among these relics of our old England.*

Going into an eating-house, the first afternoon we were in Chester, we were shown through three apartments into a kitchen, and from that into a long, narrow, irregularly-shaped room, with one little window high above our heads, and twenty-seven old wood engravings in frames about the walls. When we were ready to leave, a back door was opened, and we were told that the first opening to the left would bring us to the street. We found ourselves in one of the narrow covered ways, and instead of turning off to the street as directed, kept on in it, to go where it should happen to lead. Sometimes wide, sometimes narrow, running first, as it appeared, between a man's kitchen and his dining room; then into a dust-yard; then suddenly narrowed, and turned one side by a stable; then opening into a yard, across which a woman over a wash-tub was scolding her husband—sitting with a baby and smoking at a window; then through a black-smith's shop into a dark, crooked passage, like the gallery of a mine, at the other end of which we found ourselves on a paved street not far from the cathedral.

We entered the burying-ground, and seeing that a small door, that is cut in the large door of the cathedral, was ajar, pushed it open and went in. It was dark, silent, and chill. We felt strangely as we groped our way over the unobstructed

* Some months later than this we were at a supper party, after some old English ballads and songs had been sung, when one of the company apologized for it, saying, "We forget our American friends. It is selfish in us to sing only these national songs, in which we are peculiarly interested. Have you nothing American, now?" "Excuse me, sir," I replied, "those are our national songs as much as yours. You forget that we are also countrymen of Shakespeare, and Robin Hood, and Richard the Lion-hearted. Our mothers danced with your fathers under that same 'green-wood,' and around the 'May-pole.' Our fathers fought for their right in this land against Turk, Frenchman, Spaniard, and Pretender. We have as much pride in Old England, gentlemen, as any of you. We claim the right to make ourselves *at home* on that ground with you." "You are right; you are welcome. Give us your hand." And the whole table rose, shaking our hands with an enthusiasm that only patriotic pride will excuse among Englishmen.

stone floor, and could make nothing of it until, our eyes becoming adapted to the dimness, we discovered gilded organ-pipes, and were going towards them, when a small door in front of us was opened, and a man came out, saying impatiently, "Who are you? what do you want? Take off your hats."

"We are strangers, looking at the cathedral."

"Can't see it, now; can't see it, now. Service every day at four and ten o'clock."

As we were going out, a great bell began to toll. "What is that, sir?" said I.

"What?"

"That bell tolling—what is it for?"

"Why, that's the cuffew," and he closed and bolted the door, while we stood still without; and as the long waving boom of the bell pulsed through us, looked soberly at each other, as if America and the nineteenth century were a fading dream, slowly repeating—

"The cuffew;—to be sure—yes—the curfew."

CHAPTER XV

Chester Market—The Town Common—Race-Course—The
Yeomanry Cavalry, and the Militia of England—Public
Wash-House

THE DAY AFTER we came to Chester was market-day, and the
streets were busy at an early hour wth people coming in from
the country to sell produce, or purchase the supplies for their
families for the coming week. The quantity of butter exposed
for sale was very large, and the quality excellent. The fish-
market also was finely supplied. The dealing in both these
articles was mostly done by women.*

After walking through the market, we went to the
Roodee, and there saw the Yeomanry reviewed. They wore a
snug blue uniform, were armed with sabres, carbines, and
pistols, and were rather better mounted and drilled than any
of our mounted militia that I have seen. The active com-
mander seemed to be a regular martinet. If the lines got much
out of dress while on the trot, he would dash up, shaking his

* We noted the following as the common prices:
        Butchers' meat, 10   to 14 cents per lb.
        Best fresh butter in balls of 1½ lbs, 35 cents.
        Salmon, fresh from the Dee, 35 cents per lb.
        Turbot; 35 cents per lb.
        Soles and other fish, 16 cents per lb.

fist, and loudly cursing the squadron at fault. I noticed, also, that when pleased, he sometimes addressed them in the ranks as "gentlemen." He was probably some old army officer, engaged to drill them. The colonel of the regiment, who was constantly on the ground every day while we were at Chester, is Lord Grosvenor, heir to one of the largest estates in England. A young man in the dress of an officer, but dismounted, informed us that their number was 800, in five companies. Most of them were farmers; every farmer of a certain age in the county (as we understood him) being obliged to serve three years, but allowed to send a substitute if he chooses. They are out but once a year for training, and then continuously for eight days, and while engaged received 75 cents a day. They cannot be ordered out of the country, and are seldom called into active service, except to quell riots.

I frequently asked afterwards for more information about the yeomanry, but never found a person who seemed to know much about them. A man in the ranks of the Denbigshire yeomanry, told us the service was optional. In some counties there is no such body, and the organization, laws, and customs of it seem to vary in the different regiments. There is a regular foot-militia organization throughout England (the "train-bands"), but none of them, I believe, have been paraded for many years.

According to a parliamentary return of 1838, there were then of the mounted yeomanry 251 troops, numbering 13,594 privates; the annual expense of maintaining them was $525,-000. The enrolled militia of England in 1838 numbered 200,-000 men. The officers of these forces, when in service, rank with those of the army of the same grade. A part of the uniform and mountings of the yeomanry are paid for by the government, and some small daily compensation is allowed the privates when in service. A drill-sergeant and a trumpeter is also permanently attached to each troop, with a salary from the state.

Napier mentions that the greater part of the 16,000 British troops who gained the battle of Talavera, were men drafted from the militia at home, and that they had but very recently joined the army in Spain.

Coming up from the Roodee, we visited the Castle. It is of no importance in a military way, except as a depôt. There are 30,000 stand of arms and a large quantity of gunpowder stored in it. It is garrisoned by an Irish regiment at present, which, as well as the yeomanry, has a very good band of music, by which the town benefits.

We afterwards visited the public baths and wash-house. In its basement there are twenty square tubs, each with hot and cold water cocks, wash-board, and pounder, a drying-closet heated by steam to 212° F., etc. In the first story are the usual private baths, and a swimming tank or public bath, having a constant influx of fresh water by a jet from below, and an overflow. It is 45 by 36 feet, 2½ feet deep at one end, 6 at the other, contains 36,000 gallons, and is furnished with swings, diving-stage, life-buoys, etc. It was built by a committee of the citizens, and bought by the town very soon after it went into operation. The whole cost was $10,000, most of which was raised by a stock subscription. The water is supplied from the canal, and is all filtered—the cost of the filtering machine being $200. The principal items of current expenses are fuel and salaries. The cost of coal (very low here) is $5 a week. There are four persons constantly employed in the establishment, viz: superintendent and wife, who are paid $10 a week, and receive something besides as perquisites, (supplying bathing-dresses, for instance, at a small charge;) the bath-attendant, and the fireman, who each have $7.50 a week. Total salaries $25 a week. The charges for the use of the clothes-washing conveniences is about one cent an hour. For the baths, it varies from two to twenty-five cents, certain hours being appointed for those who choose, by paying a larger sum, to avoid a crowd. There are also commutations by the year, at lower rates: boys, for instance, have a yearly ticket for about a dollar. During the first year it has something more than paid expenses. The number of bathers the last week (in May) was over one thousand. I give these statistics, as this establishment is rather smaller than most of the kind, and they may serve the projectors of a similar one in some of our smaller cities.

CHAPTER XVI

Visit to Eaton Hall—The Largest Arch in the World—
The Outer Park—Backwoods Farming—The Deer Park—
The Hall—The Parterre—The Lawn—The Fruit
Garden—Stables

In the afternoon we walked to Eaton Park.

Probably there is no object of art that Americans of cultivated taste more generally long to see in Europe, than an
English park. What artist, so noble, has often been my
thought, as he who, with far-reaching conception of beauty
and designing power, sketches the outline, writes the colors,
and directs the shadows of a picture so great that Nature shall
be employed upon it for generations, before the work he has
arranged for her shall realize his intentions.

Eaton Hall and Park is *one* of the seats of the Marquis of
Westminster, a very wealthy nobleman, who has lately been
named "Lord High Chamberlain to her Majesty," a kind of
state-housekeeper or steward, I take it—an office which Punch,
and a common report of a niggardly disposition in his private
affairs, deems him particularly well fitted for.

We left town by the new, or Grosvenor bridge—a simple,
grand, and every way excellent work, crossing the Dee by a
single arch, which we are told is the largest in the world. It is
entirely free from decoration, and the effect of it, as seen look-

ing from the river side, imposing. It was built by the Marquis, whose family name is Grosvenor, at a cost of $180,000 (£36,-000). The designer was Thomas Harrison, an architect of note, who formerly lived in Chester.*

By the side of the road we found an oratory, or small chapel, building, and gardeners laying out grounds for a rural cemetery. Beyond this we came to the great castellated edifice that I have before spoken of, as the gateway to the park. Such we were told it was, and were therefore surprised to find within only a long, straight road, with but tolerable mowing lots alternating by the side of it with thick plantations of trees, differing little from the twenty-year old natural wood of my own farm, except that hollies, laurels, and our common dog-wood, were planted regularly along the edge. After awhile we pushed into this wood, to see if we could not scare up the deer. We soon saw daylight on the outside, and about twelve rods from the road, came to an open field, separated from the wood only by a common Yankee three-rail fence, which I had not expected to see in England; very poor it was, too.

A stout boy, leaning heavily on the stilts, was plowing stubble-ground. We jumped over and asked what crop the ground was preparing for. The horses stopped of their own accord when we spoke. The boy turned and sat upon the stilts-brace, and then answered—"Erdnow."

The same answer, or some other sounds that we could not guess the meaning of, followed several other questions. The plow had a wooden beam, bound round with hoop iron. The horses seemed to be worn-out hacks; the harness was mended with bits of rope; the furrows were crooked and badly turned. Altogether, a more unfarmer-like turn-out, and a worse piece of work, I never saw in our own backwoods. When we last saw the plowman, he had taken off his woollen cap and seemed about lighting a pipe, and the horses were beginning to nibble at the stubble, which stuck up in tufts all over the plowed

* The main arch spans two hundred feet, and its height is forty feet, and there are two dry arches, each twenty feet wide and forty feet high. From the surface of the water to the road is over sixty feet. The parapet walls are three hundred and fifty feet long, with a carriage-way and foot-path between, of thirty feet.

ground. In getting back to the road, we crossed a low spot, sinking ankle deep in mire, and noticed several trees not eight inches thick, which showed signs of decay.

We tramped on for several miles, I think, through this tame scenery and most ungentlemanly farming, until it became really tiresome. At length the wood fell back, and the road was lined for some way with a double row of fine elms. Still no deer. A little further, and we came to a cottage beautifully draped with ivy, and passed through another gate. Ah! here is the real park at last.

A gently undulating surface of close-cropped pasture land, reaching way off illimitably; very old, but not very large trees scattered singly and in groups—so far apart as to throw long unbroken shadows across broad openings of light, and leave the view in several directions unobstructed for a long distance. Herds of fallow-deer, fawns, cattle, sheep, and lambs quietly feeding near us, and moving slowly in masses at a distance; a warm atmosphere, descending sun, and sublime shadows from fleecy clouds transiently darkening in succession, sunny surface, cool woodside, flocks and herds, and foliage.

The road ran on winding through this. We drew a long breath, and walked slowly for a little way, then turned aside at the nearest tree, and lay down to take it all in satisfactorily. Then we arose and went among the deer. They were small and lean, all with their heads down feeding. Among them was one pure white fawn; none had antlers, or more than mere prongs. They seemed to be quite as tame as the sheep; but suddenly, as we came still nearer, all, as if one, raised high their heads, and bounded off in a high springing gallop. After going a few rods, one stopped short, and facing about, stood alone, with ears erect, and gleaming eyes, intent upon us. A few rods further, the whole herd halted in mass and stood in the same way, looking at us. One by one the heads again dropped; a fawn stepped out from among them; the one nearest us turned and trotted to it, and then all fell quietly to feeding again.

The sheep were of a large, coarse-wooled variety, some of them nearly as large, only not standing quite so high, as the deer—not handsome at all (as sheep) even for a mutton breed; but in groups at a distance, and against the shadows, far prettier than the deer. The cattle were short-horned, large, dapple-skinned, sleek, and handsome, but not remarkable.

We concluded that the sheep and cattle were of the most value for their effect in the landscape; but it was a little exciting to us to watch the deer, particularly as we would sometimes see them in a large herd leisurely moving across an opening among the trees, a long way off, and barely distinguishable; or still more when one, two, or three, which had been separated from a nearer herd, suddenly started, and dashed wildly by us, within pistol shot.

"I don't think they are as large as our Maine fallow-deer."

"I wonder if they'd taste as good as they did that night."

"Well, I reckon not—no hemlock to toast them over."

"Or to sleep on afterwards, eh!"

"And no wolves to keep you awake."

Following the carriage road, we came near a mass of shrubbery, over and beyond which the trees were closer and taller. It was separated from the deer park by an iron fence. Passing this by another light gate, and between thick underwood, we found ourselves close to the entrance front of the Hall.

> It is considered the most splendid specimen of the pointed Gothic. It consists of a centre and three stories, finished with octagonal turrets, connected with the main part by lofty intermediate towers, the whole enriched by buttresses, niches, and pinnacles, and adorned with elaborately carved heraldic designs, fretwork, and foliage, surmounted throughout by an enriched battlement.

So much from the Guide Book. It is not my business to attempt a criticism of "the finest specimen of the pointed Gothic" in England; but I may honestly say that it did not, as a whole, produce the expected effect upon us, without trying to find reasons for the failure. Even when we came to look at it closely, we found little to admire. There was no great simple beauty in it as a mass, nor yet vigorous original character enough in the details to make them an interesting study. The edifice is long and low, and covered with an immense amount of meaningless decoration.

Such was our first impression, and we were greatly disappointed, you may be sure. We admired it more afterwards on the other side, from the middle of a great garden, where it seems to stand much higher, being set up on terraces, and gaining much, I suspect, from the extension of architectural character to the grounds in its front. Here we acknowledged a good deal of magnificence in its effect. Still it seemed as if it might have been obtained in some other style, with less labor, and to be much frittered away in a confusion of ornament.

This garden is a curiosity. It is in the geometrical style, and covers eight acres, it is said, though it does not seem nearly that to the eye. It is merely a succession of small arabesque figures of fine grass or flower beds, set in hard, rolled, dark-colored gravel. The surface, dropping by long terraces from the steps of the Hall to the river, is otherwise only varied by pyramidal yews and box, and a few vases. On the whole, the effect of it, in connection with the house, and looking towards it, is fine, more so than I should have expected; and it falls so rapidly, that it affects the landscape seen in this direction from the house but little, and, as an enriched foreground, not disagreeably. This landscape is exquisitely beautiful, looking across the Dee, over a lovely valley towards some high, blue mountains. From other parts of the Hall, vistas open through grand avenues of elms; and there are some noble single trees about the lawn.

The English elm is a much finer tree than I had been aware of—very tall, yet with drooping limbs and fine thick foliage; not so fine as a single tree as our elm, but more effective in masses, because thicker and better filled out in its general outline.

The Hall was undergoing extensive alterations and repairs; and all the grounds immediately about it, except the terrace garden, were lumbered up with brick and stone, and masons' sheds, and in complete confusion. Being Saturday, all the workmen had left, and it was long before we could find any one about the house. We had got very thirsty, and considering that such a place would not be left without any tenants, determined that we would get a drink. After hammering for some time at a door under the principal entrance, a woman came and opened it a few inches, and learning our wish,

brought us a glass of water, which she passed out through the
narrow opening, never showing her face. We were amused at
this, which she perceiving, told us the door was chained and
padlocked, so she could not open it wider.

Soon after, while looking for an entrance to the fruit
garden, we met a gamekeeper, who was followed by a pet cub
fox. He very obligingly showed us through such parts of the
establishment as he was able to. There was nothing remarkable in the gardens or glass-houses, except some large and well-
trained fruit trees on walls. Every thing was neglected now,
however, and we did no more than glance at them. There
were some new stables nearly finished, the plans of which I
studied with interest. Each horse is to have a private box. I do
not recollect the exact size, but it is at least twelve feet square
on the floor, and more than that high. In the ceiling is a
ventilator, and in one corner an iron rack for hay (much like
a fire-grate); and there is probably intended to be a small
manger for fine and wet feed. There is a grating for drainage
in the floor, and, besides these, no other fixtures whatever.
The horse is to be left free within the walls.

CHAPTER XVII

Gamekeeper—Game Preserves—Eccleston, a Pretty Village
—The School House—Draining—Children Playing—The
Riverside Walk—Pleasure Parties—A Contrasting
Glimpse of a Sad Heart—Saturday Night—Ballad Singer
—Mendicants—Row in the Tap-room—Woman's Feeble-
ness—Chester Beer, and Beer-drinking

THE GAMEKEEPER ADVISED us to return to Chester by another
road, and following his directions, we found a delightful path
by the river side. We had not gone far before we overtook
another keeper, carrying a gun. It is hard for us to look upon
wild game as property, and it seemed as if the temptation to
poach upon it must be often irresistible to a poor man. It must
have a bad effect upon the moral character of a community for
the law to deal with any man as a criminal for an act which, in
his own conscience, is not deemed sinful. Even this keeper
seemed to look upon poaching as not at all wrong—merely a
trial of adroitness between the poacher and himself, though it
was plain that detection would place the poacher among
common swindlers and thieves, exclude him from the society
of the religious, and from reputable employment, and make
the future support of life by unlawful means almost a necessity. He said, however, there was very little poaching in the
neighborhood. Most of the farmers were allowed to shoot

within certain limits, and the laboring class were generally wanting in either the means or the pluck to attempt it.

Evidently a man has a right to foster and increase the natural stock of wild game upon his own land, that is, in a degree to domesticate it; and the law should protect him in the enjoyment of the results of the labor and pains he has taken for this purpose. The undefinable character of such property, however, makes the attempt to preserve it inexpedient, and often leads to injustice; and when the preserve is sustained at the expense of very great injury to more important means of sustaining human life in a half-starved community, the poacher is more excusable than the proprietor.

That this is often the case in England, I more than once saw evidence. A picture, drawn by the agricultural correspondent of the *London Times* of Nov. 11, 1851, represents a scene of this kind, more remarkable however than any that came under my notice:

"At Stamford we passed into Northamptonshire, obtaining a glimpse of the Marquis of Exeter's finely wooded park and mansion of Burleigh. This magnificent place, founded by Queen Elizabeth's Lord Treasurer Cecil, with its grand old trees and noble park, is just the place to which a foreigner should be taken to give him an idea of the wealth of our English nobility.

"The tenants on this estate are represented as being in the most hopeless state of despondency on account of the present low prices of agricultural produce, and as they were complaining vehemently, the Marquis offered to have the farms of any tenants who desired it, revalued. Only one on this great estate accepted the offer. There have been no farms of any consequence yet given up, and for those which do come into the market there are plenty of offerers, though men of capital are becoming chary, and will only look at very desirable farms. The estate is said to be low-rented. Small farmers, of whom there are many, are suffering most severely, as they have not saved any thing in good times to fall back upon now. Some of them are, indeed, greatly reduced, and we heard of one who had applied to his parish for relief. Others have sold every thing off their farms, and some, we were told, had not even seed corn left with which to sow their fields.

"In a fine country, with a gently undulating surface and a soil dry and easy of culture, laid into large fields moderately rented, one is surprised to hear that there is so much complaint and so much real suffering among the poorer class of farmers. It is only in part accounted for by the devastation of game, which on this and some other noblemen's estates in North Northamptonshire, is still most strictly preserved. On the 24th of January last, seven guns, as we were told, on the Marquis's estate, killed 430 head of game, a most immoderate quantity at such a late period of the season. The fields are all stuck about with bushes to prevent the poachers netting; and the farmers feel most severely the losses they sustain, in order that their landlord and his friends may not be deprived of their sport. The strict preservation of game on this and some other estates in the northern parts of the county, was described to us in the bitterest terms, as 'completely eating up the tenant farmer, and against which no man can farm or live upon the farm.' It is 'the last ounce that breaks the camel's back,' and men who might have made a manful struggle against blighted crops and low prices, are overborne by a burden which they feel to be needlessly inflicted, and of which they dare not openly complain.

"In consequence of the distress among the small farmers, any of the laborers would have been thrown out of employment had work not been found for them by the Marquis in stubbing and clearing woodland, which will thus be reclaimed for cultivation. The improvement is expected to be amply remunerative in the end, and it is one of the unlooked-for results of free trade, which are to be met with in every part of the country, that a landlord is compelled by circumstances, various in kind, to improve the neglected portions of his estate, and which, without such impelling cause, might have long lain unproductive. Every such improvement is not merely an addition to the arable land of the kingdom, but it becomes also an increased source of employment to the laborer."

I witnessed immense injury done to turnip crops by shooting over them, in Scotland. I was once visiting a tenant-farmer

there, when for a whole half day a *"gentleman,"* with three
dogs, was trampling down his Swedes, not once going out of
the field. He was a stranger, having the permission of the
owner of the property to shoot over it, probably, and the
farmer said it would do no good to remonstrate; he would
only be laughed at and insulted.

We passed near a rookery, and the keeper was good
enough to shoot one of the rooks for us to look at. It was a
shorter-winged and rather heavier bird than our crow, with a
larger head and a peculiar thick bill. At a distance the difference would not be readily distinguished. The *caw* was on a
lower note, and more of a parrot tone, much like the guttural
croak of a fledgling crow. The keeper did not confirm the
farmer's statement of their quality for the table. When they
were fat they made a tolerable pie only, he said, not as good as
pigeons. The rookery was, as we have often seen it described, a
collection of crows'-like nests among the tops of some large
trees.

We turned off from the river a little way to look at Eccleston, a village on the border of the park, and one of the
prettiest we saw in England.

The cottages were nearly all of the timber and *noggin*
walls I have described as common at Chester, covered with
thick thatched roofs, with frequent and different-sized dormers, often with bow-windows, porches, well-houses, etc., of
unpainted oak or of rustic work (boughs of trees with the bark
on), broad latticed windows opening on hinges, a profusion of
creeping vines on trellises, and often covering all the walls and
hanging down over the windows, little flower-gardens full of
roses, and wallflowers, and violets, and mignonette, enclosed
in front by a closely trimmed hedge of yew, holly, or hawthorn, sometimes of both the latter together, and a nicely-
sloped bank of turf between it and the road. I made a sketch
of one of them. An intelligent laboring man talked with me
while I was drawing it, and said it was the residence of the
schoolmaster, and the village school was kept in it. The main
part (which was covered with our Virginia creeper) was over
three hundred years old; a part of the wing was modern.

This laborer had been digging drains in the vicinity. He

said the practice was to make them from 18 to 36 inches deep, and from 5 to 7 yards apart, or "in the old *buts*"—"The *buts?*" "Ay, the buts." He meant what we sometimes call the "*'bouts*" (turnabouts) or furrows between the *lands* in plowing, which here are often kept unaltered for generations for surface drainage, and, oddly enough, considering the many manifest inconveniences of retaining them, as we were often told, on account of the convenience of measuring or dividing fields by them, (as our farmers are often guided in their sowing by the *lands*, and estimate areas by counting the panels of fence.) Tiles, such as are being now introduced with us, an inch or an inch and a half in diameter (without collars), were laid in the drains to conduct the water. The usual crop of potatoes in the vicinity he thought about three *measures* to a rood, or 225 bushels to an acre; of wheat, 30 bushels.

We went into a stylish inn to get some refreshment, and while waiting for it, watched some little girls playing in the street. They stood, four holding hands, dancing and singing round one ("Dobbin") lying on the ground:

> *"Old Dobbin is dead,*
> *Ay, ay;*
> *Dobbin is dead,*
> *He's laid in his bed,*
> *Ay, ay.*
>
> *There let him lie,*
> *Ay, ay;*
> *Keep watch for his eye.*
> *For if he gets up*
> *He'll eat us all* UP—"

and away they scampered and Dobbin after them. The one he first catches lays down again for "Dobbin," when it is repeated.

The Church was a little to one side of the village on an elevation, and so hidden by trees that we only saw a square tower and vane. Near it a neat stone building, I thought likely to be the parsonage, and pointing towards it soon after, asked a man who lived in it? His reply was, "Why, there's none but poor peoples' houses there, sir!" The vicarage he showed us in another direction—a fine house in spacious grounds.

From Eccleston we had a delightful walk in the evening to Chester. There is a good foot-path for miles along the river bank, with gates or stiles at all the fences that run down to it, and we met great numbers of persons, who generally seemed walking for pleasure. There were pleasure boats, too, with parties of ladies under awnings, rowing up and down the river, sometimes with music.

We were stopped by some laboring people going home, who asked us to look after a poor woman we should see sitting by the water side over the next stile, who, they feared, had been unfortunate, and was going to drown herself. She had been there for an hour, and they had been for some time trying to prevail on her to get up and go home, but she would not reply to them. We found her as they had said—a tall, thin woman, without hat or cap on her head, sitting under the bank behind some bushes, a little bundle in a handkerchief on her knees, her head thrown forward resting upon it, her hands clasped over her forehead, and looking moodily into the dark stream. We drew back and sat on the stile, where we could see if she stepped into the water. In a few minutes she arose, and avoiding to turn her face towards us, walked rapidly towards the town. We followed her until she was lost in a crowd near the gate.

We found the streets within the walls all flaring with gas light, and crowded with hawkers and hucksters with donkey carts, soldiers, and policemen, and laboring men and women making purchases with their week's earnings, which, until lately, it has been a universal custom in England to pay on Saturday night. We heard a ballad-monger singing with a drawling, nasal tone, on a high key, and listened for awhile to see what he had. One after another he would hold them up by a gas light, and sing them. The greater number were protection songs, with "free trade" and "ruin" oft repeated, and were the worst kind of doggerel. One (sung to "Oh, Susannah!") I recollect, as follows:

> *"Oh, poor farmers,*
>   *Don't wait and cry in vain,*
>   *But be off to Californy,*
>   *If you cannot drive the wain."*

He read also choice scraps from confessions of murderers; parts of the prayer-book travestied so as to tell against free trade; and other such literature. In another place we found a crowd about a man with a flute, a woman with a hurdy-gurdy, and three little children singing what we guessed must be Welsh songs—regular wails. The youngest was a boy, not appearing to be over five years old, and was all but naked.

In front of our inn a man held in his arms a fine, well-dressed little boy, and cried in a high, loud, measured, monotonous drawl, continuously over and over—"His mother died in Carlisle we have traveled twenty-seven miles today I have no money she left this boy yesterday he walked eighteen miles I have no supper he is five years old I have walked two hundred miles this is no deception I have seen better days friends his feet are lacerated I am in search of work I am young and strong he cannot walk his mother died in Carlisle help me in my lamentations I have but sixpence for myself and boy friends I am compelled to beg I am young and strong his mother died in Carlisle I am in search of work his feet are lacerated"—and so on. We watched him from the rows perhaps two minutes, and saw seven persons drop coppers into his hat: two little girls whom a man was leading, a boy, a German lace-peddler, a woman with a basket of linen on her head, another woman, and a well-dressed man.

The rest of the evening we sat round a bright coal fire, in what had been the great fireplace of the long back parlor. We are the only inmates of the inn except Mrs. Jones, the landlady, and her maid. About eleven o'clock we were disturbed by some riotous men in the tap-room, which is the other side of the big chimney. Mrs. Jones seemed trying to prevail on them to leave the house, which they refused to do, singing, "We won't go home till morning." Mrs. Jones is a little, quiet, meek, soft-spoken woman, and we were apprehensive for her safety. I was about to go to her assistance, when the maid entered and said, "If you please, sir, my mistress would like to see you." I went hastily round into the tap-room, and found two stout, dirty, drunken men, swinging pewter mugs, and trying to sing "There was a jolly collier." Mrs. Jones stood between them. I pushed one of them aside, and asked her what she wished—expecting that she would want me to try to put him into the street. The men made such a noise that I could not hear her mild voice in reply, which, she perceiving, turned again and said, in a tone that at once quelled them, "Stop your noise, you brutes!"—and then to me, "will you please step into the kitchen, sir?" She only wished to know what we would like to have for our breakfast and dinner, as the shops would close soon, and, tomorrow being Sunday, they would not be open before noon.

The next morning, when we were going out, she came to unlock the door of the passage or entry, and told us she was obliged by law to keep it locked till two o'clock. At two o'clock we found it open, and immediately after saw a man drinking beer in the tap-room again.

There is a continual and universal beer-drinking in Chester. Mrs. Jones tells us that the quality of the beer made here has long been a matter of town pride, though now there is very little brewed in families, every one almost being supplied, at a great saving of trouble, from the large breweries. She says there used to be a town law that whoever brewed poor beer should be publicly ducked. Sunday night, young men with their sweethearts and sisters, of reputable appearance, and quiet, decent behavior, came into our back parlor, and sitting by the round-table, ordered and drank each their glass or two of beer, as in an American town they would take ice-cream. Now and then a few remarks would be made about the sermon and who had been at church, or about those who had been, or were soon going to be, married, or other town gossip; but for the most, they would sit and drink their beer in silence.

CHAPTER XVIII

Character of the Welsh—The Cathedral: The Clergy,
Service, Intoning, the Ludicrous and the Sublime—A Re-
verie—A Revelation—The Sermon—Communions—Other
Churches—Sunday Evening—Character of the
Townspeople

Sunday, June 2d

WE WERE AWAKENED this morning by a sweet chiming of the
cathedral bells.

After breakfast, Mrs. Jones introduced us to a young
Welsh woman, who had come to visit her. She was intelligent
and handsome, having a clear, though dark complexion, thick,
dark hair, and large eyes. This style of beauty seems common
hereabouts, and is, I judge, the Welsh type.

She lived among the mountains near Snowdon, and told
us the country there was bleak and sterile, and agriculture
confined mostly to grazing. She spoke highly of the character
of the peasantry in many respects, but said they had strong
prejudices, usually despising the English and refusing to associate with them. Many of them could not speak English, and
those who could would often affect not to understand, if they
were addressed by an Englishman. Among themselves they
were neighborly, clannish, honest, and generous, but strangers

they would impose upon shamelessly. She had known very few to emigrate, and those that did usually went to Australia. In her neighborhood they were mostly dissenters—Methodists and Baptists, and, with the exception of deceit to strangers, were of much better character than the English laborers. They had, however, many traditional superstitions.

We attended service in the morning at the cathedral. The comparative lowness and depth of its walls, strengthened by thick, rude buttresses, and its short, square massive tower, together with its general time-worn aspect, impressed me much as an expression of enduring, self-sustaining age. Like the stalwart trunk of a very old oak, stripped by the tempests of much of the burden of its over-luxuriant youth, its settled, compact, ungarnished grandeur, was much more imposing than the feeble grace and pliant luxuriance of many more celebrated structures. The raggedness of outline, the wrinkles and furrows and scars upon the face of all the old masonry, are very remarkable. The mortar has all fallen from the outside, and the edges of the stones are worn off deeply, but irregularly, as they vary in texture or are differently exposed. The effect of rain and snow and frost, and mossy vegetation and coal smoke, for six hundred years upon the surface, I know of no building in America that would give you an idea of. The material of construction is a brown stone, originally lighter than our Portland sandstone, but now darker than I have ever seen that become. It has had various repairs at long intervals of time, and is consequently in various stages of approach to ruin—some small parts, not noticeable in a cursory view, being in complete and irreparable demolishment, and others but yesterday restored to their original lines and angles, with clean-cut, bright-colored stone and mortar—bad blotches, but fortunately not prominent.

It was once connected with an abbey, and other religious houses that stood near it, and by the long under-ground passage with the nunnery at the other side of the town. Think of the poor girls walking, with a wailing chant through that mile of darkness, to morning service at the cathedral!

Our approach to it this morning was by a something less gloomy and tedious way. We were accidentally in an alley in the vicinity, when we saw a gentleman in a white gown, and a square or university cap on his head, with a lady on his arm, enter an old, arched, and groined passage. We followed him adventurously, not being sure that it was not the entrance to his residence. After passing to the rear of the block of buildings that fronted on the alley, we found ourselves in a kind of gallery or covered promenade attached to the outside of the cathedral. (The cloisters.) From this we passed into the nave (or long arm of the cross). Its length, its broad, flat stone floor, entirely free from obstruction, except by a row of thick clustered columns near the sides, and the great height and darkness of its oak-ceiled roof, produced a sensation entirely new to us. Its dignity was increased by a general dimness, and by the breadth of the softened, colored light, that flowed in one sheet through a very large stained-glass window at one end. In the end opposite this were wide piers that support the tower, and between the two central ones of these were the gilded organ-pipes that we had seen in our nocturnal visit.

Under these was an arched door, on each side of which stood about thirty boys, from ten to fifteen years old, dressed in white robes—the "singing boys," or "choristers." Walking leisurely up and down the otherwise vacant floor of the nave, were "my Lord Bishop of Bath and Wells" (I believe that is the title), the dean and canons, etc.; a squad of ecclesiastical dignitaries, whose very titles were strange to me, but altogether forming, what Mrs. Jones said we should see, "a very pretty pack of priests." The bishop was a thin man, with an insignificant face, and crisp hair brushed back from his forehead, dressed in a black gown with white lawn sleeves, and a cap on his head. The dean, a burly man, strikingly contrasting with the bishop, particularly when they laughed, in white gown with a sort of bag of scarlet silk, perhaps a degenerate cowl, tied around his neck, and dangling by strings down his back. The others had something of the same sort, of different colors. We were told afterwards, that these were university badges, and that the color was a mark of rank, not in university honors, but in the scale of society—as nobleman or commoner—(a pretty thing to carry into the worship of the Father, is it not?) The others were in black.

We walked about for a few minutes outside the columns, reading the inscriptions on the stones of the floor, which showed that they covered vaults for the dead, and looking at the tablets and monumental effigies that were attached to the walls and columns. They were mostly of elaborate heraldic design, many with military insignia, and nearly all excessively ugly and inappropriate to a place of religious meditation and worship.

After a while the great bell ceased tolling, and some men in black serge loose gowns, two bearing maces of steel with silver cups on the ends, the rest carrying black rods, entered the saluted the bishop. A procession then formed, headed by the boys, in double file, followed by the bishop, dean, sub-dean, canons major and minor, archdeacon, prebendaries, etc., and closed by three Yankees in plain clothes; passed between the "vergers," who bowed reverently and presented arms, through the door under the organ into the choir—a part of the edifice (in the centre of the cross) which is fitted up inconveniently for public worship.

It is a small, narrow apartment, having galleries, the occupants of which are hidden behind a beautiful open-work carved wood screen, and furnished below with three or four tiers of pews and a few benches. Under the organ loft were elevated armed seats, which were occupied indiscriminately by the unofficiating clergy and military officers in uniform; the governor of the castle; Lord Grosvenor (as "colonel of the militia"), Lord de Tapley, and others. Stationing soldiers among the canons, it struck us, was well enough for a joke, but objectionable as part of a display of worshiping the God of Peace.*

Half way between these elevated seats and the chancel was the reading desk and pulpit, and on each side of this the

---

* I remember when I was a child, seeing on the Sunday preceding the first Monday in May—the annual *training day*—in one of the most old-fashioned villages in Connecticut, the officers of the militia come into the meeting-house in their uniforms. The leader of the choir was a corporal, and the red stripes on his pantaloons, the red facings and bell-buttons of his coat, as he stood up alone and pitched the psalm tunes, was impressed irretrievably on my mind.

choristers were seated. Several persons rose to offer us their seats as we approached them, and when we were seated, placed prayerbooks before us. The pews were all furnished with foot-stools, or hassocks of straw rope, made up in the manner of a straw beehive.

Much of the service, which in our churches is read, was sung, or, as they say, *intoned*. Intoning is what, in school-children, is called *"sing-song"* reading, only the worse kind, or an exaggerated sing-song. I had never heard it before in reli-gious service, except in a mitigated way from some of the old-fashioned Quaker and Methodist female exhorters, and I was surprised to hear it among the higher class of English clergy, and for a moment perplexed to account for it. But I remem-bered that nearly all men, in reading Scripture, or in oral prayer, or in almost any public religious exercises, use a very different tone and mode of utterance from that which is usual or natural with them, either in conversation or in ordinary reading. And this is more noticeable in persons of unculti-vated minds; so it is probably an impulse to distinguish and disassociate religious exercises from the common duties of life, that induces it. The effect is, that the reading of the Bible, for instance, instead of being a study of truth, or an excitement to devotion and duty, as the individual may intend, becomes an *act of praise* or prayer—the real, unconscious purpose of the reader finding expression in his tone and manner. So we may often hear the most arrant nonsense in oral prayers; a string-ing together of scriptural phrases and devout words in confus-ing and contradicting sentences, while the tone and gesture and the whole manner of the devotee show that he is most sincerely, feelingly, enthusiastically in earnest supplication. What for? Not for that which his words express, for they may express utter blasphemy, as in fact, it seems to me, they gen-erally do. It is simply an expression or manifestation by the act of uttering words in a supplicating tone—of the sense of dependence on a superior being—of love, of gratitude, and of reverence. David did the same thing by dancing and playing upon the harp. It is done now, as it seems to us, more solemnly in playing upon church organs. It is done by monuments, and in the decorations of churches. It is done by the Catholics, in listening and responding to prayers in a language which they don't pretend to understand, and in mechanically repeating others, the number of them counted by beads, measuring the importance or intensity of their purpose. It is done by abstaining from meat on Friday, and by confession to one another, in the form prescribed by their church government. It is done by the Japanese, in twirling a teetotum; by the Chinese, in burning Joss-sticks; by the Fakirs, in standing on one leg; by the Methodists, in groans and inarticulate cries; by the Shakers, in their dance; by the Baptists, in ice-water immersions; by Churchmen, in kneeling; by Presbyterians, in standing; by New Englanders, in eating a cold dinner and regularly going to meeting on Sunday; by the English, in feasting; and the Germans, in social intercourse on that day, as well as by more distinctly devout exercises.

It was plain to me that the tone of the reader was meant to express—"Note ye that this reading is no common reading, but is the word derived from God, not now repeated for your instruction, plainly and with its true emphasis, but markedly otherwise, that we may show our faith in its sacred character, and through it acknowledge our God; I by repeating its words, as men do not those of another book—you by your presence and reverent silence while I do so."

It was evident, too, by the occasional difficulties and consequent embarrassment and confusion of our reader, causing blushing and stammering, that it was not with him a natural expression of this purpose, as was the nasal tone of the Puritan, but a studied form, which had originated in some person more musically constituted.

Whether I was right with regard to the theory or not, there was no room for doubt that, practically, such was the operation of much of the service. The portion of the Old Testament read was one of those tedious genealogical registers that nobody but an antiquary or a blood nobleman would pretend to be interested in. The psalm, one of the most fearful of David's songs of vengeance and imprecation, alternately sung by the choristers and intoned by the reader, one often running into the other with most unpleasant discord. The same with the Litany. Even the prayers could with difficulty be understood, owing partly to echoes, in which all distinctness was lost.

Despairing of being assisted by the words of the service, I endeavored to "work up" in myself the solemnity and awe which seemed due to the place and the occasion, by appropriate reflections. Under this vaulted ceiling, what holy thoughts, what heavenly aspirations, have been kindled—what true praise of noble resolution has, like unconscious incense, grateful to God, ascended from these seats! On these venerable walls, for hundreds of years, have the eyes of good men rested, as from their firm and untottering consistency they gained new strength and courage to fight the good fight,—and again I raised *my* eyes to catch communion with them. They fell upon a most infamous countenance, like to the representations of Falstaff's—a man with one eye closed and his tongue tucked out the side of his mouth—his body tied up in a sack, his knees being brought upon each side of his chin to make a snugger bundle. I turned away from it immediately; but there was another face in doleful grimace, as if a man who had been buried alive had suddenly thrust his head out of his coffin, and was greatly perplexed and dismayed at his situation. Again I turned my eyes—they fell upon the face of a woman under the influence of an emetic; again, upon a woman with the grin of drunkenness. Everywhere that any thing like a boss would be appropriate to the architecture, were faces sculptured on the walls that would be capital in a comic almanac.

I closed my eyes again, and tried to bring my mind to a reverent mood, but the more I tried the more difficult I found it. My imagination was taken possession of by the funny things, and refused to search out the sublime. Not but that the sublime, the grand, and the awful were not apparent also, all over and around—ay, and consciously within me; but, like a stubborn child, my mind would resist force. I gave it up, envying those who would have been so naturally elevated by all these incitements and aids to devotion.

I could not understand a sentence of the service, but sat, and rose, and kneeled; thus only being able to join in the prayer, and praise, and communion of the congregation.

Soon my thoughts, now wandering freely, fell to moving

in those directions of reverie that I have found they are apt to take when I am hearing what those who listen with critical ear shall call fine music: doubtless it is the best and truest that can effect this. I had been wandering in a deep, sad day-dream, far away, beyond the ocean—beyond the earth . . . dark—lost to remembrance—when I was of a sudden brought back and awakened again, in the dim old cathedral, with such emotion, as if from eternity and infinity, I was remanded to mysterious identity and sense of time, that I choked and throbbed; and then, as the richest, deepest melody I must ever have heard passed away, softly swelling through the vaulted ceiling, caught up tenderly by mild echoes in the nave, and again and again faintly returning from its deepest distances, I kneeled and bowed my head with the worshipers around me, acknowledging in all my heart the beauty and sublimity of the place and the services.

The sermon was from an elderly man, with a voice slightly broken, and an impressive manner, whom we were afterwards told was Canon Slade, a somewhat distinguished divine. It was one of the best, plain, practical, Christ-like discourses I ever heard from a pulpit. It was delivered with emphasis and animation, in a natural, sometimes almost conversational tone, directly to *individuals,* high and low, then and there present, and of course was listened to with respectful attention. The main drift of it was to enforce the idea, that a knowledge of the truth of God was never to be arrived at by mere learning and dry study; that these were sometimes rather encumbrances; that love was of more value than learning. He had been describing the Pharisees of old, and concluded by saying, that the Pharisees, satisfied with their own notions, and scorning new light, were not scarce in our day. "There are some of them in our Church of England: would that there were fewer; that there were less parade and more reality of heavenly knowledge." He made but little use of his notes, and pronounced an extemporaneous prayer at the conclusion with extreme solemnity.

I remained in company with a large proportion of the women present, and half a dozen men, at the communion service. The Church of England service, which has always

seemed to me more effective than most others to the practical
end of the ceremony, never was so solemn, impressive, and
affecting. It was administered by the bishop, unassisted, with
great feeling and simplicity. There was not the least unnecessary parade or affectation of sanctity; but a low, earnest voice,
and a quiet, unprofessional manner, that betokened a sense
of the common brotherhood of us all "united by God in
Christ." The singing was "congregational," the choristers having left, and without assistance from the organ.

A considerable proportion of the congregation were servants in livery; and besides these and the soldiers and clergy,
the men present were generally plainly, and many shabbily,
dressed. The women, many of them, seemed of a higher class,
but were also simply dressed, generally in dark calicoes.

In the south transept (or short arm of the cross) of the
cathedral another congregation were assembling as I came out.
I followed in a company of boys, marching like soldiers,
dressed in long-skirted blue coats, long waistcoats, breeches,
and stockings, and with the clerical bands from their cravats.
Within were several other such companies—boys and girls in
uniform, from charity schools, I suppose. The girls were
dressed in the fashion of Goody Two-Shoes, with high-backed
white caps, and white "pinafores" over blue check gowns.

This transept is a large place of worship in itself, though
but a small part of the cathedral, and is occupied by the
parish of St. Oswald—morning and evening service being held
in it immediately after that of the cathedral church. On the
doors were notices, posted in placards, addressed to persons in
certain circumstances—among others, to all who used hair-
powder—to give notice to the appointed officers, that they
might be rightfully taxed.

In the afternoon we visited a Sunday-school of the Uni-
tarians, where we saw about sixty well-behaved children—
the exercises much the same as in ours. Afterwards we heard a
sensible sermon in the Independent chapel. The clergyman,
who has been a missionary in the East, and has also traveled in
America, was good enough to call on us and invite us to his
house the next day. The congregation seemed to be of a higher
grade than most of that we had seen at the cathedral—more

intelligent and animated, and more carefully dressed, yet very much plainer, more modestly and becomingly, and far less expensively, than you could often see any congregation with us.

We had a delightful walk, later in the afternoon, on the walls, where we met a very large number of apparently very happy people. I never saw so many neat, quiet, ungenteel, happy, and healthy-looking women, all in plain clean dresses, and conversing in mild, pleasant tones; hundreds of children, too, dressed ridiculously bright and clean and stiff, not a dirty one among them, and as well behaved as dolls, comically sober and stately. The walls form a good promenade, elevated and dry. The landscape view across the river, in the sunset haze, seemed in communion with the minds of the people, tranquil and loving. An hour later, and we found the streets lighted up and almost as crowded as on Saturday night, yet very quiet, and no impudence, black-guardism, or indecency. On the whole, spite of the universal beer-drinking, we obtained a high opinion of the character of Chester people, quite as high in respect to morality and courtesy at least, as a stranger passing a Sunday in a New England town of the same size would be likely to form of its inhabitants.

CHAPTER XIX

Clandestine Architectural Studies—A Visit to the Marquis
of Westminster's Stud—Stable Matters

Monday, June 3d

EARLY IN THE MORNING we visited the old church of St. John's,
and afterwards several curious places, relics of Romans,
Saxons, and Normans, in the suburbs—after all, nothing so
interesting to me as the commonest relics of Englishmen but
two or three centuries old. As we returned through the town
at seven, the early risers seemed to be just getting up. Passing
the cathedral as the bell tolled for morning prayer, we turned
in. There are services every day at 7, 11, and 3 o'clock. The
service was performed in the Lady Chapel, which we did not
enter. The attendance must have been rather meagre, as we
saw no one going to it but two ladies with an old man-servant.
We remained some time hunting on tip-toe for traces of the
"Norman transition" in the architecture, and found we had
had already practice enough to readily detect it in various
parts. Stealing softly into the choir, from which the Lady
Chapel opens, we examined the bishop's throne. It is adorned
with many figures of saints and angels, kings and queens, and
having been once broken to pieces, in the repairs upon it the
old heads were generally put on young shoulders, and *vice
versa,* producing in some instances a very ludicrous effect, par-

ticularly where the men's heads, beards and all, are set on female bodies. We then got out into the cloisters, and from them into the chapter-house, in which heavy-groined arches, simple, and without the slightest ornament, have a fine effect. The date is about 1190. We saw here some very strongly marked faces which, in stone, represent certain Norman abbots whose graves were under us.

Without the cathedral yard, the ruins of the old abbey appear frequently among the houses—the old black oak timber and brick work of the time of Cromwell, mingling picturesquely with the water-worn carvings of the older, old masonry. This morning we saw a stout, round, old Saxon arch giving protection to a fire-engine, which brought to mind the improbability of the present race of New Yorkers sending down to posterity such memorials of itself. Well, it will send better perhaps, and more lasting than stones—or stocks.

On the town-hall is a large statue, said to be of Queen Anne, but so battered and chipped, that it might stand for anybody else, in a long dress. The hands and nose, and all the regalia, are knocked off. And how, do you suppose? By the *super*-sovereign people in election demonstrations. Thank God, we may yet boast that, in our thoroughly democratic elections, where the whole national policy is turning, and the most important private and local interests are at issue, we leave no such memorials of our time. (I beg pardon of the "bloody Sixth.")

Going into a book-shop for a direction, we saw Emerson's "Representative Men," and Irving's "Sketch Book," on the counter, with newspapers and railway guides, and the proprietor told us he had sold many of them.

We passed through a crockery shop to see a Roman bath, which had been discovered in excavating a cellar in the rear of it. Such things are every year turning up.

After breakfast we once more took our knapsacks, and left Chester by the foot-path on the bank of the Dee.

The Marquis of Westminister owns some of the finest horses in the kingdom: in passing through Eccleston, we asked a man if he could direct us where we could see some of them.

He informed us that he was himself head groom of the stud, and would take pleasure in showing it to us. He took us first to "the paddocks," which are fields of from two to five acres, enclosed by stone walls, ten feet high, some of them with sheds and stables attached, and some without. In these were thirty or forty of the highest bred and most valuable mares and fillies in the world. Unfortunately I am not a horse-*man*, and cannot attempt to describe them particularly. It needed but a glance, however, to show us that they were almost any of them the most beautiful animals we had ever seen. The groom, whose name is Nutting, and whose acquaintance I recommend every traveler this way to endeavor to make, was exceedingly obliging, not only taking us into every paddock and stable, and giving us an account of the pedigree, history, and performances of every horse, but calling our attention to his "points," all the peculiarities of form which distinguished each individual. It was evident his heart was in his business, and that his regard was appreciated, for as soon as he unlocked the gate and showed himself within the enclosure, some of the older mares would trot up to be caressed with the most animated, intelligent, and gratified expression. The most celebrated among them was *Bee's-wing*. She is seventeen years old, and very large, but perfect in form; I should think better than her daughter, *Queen-Bee*, who is lighter and more delicate. The extraordinary beauty of "Ghuznee" and "Crucifix," both distinguished on the turf, was also obvious. These, I think, do not belong to the Marquis. In one of the paddocks were a number of foals, pretty, agile, fawn-like creatures. They came around us dancing and capering, catching our knapsacks with their teeth, then springing off and coming back again, like dogs at play. The mares, fillies, and colts were all of dark bay color but one, which was dark iron-grey, nearly black.

Just as we left the colts, a great cart-horse, belonging to the Marquis, was passing on the road. The contrast was striking. He was seventeen hands and one inch high (within a trifle, six feet), and putting both my thumbs to the smallest part of his leg, I could not make my fingers meet around it.

From the paddocks we went to the stables to see the stallions. They were all loose boxes (no stalls), thirteen feet by sixteen, some with rack and manger across the side, some with the same in a corner. *Touchstone* is a magnificent creature. It is impossible to imagine higher condition, indicated not less in the happy and spirited expression and action, than in the bright, smooth, supple, and elastic *feel* of his skin. I never saw any thing to equal it; and it was nearly as remarkable in the mares. Five thousand guineas (over $25,000) have been offered and refused for Touchstone. *Springy-Jack* is a younger stallion; by Nutting esteemed even higher than Touchstone. Nothing in the world of animal life can be finer than the muscular development of his neck. Touchstone is thought a little coarse in the withers. They were intending to put him in pasture the next week, and in preparation for it, he had some fresh grass mixed with hay to eat. He stood in a deep bed of straw, and was not curried—groomed merely with a cloth—yet he was so clean that it would not have soiled a white linen handkerchief to have rubbed it upon him.

In the granary we saw some very plump and bright Scotch oats; they were bought for 42 lbs. to the bushel, but would overweigh that. The common feed was oat and bean meal, mixed with cut hay. The hay was cut very fine (not more than ⅛ inch lengths) by a hand machine. I believe, cut as it usually is by our machines (½ inch to 1 inch), it is more thoroughly digested. I use Sinclair's, of Baltimore, which is intended for cornstalks, driven by horse-power, and cuts hay and straw from one to three inches, which I prefer to the finer.* The machine here cost £6 ($30), and was in no way superior, that I could see, to Ruggles's, of Boston, which is sold at half that price.

The farm buildings were not fine or in good order; manure wasting, old carts and broken implements thrown carelessly about, and nothing neat. Nor were the cattle remarkable—most of them below the average that we have seen on the roadside. It is evident that the Marquis is more of a horse-jockey than a farmer.

The groom's house, which we entered, was very neat and

* I do not wish to recommend this machine for hay and straw, which it does not cut as rapidly as some others, but for stalks it cannot be surpassed—cutting and *splitting* them in small dice.

handsomely built of stone. All the cottages hereabout are floored with tiles, nine inches square.

Nutting showed us a cow of his own, which I took to be a direct cross of Devon and Ayrshire, and which had as fine points for a milker as I ever saw. She was very large, red and white, and a good feeler. He assured us that she was giving now on pasture feed thirty-two quarts a day.

The hay was partly stored under slate roofs, supported by four strong stone columns, the sides open. This plan differs from the hay "barracks," common where the Dutch settled in America, in which the roof, thatched or boarded, is attached to posts in such a way that it can be easily set up or down, and adjusted to the quantity of hay under it. These erections are here called Dutch barns. Nutting thought hay was preserved in them better than in any way he knew, and this has been my opinion of that from our barracks. Close barns he particularly objected to. Probably hay suffers more in them here than it does in America.

After showing us all about the farmery, he walked on with us to a shady pasture by the riverside, where was a herd of fine mares. We sat here under an old elm for some time, looking at them as they clustered around us, and talking with him about the agriculture of the district. He was so easily good-natured, and conversed so freely, asking as well as answering questions, that we were greatly puzzled to tell whether he expected a fee, or would be offended by our offering it. At length, when he was about to leave, we frankly stated our difficulty, explaining that we were foreigners, and not familiar with the English customs. He answered pleasantly, that he was always glad of a chance to converse with gentlemen on such subjects as we appeared to be interested in; if they liked to give him something he did not refuse it, but he did not wish any thing from us. We assured him that we were much in-debted to him, handing him a half crown, which he dropped into his pocket without thanking us, but politely replying that he considered himself fortunate in having met us. He then said he would walk on a little further, to direct us on a path much pleasanter than the regular travel, and from which we might see one of the best dairy farms in the country, with an excellent herd of one hundred and fifty cows. The path would run through the park, and was not public, but if we would mention his name at the lodges they would let us pass.

We soon came in sight of the cows. They were large, half-bred Ayrshires, which seem to be the favorite dairy stock throughout the county. Pure bred stock of any breed is not in favor, but the Ayrshire blood is most valued.

CHAPTER XX

The Cheshire Cheese District and English Husbandry upon Heavy Soils—Pastures; Their Permanence—The Use of Bones as a Manure in Cheshire—A Valuable Remark to Owners of Improved Neat Stock—Breeds of Dairy Stock—Horses

THE SOIL OF a considerable part of this county being a tenacious clay, favorable to the growth of grasses, and difficult of tillage, its inhabitants are naturally dairy-men, and it has been particularly distinguished for many centuries for its manufacture of cheese. Its distinction in this respect does not appear to be the result of remarkable skill or peculiar dairy processes, but is probably due to the particular varieties of herbage, to the natural production of which, the properties of its soil, and perhaps of its climate, are peculiarly favorable.*

The grounds for this conclusion are the general value placed by the farmers upon their old pastures, where the natural assortment of herbage may be considered to have entirely obtained and taken the place of the limited number of

* The best cheese is made on cold, stiff, clay soils (but not on the purest clays), and from the most *natural* herbage, even from *weedy*, sterile pastures; but much the largest quantity is made from an equal extent of more moderately tenacious and drained or permeable soils, spontaneously producing close, luxuriant, fine (not rank) grasses and white clover.

varieties which are artificially sowed; the fact that the butter of the district is not, as a general rule, highly esteemed; and that I cannot learn that the process of cheese-making differs any more from that of other districts in England or the United States, than between different dairies producing cheese of equal value, in this district itself.

It is by no means to be inferred, however, that the quality of cheese is not affected by the process of manufacture. There is no doubt that the skill and nicety of a superior dairy-maid will produce cheese of a superior quality, on a farm of poor herbage, while an ignorant and careless one will make only an inferior description, no matter what the natural advantages may be. The best cheese made in the United States is quite equal to the best I have tasted here, but the average quality is by no means equal to the average quality of Cheshire cheese.

Superiority in the manufacture seems not to depend, however, upon any describable peculiarities of the process, which differs in no essential particular from that common in our dairies. Excellence is well understood to depend greatly upon extreme cleanliness in all the implements employed, and upon the purity and moderate temperature of the atmosphere. Means to secure the latter are used much the same as with us. Stoves and hot-water pipes are sometimes employed in the cheese-room, and where this is in a detached building of one story, it is considered essential that it should have a thatched roof. In some cases where the roof has been slated, it has been found necessary in the warmest weather to remove the cheese to the cellar of the farm-house. Plank shelves are more generally used, and are esteemed better than stone.

Not only is there no uniformity in the methods of the different dairies, to distinguish them from those of the United States, but rarely in any single dairy are there any exact rules with regard to the time to be employed in any parts of the process, or as to the temperature or the measure of any ingredients. Thus the degree of heat at setting the milk, although the skill to *feel* when it is right is deemed highly important, is almost never measured, even in the best dairies. The quantity of rennet is guessed at, and its strength not exactly known. The quantity of salt used is undefined, and the time of *sweating* or curing of cheese, when made, is left to accident.

With regard to some of these points, however, it has been found (as reported to the Royal Agricultural Society) that in some of the best dairies, the milk, when judged to be of the right temperature for coagulating, was by the thermometer at 82° F. (variations from 76° to 88°). From four to sixteen square inches of rennet skin in a pint of water (generally four square inches), were used to make the cheese from fifty gallons of milk, and 1 lb. to 1 lb. 4 ounces salt to the same quantity. It is thought that the best cheese is made with less salt than this. The heat of the milk-room was found to vary from 64° to 78° in August, and it was thought desirable that it should be cooler than this. The reporter thought that a temperature of 50° would be most approved throughout the year. I never heard of ice being used in any way in a Cheshire dairy.

Some of the best dairy-maids claim to have "secrets" by which they are enabled to surpass others; but it is certain that they do not lessen the necessity for extreme cleanliness, nicety, and close observation and judgment, and that with this, in addition to what is everywhere known and practiced, there is no mystery necessary to produce the best.*

The Cheshire cheese in market always has an unnaturally deep yellow color, though of late less so than formerly. It is given by the addition of "coloring" to the milk, immediately before the rennet steep is applied. This "coloring" is manufactured and sold at the shops for the purpose. It is an imitation

---

* "A cheese dairy is a manufactory—a workshop—and is, in truth, a place of hard work. That studied *outward neatness,* which is to be seen in the show dairies of different districts, may be in character where butter is the only object, but would be superfluous in a cheese dairy. If the room, the utensils, the dairy-woman and her assistants be sufficiently *clean* to give perfect sweetness to the produce, no matter for the *color* or the *arrangement.* The scouring-wisp gives an *outward fairness,* but is frequently an enemy to *real cleanliness.*"—MARSHALL's VALE OF GLOUCESTER. Besides the means of securing this *inner* cleanliness, sweetness, and purity, which must be of the air too, as well as of the utensils, etc., it is probable that the dairy-maids' secrets are in a knowledge of the best temperature, particularly of that at which the milk should be curdled.

of annatto, formed chiefly of a small quantity of real annatto, mixed with tumeric and soft soap. I think it is never used in sufficient quantity to affect the flavor at all; but I observe that the farmers and people in the county prefer cheese for their own use that is not colored.

Whey Butter.—It is common in Cheshire to make butter from the whey. It will probably surprise many to learn that there is any cream left in whey; but there undoubtedly is, and it may be extracted by the same means as from milk. The only difference in the process is, that it is *set* in large tubs instead of small pans, and that the whey is drawn off by a faucet from the bottom after the cream has risen. If allowed to remain too long it will give a disagreeable flavor to the cream. One hundred gallons of milk will give ninety of whey, which will give ten or twelve gallons of cream, which will make three or four pounds of butter. So that besides the cheese, twenty to twenty-five pounds of butter are made in a year from the milk of each cow—an item of some value in a large dairy. The butter is of second-rate quality, but not bad—worth perhaps three cents a pound less than milk butter.

The farms in the country over which we walked in Cheshire were generally small—less, I should think, than one hundred acres. Frequently the farmer's family supplied all the labor upon them—himself and his sons in the field, and his wife and daughters in the dairy—except that in the harvest month one or two Irish reapers would be employed. The cows, in the summer, are kept during the day in distant pastures, and always at night in a home lot. During the cheese-making season, which on these small farms is from the first of May till November, they are driven home and fastened in *shippens,* or sheds, between five and six o'clock, morning and night, and then milked by the girls, sometimes assisted by the men. On a farm of one hundred acres, fifteen to twenty cows are kept, and three persons are about an hour in milking them. From twenty to thirty gallons of milk (say six quarts from each cow) is expected to be obtained on an average, and about one pound of dried cheese from a gallon of milk. From two to five cwt. (of 112 lbs.) of cheese may be made from the milk of each cow during the year. Three cwt. is thought a fair return on the best farms. In a moderately dry and temperate summer, more cheese is made than in one which is very wet.

The pastures are generally looked upon as permanent; the night pastures are sometimes absolutely so, as it is supposed that they have not generally been broken up for many hundred years. During the last ten years the pasture lands have been very greatly, and, as they tell me, almost incredibly improved by the use of bone-dust. It is applied in the quantity of from twenty to forty cwt. on an acre, as top-dressing; and I was told that pastures on which it had been applied at the rate of a ton to an acre, eight or nine years ago, had continued as good (or able on an average of the years to bear as many cows) as similar land top-dressed with farm-yard dung every two years, probably at the rate of thirty cubic yards to an acre. There seems to be no doubt at all that lands, to which *inch* bones were applied ten years ago, are yet much the better for it. They are usually applied in April, and the ground is lightly pastured, or perhaps not at all, until the following year. The effect, the farmers say, is not merely to make the growth stronger, but to make it sweeter; the cattle will even eat the weeds, which before they would not taste of. However, in poor land especially, it is found to encourage the growth of the more valuable grasses more than that of the weeds; so that the latter are crowded out, and a clean, thick, close turf is formed. If the ground has been drained, all these improvements are much accelerated and increased. Upon newly *laid down* lands, however, the effect is not so great; it is especially on old pastures (from which the extraction of the phosphates in the milk has been going on for ages sometimes, uninterruptedly) that the improvement is most magical. The productive value of such lands is very frequently known to have been doubled by the first dressing of bones.

Both boiled and raw bones are used, and though there is a general belief that the later are more valuable, I do not hear of any experience that has shown it; on the contrary, I am told of one field which was dressed on different sides equally with each sort, and now, several years after, no difference has been observed in their effect. A comparison must, of course, be made by measure, as boiled bones are generally bought wet, and overweigh equal bulks of raw about 25 percent. Dry bone-dust weighs from 45 to 50 lbs. to a bushel.

I have not heard of *super-phosphate of lime,* or bones dissolved in sulphuric acid, being used as a top-dressing for pastures.

I quote the following from the journal of the Royal Agricultural Society, as a mark of deep significance to American farmers, beyond its proof of the value of bones:—"Before bones came into use in this country, the farmers made a point of selecting a *hardy* and *inferior* description of stock for their clay lands, farmers finding that *large, well-bred cows did not at all answer upon them;* but now they find" (*in improved pasture*) "that the best of stock find ample support, not only to supply the cheese-tub freely, but also to *do justice to their lineage,* by retaining, if not improving, their size and symmetry; so that the farmer has not only the advantage of making considerably more cheese, but also of making more money by his turn of stock."

I cannot now ascertain the amount of bones annually exported from the United States to England, but it must be very great, as I know one bone-miller, near New York, that has a standing order to ship all he can furnish at a certain price, and who last year thus disposed of 80,000 bushels.

Breeds of Dairy Stock.—I have already described most of the dairy stock that we have observed along the road. We have seen scarcely any pure bred stock of any kind. Ayrshire blood seems to predominate and be most in favor on the best farms. The points of the short-horns are also common, and in the south we saw some Herefords. The best milkers seemed to be a mixed blood of Ayrshires, and some other large and long-horned cattle, with a smaller red and black breed, probably Welsh. I incline to think that experience has taught the dairy-men to prefer half or quarter bred stock to full bloods of any breed. For beef-making it is otherwise. I have seen no working oxen. Horses are the only beasts of draught on the farms; they vary greatly in quality, but are generally stout, heavy, hardy, and very powerful. On a farm of one hundred acres, three will be kept, sometimes four, and at about that rate on the larger farms, with an additional saddle-horse or two for his own use, if the farmer can afford it. Farmers generally raise their own cows, choosing heifer calves from their best milker for the purpose. Cattle are not commonly reared for sale here. Few sheep are raised; but many are brought lean from Wales and Ireland, and fatted here.

CHAPTER XXI

Tillage—Size of Farms—Condition of Laborers—Fences—
Hedges—Surface Drainage—Under Drainage—Valuable
Implements for Stiff Soils, Not Used in the United States

I SHOULD THINK that more than three-quarters of the land we
have seen is in grass and pasture. I suppose that it would be
more productive of human food, and support a much larger
population, if it were cultivated; but the farmers being generally men of small means, barely making a living, are indis-
posed to take the trouble to break up and till the tough sward
and stiff soil, from which, while it is in pasture, they are always sure to realize a certain product of cheese without any
severe labor. The cultivation is not, either, very thorough,
because the strongest and most efficient implements and great
brute forces are needed to effectually act upon such a soil.
Accordingly we have observed on the large farms, where the
extent of ground to be, of necessity, cultivated, warranted the
purchase of clod-crushers and other strong and expensive
implements, and made it necessary to employ a considerable
number of laborers, the proportion of land under tillage was
more extensive, and much more thorough work was made with
it.

I wish I could say that the condition of the laborers appeared to be elevated with that of agriculture, by the leasing

of the land in larger tracts, and to men of larger capital. It is true that the tendency is to increase the rate of wages and give employment to more hands; but it is also evident that, by the engrossment of several small farms in one large one, a number of persons must be reduced from the comparatively independent position of small farmers to that of laborers, and I cannot see that for this there is any compensating moral advantage.

Another evil of the small farms (not exclusively however), is the quantity of land injured or withdrawn from cultivation by the fences. These are almost universally hedges; and not only are they left untrimmed and straggling, thereby shading and feeding upon the adjoining land, but a great many large trees have been allowed to grow up in them, of course to the injury of any crops under their branches. These are sometimes kept low, the limbs being trimmed off for firewood (in which case they are called *pollards*), or are left to grow naturally. In the latter case, of course, they add exceedingly to the beauty of the landscape, and eventually become of value for timber; but high as this is here, I cannot at all believe it will ever compensate for the loss occasioned to the farm-crops. Where every five or ten acres is surrounded by a hedge and ditch, the damage done cannot be slight. By way of improvement, we have seen where lately some hedges have been grubbed up, two old fields being thrown together. We have also seen a few wire fences in use. These latter were very slightly set up, and could hardly be intended for permanence. We have also seen some fine, low, narrow hedges, taking up but little room, and casting but little shade. When a hedge is thus well made and kept, I am inclined to esteem it the most economical fence. The yearly expense of trimming it is but trifling (less than one cent a rod), and it is a perfect barrier to every thing larger than a sparrow. The farmers seem to set much value upon the shelter from cold winds which the hedges afford.

Drainage.—The need of thorough draining is nowhere so obvious as upon clay soils with stiff sub-soils. There will be but a few weeks in a year when such soils are not too wet and mortary, or too dry and bricky, to be plowed or tilled in any way to advantage. In the spring it is difficult to cart over them, and in the summer, if the heat is severe and long-continued, without copious rain, the crops upon them actually dwindle and suffer more than upon the dryest sandy loams. To get rid of the surface-water, the greater part of the cultivated land of Cheshire (and, I may add, of all the heavy land of England) was, ages ago, plowed into beds or "butts." These are commonly from five to seven yards wide, with a rise, from the furrows (called the "reins") to the crown, of three or four inches in a yard. The course of the butts is with the slope of the ground; a cross butt and rein, or a wide, open ditch by the side of the hedge, at the foot of the field, conducting off the water which has collected from its whole surface. When the land is broken up for tillage, and often, even after thorough under-drainage, these butts are still sacredly regarded and preserved.

Thorough under-draining, by which all the water is collected after filtering through the soil to some depth, was introduced here as an agricultural improvement within the last eight years. The great profit of the process upon the stiff soil was so manifest that it was very soon generally followed. The landlords commonly furnished their tenants with tile for the purpose, and the latter very willingly were at the expense of digging the drains and laying them. Wishing, however, to do their share of the improvement at the least cost, the tenants have been too often accustomed to make the drains in a very inefficient manner, being guided as to distance by the old reins, and laying their tile under these, often less than eighteen inches from the surface. The action of the drains was thus often imperfect. It is now customary for the landlords, when they furnish tile, to stipulate the depth at which they shall be laid. They sometimes also lay out the courses and distances of the drains. The Marquis of Westminster employs an engineer, who appoints foremen, and, to a certain extent, suitably-trained laborers, to secure the drainage of his tenant-lands in the most lastingly economical and beneficial manner. Last winter he had two hundred men so employed, in addition to the labor furnished by the tenants themselves, and over one million tiles were laid by them. I heard nowhere any thing but gratification and satisfaction expressed with the operation of the thorough-drains.*

Implements.—After breaking up the sward of these heavy lands with a deep, narrow furrow-slicing plow, an admirable instrument, quite commonly in use and everywhere spoken well of, for crushing and pulverizing the soil in a much more effectual and rapid manner than the harrow, is Croskill's Patent Clod-crusher Roller.

"This implement," according to the inventor's advertisement, "consists of twenty-three roller parts, with serrated and uneven surfaces, placed upon a round axle, six feet wide by two and a half feet in diameter. The roller-parts act independent of each other upon the axle, thus producing a self-cleaning movement. Of course the roller must only be used when the land is so dry as not to stick.

"The following are the various uses to which this implement is applied:

"1. For rolling corn as soon as sown upon light lands; also upon strong lands, that are cloddy, before harrowing.

"2. For rolling wheats upon light lands in the spring, after frosts and winds have left the plants bare.

"3. For stopping the ravages of the wire-worm and grub.

"4. For crushing clods after turnip crops, to sow barley.

"5. For rolling barley, oats, etc., when the plants are three inches out of the ground, before sowing clover, etc.

"6. For rolling turnips in the rough leaf before hoeing, where the plants are attacked by wire-worm.

"7. For rolling grass lands and mossy lands after compost.

"8. For rolling between the rows of potatoes, when the plants are several inches out of the ground.

"Cash prices, with traveling wheels complete, 6 feet 6 inches, £21; 6 feet, £19 10s.; 5 feet 6 inches, £18."

For still more deeply stirring, and for bringing weeds to the surface of soil recently plowed, a great variety of instru-

---

* A careful account was kept with one large farm, drained eight years ago by the Marquis of Westminster. The increased production attributed to the operation is now equal to 27 per cent. per annum on the expenditure, and it was lately leased with a corresponding improved rental.

ments entirely unknown in America are in common use here. They all consist of sets of tines, or teeth, placed between a pair of wheels, and so attached to them that, by means of a lever, having the axletree of the wheels for a fulcrum, the depth to which they shall penetrate is regulated; and they may at any time be raised entirely above the surface, dropping and relieving themselves from the weeds and roots which they have collected. Thus, they may be described as combining the action of the harrow, the cultivator, and the horse-rake. (The wire-tooth horse-rake is used as an instrument of tillage by Judge Van Bergen, at Coxsackie, N.Y.) They are designated variously by different manufacturers—as grubbers, scarifiers, extirpators, harrows, and cultivators. The "Uley Cultivator" is one of the simplest and most efficient. In this the tines are raised by turning a crank, each complete turn of which raises or depresses them one inch. The depth to which they are penetrating at any time, is marked by a dial near the handle of the crank. Something of the kind, more effectual than any thing we yet have, is much needed to be introduced with us. Clean and thorough culture of stiff clay soils can hardly be performed without it.

I should remark of English agricultural implements in general, that they seem to me very unnecessarily cumbrous and complicated.

CHAPTER XXII

The General Condition of Agriculture—Rotation of Crops—Productiveness—Seeding down to Grass—Comparison of English and American Practice—Practical Remarks—Rye-grass, Clover—Biennial Grasses—Guano—Lime—The Condition of Laborers, Wages, etc.—Dairy-Maids—Allowance of Beer

I MUST SAY that, on the whole, the agriculture of Chesire, as the first sample of that of England which is presented to me, is far below my expectations. There are sufficient reasons to expect that we shall find other parts much superior to it; but what we have seen quite disposes of the common picture which our railroad and stage-coach travelers are in the habit of giving to our imagination, by saying that "all England is like a garden." Meaning only a "landscape garden," a beautiful and harmonious combination of hill and dale, with the richest masses of trees, and groups and lines of shrubbery, the greenest turf and most picturesque buildings, it might be appropriately said of many parts; but with reference to cultivation, and the productiveness of the land, it might be quite as truly applied to some small districts of our own country as to this part of England.

In commencing the cultivation of land that has been in

grass, the first crop is usually oats; and the most approved practice upon the stiff soils seems to be, to plow deeply in the fall or winter, and in the spring to prepare the ground with some strong implement of the cultivator sort. Oats are sowed much thicker than is usual with us. I hear of six bushels to the acre; but with regard to this there is much difference of opinion. The crop of oats is not often large (from thirty to forty bushels from an acre is common); but oats seldom make a large crop upon clay soils. The next year the ground will be summer-fallowed, or, by the more enterprising farmers, cropped with turnips, beets, or with potatoes. The potatoes are sold, the turnips and beets fed to the cows during the winter. On the poorer farms, the cows get little but hay from December to April; and cheese-making is given up during the winter. Others, by the help of turnips, beets, and linseed cake, keep a constant flow of milk, and cheese-making is never interrupted. (Of course the milking of each cow is interrupted for awhile at her calving time, which they try to have in March.)

The crop after roots is commonly barley; after fallow, wheat, of which twenty-five to thirty bushels is a common crop, and forty not uncommon. After wheat, oats again, and perhaps after the oats another crop of wheat; if so, the land is manured with bones or boughten manure, and sometimes limed at the rate, say of four tons to the acre of stone lime.

Grass.—With the last crop of oats or wheat, clover and grass seeds are sowed. Grass was thought to come better after wheat upon under-drained land. The best farmers sow a very great variety and large measure of grass seeds; the poorer ones are often content with what they can find under their hay bays, sowing it, weeds and all, purchasing only clover seed.

The quantity of grass seeds sowed is always much greater here than in America. I should think it was commonly from a bushel to three bushels on an acre; rarely less than one, or more than three. I do not think more than one quarter of a bushel, or perhaps half a bushel of the lighter seeds, is often sowed in the United States. I should attribute the more general evenness and closeness of the English meadows in a great degree to this, though, doubtless, much is due to the moister climate. Land intended for permanent pasture receives much more seed, and a larger variety, than that which is intended to be mown only for a few years, and then be brought to tillage again. Of the good policy of the English practice for pastures (and the same applies to lawns and public greens) I have no doubt. Among the great variety of grasses in an English meadow, there will be one that springs up and grows strongly, furnishing a wholesome and delicious bite to the cattle, as early after the first warm breath of spring as the ground will be dry enough to bear a hoof (and on drained lands it is rarely not so). This will be succeeded by others, and in May by others; and in July, those natural to the dryest and warmest soils will be in perfection; and so through the year there is a constantly renewing perfection. A ranker sward, and one that would for a season support more cattle, I think would be obtained from sowing a smaller quantity and less variety of seed.

I am not prepared to recommend the English practice for mowing lands. To obtain the largest quantity of grass hay from an acre, without regard to quality, plow deep, manure deep, and sow one variety of seed in such quantity that when it comes up it will speedily *tiller,* and occupy the whole ground, yet not stand so closely as to greatly crowd and compress the stools, thereby dwarfing the reeds from their natural size, and obstructing the flow of sap in their vessels. Cut it when it has attained to its greatest size, while it is yet entirely succulent, just at the time that the *blood* of the plant begins to be drawn up into the forming seed, and the bottom dries into such tough, close, ligneous fibre that nourishment can no longer ascend from the root. The right quantity of seed for this will vary in different soils—a very rich, deep soil needing less than a more sterile one, because in the latter the roots cannot extend far enough to collect the requisite food and drink to make a large, strong, open stool, and more herbage will grow upon the same space by having the stools stand closer.

In some degree proportionately to the closeness of the fibre and the fineness of the grass, will be its nourishing quality, so that ninety pounds of fine, close-grown hay, from a thick-seeded meadow, may be of equal value with a hundred pounds of a coarser, ranker quality. But the nourishment is by no means in the inverse ratio of size; so that for all ordinary purposes, with all the usual hay-grasses, the farmer will find his profit in studying to obtain the largest burthen of grass. For this end, I am inclined to think English farmers often sow too much seed—Americans not enough. It seems, however, to be the best farmers in other respects that sow the most seed in England.

There is one consideration that I have omitted to mention, against the common practice on American farms, where hay is an important staple crop: it is generally an object to retain a clean sward of grass as long as possible, without the necessity of breaking up, from the grass having *run out,* that is, given place to weeds, or to finer and less profitable grasses. Where the seed has been thickly sown, the grass takes more entire possession of the surface, and retains it longer. The thicker grass seed is sown, therefore, other things being equal, the longer it will *lay.*

I have known, in a district where it was the custom to sow four to eight quarts of timothy seed, on two occasions, twenty quarts sowed. The result was a finer grass in both cases; in one it was thought the crop was much larger, and in the other that it was somewhat smaller, than where ten quarts was sowed alongside. The probability is, that in an average of ten years it will prove the larger crop on the thickest sown, in both fields.

The commonest grass seed sowed in England is rye-grass, or ray-grass (perennial). It is a much smaller, closer-growing grass than our timothy; I think it has a sweeter taste, is probably bulk for bulk, considerably more nutritious, and perhaps so pound for pound; but I think more fat and muscle can be made from an acre, if sowed with timothy, than with rye-grass. A valuable quality of rye-grass is its early spring growth. A field of rye-grass will be up some inches, offering a tempting bite to cattle, before a field of other grasses will begin to show a green surface. I believe that it ripens earlier too than timothy, and is better for mowing-ground on that account, to be sown with clover, which is much injured by over-ripeness, if not cut till timothy is in its best state to make hay. I have seen no timothy in England, but I know that it is sometimes sowed.

Rye-grass has stood at the head of the mowing grasses in some parts of England for centuries. In districts of light and dry soil, it is less in favor than elsewhere, but, I judge, becomes of more value with the improvement of husbandry generally. Marshall (1796), writing from Gloucestershire, speaks of the general strong prejudice of the farmers against ray-grass, "smothering every thing and impoverishing the soil, until it will grow nothing!" they say; and, arguing against them, he makes an observation of value with reference to the question of quantity of seed. "If *real* ray-grass has ever been tried alone, and without success, it has probably risen from too great a quantity having been sown. Be it ray-grass or rubbish, I understand seldom less than a sackful" (three heaped bushels) "an acre is thrown on, whereas *one gallon* an acre of *clean-winnowed real ray-grass seed* is abundantly sufficient on such soil as the vale in general is covered with." The soil is "a rich, deep loam."

Clover (red and Dutch) is more sowed here for hay than with us, though it is much more difficult to make good hay of it in this climate. It is sowed in the spring, as with us, perhaps 20 lbs. to the acre. We commonly sow 5 to 10 lbs. Arthur Young tried about a dozen experiments to ascertain the most profitable quantity of clover seed to sow, and concluded his record of them as follows:

"The more seed, as far as 20 lbs. per acre, undoubtedly the better. This is a plain fact, contradicted by no part of the experiment; and the great inferiority of 5 to 7 lbs. shows equally clear that such portion of seed is too small for an acre. Where land is well manured, less seed is required; 12½ lbs. seems the proper quantity" (on very rich, gravelly soil).

A bushel of clover seed weighs 60 to 64 lbs.

In ground intended for mowing but one or two years, biennial varieties of the rye-grass are sown, which are of stronger growth than the perennial. They are also sowed sometimes with permanent grasses, giving, on a deep, rich soil, a heavier burthen of grass the first year of cutting than these would do. For this purpose, I have thought it might be well to sow the biennial or sub-perennial rye-grass seed with timothy, which does not usually yield a fair crop at its first cutting, and have twice attempted to make trial of the Italian rye-grass, but in both cases the seeds that I had procured failed of germination.

I may hereafter notice several species of herbage that are much valued in England, that have not been generally introduced in the United States.*

The grass is mowed for hay for a longer or shorter course of years; sometimes broken up after one or two seasons, sometimes becoming permanent or perennial pasture, and so running on indefinitely; and sometimes being mowed for a number of years. One field I saw that had been mowed eight years, and having received a dressing of 30 cwt. of bones, promised fair yet to bear heavy swaths. Mowing lands are usually top-dressed at the end of the second year, and afterwards every second or third year. All the homestead dung is commonly reserved for this purpose, and all other manure is purchased from the towns. Guano for turnips and wheat is coming into general use; some think very profitably, others have been disappointed. For wheat, it is applied at the seed sowing, and sometimes again as a top-dressing in the spring; but in a dry season it is thought that this second application has done more harm than good. Guano has been a good deal tried as a top-dressing for pastures, and it has been said to improve the quality of cheese when so used. The immediate effect upon grass, when applied in the spring, is always very advantageous; but later in the summer, particularly if the season is dry, the good effect disappears, and sometimes the result is unfavorable.

Of course the round of crop varies according to every farmer's notion. What I have described is as common as any, though not probably among the best farmers. Another crop is beans, which is introduced between either of those I have mentioned, sometimes at the head. Not uncommonly the first crop is wheat, the ground having been summer-fallowed.

* Fifteen or twenty varieties of grass seeds are sowed together, and the expense for seed in laying down for pasture is often ten or twelve dollars an acre.

Wheat is drilled or sowed broadcast—most commonly sowed in this county—and is either plowed or harrowed in, opinions varying as to which is best. My own experience on a stiff soil is decidedly in favor of plowing in.

Laborers.—Wages, as they have been reported to me, vary much, and unaccountably. I should think the average for able-bodied men as day-laborers, working and receiving pay only in days that commence fair, was $2.25 a week, perhaps averaging thirty-three cents a day. The rent of a laborer's cottage, with a bit of garden attached (less than a quarter of an acre), is from $15 to $25. In addition, they have sometimes a few perquisites from the farmers who regularly employ them. A great many laborers in winter are without work, and wages are then a trifle less than I have mentioned, as in harvest time they are also a trifle more. The reader will understand that out of this thirty-three cents, which I have supposed to be the average receipts of a laborer per day, he has to pay his rent, and provide food and raiment for his family. Of course his diet cannot be very sumptuous (the cost of provisions being, perhaps, ten per cent higher than with us), but I have not learned particulars.

The wages of farm servants, hired by the month or year, and boarded in the family, are for men, from $45 to $65 a year; for boys, $15 to $25; maid-servants, $30 to $40; dairy-maids, greatly varying, saying from $50 to $100.*

It is customary to give all laborers and servants a certain allowance of beer besides their wages. It is served out several times a day, and may be supposed to cost, on an average, ten cents a day for each person. One farmer estimated it at twice that.

---

* Wages have since advanced considerably, while provisions have fallen in price. Agriculture is nevertheless more profitable, agricultural improvement having been very great.

CHAPTER XXIII

Remarks on the Cultivation of Beet and Mangel-wurzel

I FOUND THE BEST farmers in all the south of England, and throughout Ireland, where the soils were at all stiff, increasing their crops of these roots. For the production of milk they are, undoubtedly, a more valuable crop than turnips or ruta-bagas, though it is asserted that the milk is more thin and watery. Some thought them equal, and even superior, weight for weight, for fattening cattle. I think it is certain that, in such soils, a larger amount of nutriment can be obtained from a crop of them on an equal measure of ground. Donaldson says the beet yields a larger weight per acre, both in roots and leaves, than any other root crop known. I have heard of crops of from fifteen to thirty-five tons an acre; and in one instance, near New York, at the rate of forty-four tons an acre, from one quarter of an acre. Chemical analyses and practical experiments in feeding, to ascertain their value as compared with other roots, or with hay, differ so very greatly, that nothing can be said with any certainty about it. The climate of the United States, like that of France, is much better adapted to the beet, and much less favorable to the ruta-baga, than that of England. The beet is much less liable to be injured by insects or worms than the turnip or ruta-baga, though I incline to think the latter is much more favored with us than in England in this respect.

The ground for beet crops is prepared the same as for turnips; that is, it is finely and deeply tilled (and there is no crop which will better show the value of draining and subsoil plowing), and manured with well-decomposed dung, compost, bones, or guano, in drills from twenty-seven inches to three feet apart. The seed is usually prepared by steeping for from twenty-four to forty-eight hours, and is then rolled in lime. As rapidly as possible after the manure is deposited, it is covered with soil and the seed dropped, sometimes being drilled like turnip seed, but more commonly dibbled. There are two simple machines used here for dibbling. Whatever way the seed is planted, it must be expected that a large part will fail to germinate.

I have found dibbling by hand not very tedious, as follows: One man making holes an inch deep, and six or eight inches apart, with a round stick an inch in diameter, another following and dropping three seeds in a hole, and a third covering by a single stroke, and pressing, with a hoe. I have obtained a large crop, planting so late as the middle of July, in the climate of New York.

A rapid, early growth of the plant is important. When the weeds come up, the horse-hoe or cultivator is run through, and as often afterwards as there is need, while the size of the beets will permit it, they are horse and hand-hoed. It is found that earthing-up with a plow is injurious. When two or three inches high, the plants are thinned to twelve inches apart. When two or three plants come up in a bunch one only of them must be left. It will wilt down flat upon the ground at first, but soon recovers.

The outer leaves begin to dry and decay early in the fall, and may then be plucked and fed to cows with profit, and without retarding the continued growth of the root. The root may be pulled by hand, and is harvested more readily than any other. It will keep (at New York) in the open air, in stacks four feet wide and high, covered with straw and six inches of earth, a small hole being left in the top for ventilation, until

April, and is then of great value to new milk-cows and ewes with lambs.

I particularly recommend the cultivation of the sugar and mangel-wurzel beets to cottage-farming gentlemen, who wish to keep a small dairy with a limited extent of land.

CHAPTER XXIV

Delightful Walk by the Dee Banks, and Through Eaton
Park—Wrexham—A Fair—Maids by a Fountain—The
Church—Jackdaws—The Tap-room and Tap-room Talk
—Political Deadness of the Laboring Class—A Methodist
Bagman

FOLLOWING NUTTING'S DIRECTIONS, we had a most delightful
walk along the river bank and under some noble trees, then
through thick woods and over a bit of low, rushy land, where
some Irishmen were opening drains, and out at length into the
private park-road—a pleasant avenue, which we followed
some miles. The park here was well stocked with game; rabbits
were constantly leaping out before us, and we frequently
started partridges and pheasants from a cover of laurels, holly,
and hawthorn, with which the road was lined.

We came out at Pulford, when we lunched at the Post
Office Inn; and thence walked by an interesting road, through
a village of model cottages not very pretty, over a long hill,
from the top of which a grand view back, and by a park that
formerly belonged to Judge Jeffreys, of infamous memory, to
Wrexham.

Wrexham is a queer, dirty, higgledy-piggeldy kind of
town, said to be the largest in Wales (it is about as large as
Northampton). It was the latter part of a fair-day, and there

had been a mustering of the yeomanry of the shire, so that the streets were crowded as we entered. In the balcony of a hotel in the market-place, a military band was playing to a mass of up-turned, gaping faces, through which we worked our way. The inns were generally full of guzzling troopers, dressed in a very ugly fashion; but we finally found one, some color of the bear family—blue, I believe—which seemed tolerably quiet, where we stopped for the night.

After dining and resting awhile, we took a walk about the town. Most of the houses out of the market-place are very mean and low, the walls plastered with mud and whitewashed, and the roofs thatched. Noticing a kind of grotto in a back street, about which a pretty group of girls in short blue dresses, engaged in lively talk, were standing with pitchers, we approached it. We came close upon them before they noticed us, but instead of showing any timidity, they glanced at our hats and laughed clear and heartily, looking us boldly in the face. Catching one alone, however, as we descended to the fountain, and asking her to let us take her mug to drink from, she handed it to us, blushing deeply, and said nothing; so we were glad to leave quickly to relieve her. There was a spring and pool of remarkably clear, cool water within the grotto, from which all the neighborhood seem to be supplied. Our California hats attracted more attention at Wrexham than anywhere else in Europe, but we met with no incivility or impertinence beyond a smile or laugh.

The church at Wrexham is curious, from the multitude of grotesque faces and figures carved upon it. It is a large and fine structure, and the tower is particularly beautiful, as seen from the village. There were jackdaws' nests in it, and a flock of these birds, the first we have seen, were hovering and screeching around them. They are of the crow tribe, black, and somewhat larger than a blue-jay.

Returning to our inn, we found in the parlor a couple of lisping clerks, who were sipping wine in a genteel way, and trying to say smart things while they ogled the landlady's daughter. Retreating from their twaddle, I called for a pipe and mug of ale, and joined the circle in the tap-room. There was a tall, scarlet-coated fellow, who told me he was a sergeant of the Guards, recruiting here; an older man, who had been in India; a half-tipsy miller, with a pleasant-speaking, good-natured wife trying to coax him to come home; and half a dozen more rustics, all muddling themselves with beer and tobacco.

The conversation was running on politics, and was not at all interrupted by my entrance; on the contrary, I thought the old Indian was glad of a stranger to show himself off before. He was the orator of the night, and the others did little but express assent to his sentiments, except the miller, who every few moments interrupted him with a plain and emphatic contradiction. The sergeant said very little either way except he was appealed to, to substantiate some assertion "as a military man," but leaned on the bar, drinking hot gin-and-water, and whispering with the bar-maid.

There was news that the French minister had taken diplomatic offense and demanded his passports, and war was threatened. War there certainly would be, according to the ex-soldier, and a terrible time was coming with it. England was going to be whipped-out—it was inevitable. Every body assented "it was inevitable" except the miller, who said it was fol-de-rol. "Why," continued the Indian, "isn't every country in Europe against England?—don't they all hate her? and isn't every Frenchman a soldier?" Then he described the inefficient state of the national defenses, and showed how easy it would be for a fleet of steamers, some dark night the next week, to land an army somewhere on the coast of Wales, and before they heard of it, it might be right there amongst them! He would like to know what there was to oppose them. The miller said there was—"gammon." The sergeant, on being asked, admitted that he was not aware of any respectable force stationed in that vicinity, and the miller told him he was a "traitor then." Indian said miller knew nothing about war, and the company unanimously acquiesced. Indian then resumed his speech—asked if government would dare to give arms to the people, and pictured an immense army of Chartists arising in the night, and, with firebrands and Frenchmen, sweeping the government, Queen and all, out of the land, and establishing "a republican kingdom," where the poor man was as good as the rich. The company all thought it very probable, and each added something to make the picture more vivid. A coarse joke about the Queen's bundling off with her children produced much laughter; and the hope that the parsons and lawyers would have to go to work for a living, was much applauded.

It was strange what a complete indifference they all seemed to have about it, as if they would be mere spectators— not in any way personally interested. They spoke of the government and the Chartists, and the landlords and the farmers, but not a word of themselves.

Late in the evening there was some doleful singing, and a woman came in and performed some sleight-of-hand tricks, every one giving her a penny when she had concluded. We were obliged to sleep two in a bed, one of us with a Methodist young man, who traveled to make sales of tea, among country grocers and innkeepers, for a Liverpool house. He said that what we had seen in the tap-room would give us a very good notion of the character of a large part of the laboring class about here. He thought their moral condition most deplorable, and laid it much to the small quantity and bad quality of the spiritual food that was provided for them. He seemed well informed about America, and, excepting for slavery and steamboat explosions, greatly to admire our country. He had some idea of going to it; and said his present business was exceedingly disagreeable, as it compelled him to be so much at inns, where he rarely found any one with whom he could pleasantly associate.

CHAPTER XXV

Morning Walk Through a Coal District—Ruabon—An
Optimist with a Welsh Wife—Graveyard Notes—A Stage-
Wagon—Taxes—Wynstay Park—Thorough Draining—A
Glimpse of Cottage Life—"Sir Watkins Williams Wyn"

June 4th

THE MOST AGREEABLE CHIMES from the church tower we had
ever heard, awoke us this morning at three o'clock. It is light
enough here at that time to read or write, and the twilight at
evening does not seem to be over at half-past ten. I felt stiff
and sore, but arose and wrote till half-past six, when we got
the bar-maid up, paid our bill (we were charged only sixpence
a piece for our lodging), and were let out into the street; no
signs that any one else in the town was yet stirring.

Our road ran through a coal district, tall chimneys throwing out long black clouds of smoke, and pump-levers working
along the hill-tops; the road darkened with cinders; sooty men
coming home from the night-work to low, dirty, thatched cottages—the least interesting and poorest farmed country we
had yet traveled over. After walking six miles, we stopped at
the Talbot Inn, Ruabon, to breakfast.

In the tap-room, over his beer, was a middle-aged man, a
currier by trade, who told us he had come hither nine years
ago from Staffordshire, had married a nice Welsh girl, and

151

settled himself very comfortably. He said wages were good here, and it did not cost so much to live as it used to. He had a cottage in the village; the landlord, Sir Watkins Wyn, was an excellent man, and his agent was very kind to poor people. He did not see any need of grumbling, and, for his part, thought the world a pretty fair world.

After a good breakfast, in a room adorned with sporting pictures and a likeness of Sir Watkins Wyn, as colonel of the local yeomanry, I returned to talk with him. When he had work, his wages were six dollars a week, but just now he was out of work. The rent of his cottage and four roods of land was one hundred and twenty dollars, and Sir Watkins paid the poor-rates. Sir Watkins was not very generally liked by his tenants, because he was not so liberal with them as his father; but his father had been extravagant, and run the estate deeply in debt, and he had need to be more particular; and he was sure he was always very easy with poor folks. He had had a deduction made on his rent more than once when the times were hard with him, and this year the farmers all were allowed ten per cent of their rents, because corn is so low.

I had told him I was from America, and he was asking me some questions about it, when he suddenly stopped, fidgeted about a moment, and then, looking at a woman coming across the street, said, with a laughing, swaggering air, "There's my wife coming; now you'll see a specimen of a Welsh girl!" His wife, a stout, hard-looking woman, walked briskly in, stood up straight before him, folded her arms, and, in a deep, quiet, determined way, gave him a regular *Caudling*. He tried for awhile to make a joke of it, and to appease her. "Come now, missus, don't be hard upon un'; sit ye down now, and take a pint; these gentlemen be from Ameriky, and I talks with 'um about going there. Come now, how'd thee like to go to Ameriky?" As we were thus introduced, she glanced fiercely at us, and we retreated at once without the door. He tried for a moment longer to brave her, and called loudly for another mug of ale. She turned her head to the bar-maid, and said, "You'll get no more ale!" and the bar-maid minded her.

She said he has been there before this morning, and when

he began drinking in the morning, it was always the last of him for the day. He whimpered out that he had come home and breakfast wasn't ready, and he hadn't anything else to do but to come back here. It was ready, she said, and he might have been looking for some work, and so on. In a few minutes they went off, arm in arm.

Opposite the inn was an old church and a graveyard. There were more monkey-faces on the church, and two effigies in stone, of knights—the forms of their bodies, with shields, barely distinguishable, and their faces entirely effaced. Many of the gravestones had inscriptions in Welsh, and both here and at Wrexham I noticed the business of the deceased person was given; as, *John Johnes, Wheelright; William Lloyd, Tanner,* etc. On a flat stone near the church, the following was inscribed (letter for letter), perhaps by a Welsh stone-cutter following an English order, given verbally—*"This his the end of the vault."*

Returning from the church, we found the currier again drinking beer in the tap-room, with a number of other men, a drunken set, who probably had come passengers by a "stage-wagon" that stood in the road. This was an immense vehicle, of pre-railroad origin, like our Pennsylvania wagons, but heavier and higher. It had a heavy freight of barrels, cases, and small parcels, on the top of which, under the canvass-hooped cover, a few passengers were cheaply accommodated, there being a ladder in the rear for them to ascend by. Behind one of the hind-wheels was a roller, attached by chains on either side the wheel to the axletree, so that if the wagon fell back any, it scotched it—a good idea for heavy loads in a hilly country. There were six stout cart-horses to draw it, and all in a line, the wheeler being in shafts. The driver said he had a load of eight or ten tons, and drove three miles an hour with it. He paid about sixteen dollars a year taxes for his horses, and two dollars for a very ugly bull-dog, that stood guard over the establishment for more than an hour, while he was refreshing himself in the inn. At length we saw the whole company come out, and the wagon started again, all very jolly; the currier and another man, with their hands on each other's shoulders, staggered across the street, singing "Oh, Susannah!"

At the churchyard gate both fell, rolled over and embraced each other, once or twice tried ineffectually to get up, and then both went to sleep there on the ground. No wonder the sample Welsh girl had a hard look.

After finishing our letters to send by the steamer, we visited Wynstay Park. It is much more picturesque than Eaton, the ground being diversified and the trees larger. The Hall, which is a plain building, was undergoing repairs.

We separated here for a few days, my friends wishing to see more of Welsh scenery, and going to the vale of Llangollen (pronounced Langothlan), while I had a letter I wished to deliver in another direction.

The park was covered with lines of recently-made under-drains, and I hunted over it in hopes to find men at work, that I might see the manner in which they were constructed. Going to a pretty checkered timber house to make inquiries, I was so fortunate as to meet the foreman of the draining operations, Mr. Green, an intelligent Warwickshire man, who kindly took me to a field a mile or two distant, where he had thirty men at work. The soil was a gravelly loam, with a little heavier subsoil. The drains were laid twenty-seven feet apart, and dug three feet deep (ordinarily), and one foot wide from top to bottom; in the middle of the bottom a groove was cut for the pipe, so the top of it would be three feet from the surface. No narrow tools were used, except to cut the grooves for the pipe. The foreman said that, though a man could work to much better advantage in a wider-mouthed drain, the extra dirt to be moved compensated for it, and made this plan the cheapest.

I thought then, and since, until I came to try it in gravelly and stony land, that the work might be done much more rapidly with the long, narrow tools described by Mr. Delafield,* making the bottom of the drain only of the width of the pipe intended to be laid; but I find these can only be used to advantage in free ground. The method here described is probably the best for draining soils, where many stones larger than a hen's egg are to be met with.

Cylindrical pipes, of either one or one and a half inch

* Transactions N. Y. State Agricultural Soc., 1848, p. 232.

bore, were laid in the grooves at the bottom of the drain; *collars,* connecting them, were only used in the loosest soils. The *mains* were laid one foot deeper than the collecting drains, and the pipes in them were from two to six inches bore. No series of drains were run more than seventy yards in length without a main, and all the mains emptied into an open ditch at the lowest side of the field, which was made deep enough to allow of a drop of one foot from the mouths of the pipes. Where such a ditch was likely to gully, the sides were sloped and turfed.

The wages of the men employed at this work averaged $2.25 a week; boys, 16 cents a day.

Mr. Green sent a lad to guide me across the park to the road I wished to take—a remarkably bright, amiable boy, with whom I had a pleasant talk, as he led me on by the most charming way among the old oaks, and through herds of deer. He could read and write, and knew something of geography and arithmetic, having been instructed by the curate of Ruabon, whom he seemed to have much loved. (I think he had died lately.) He also spoke kindly of Sir Watkins and lady, to whom his father was shepherd, and said that all their servants and poor people were much attached to them. Passing near the Hall, I asked for some water, and he took me into one of the servants' cottages to get it. There was an old woman rocking a cradle, and a young woman ironing linen, both very neatly dressed; the furniture plain and meagre, but every thing clean, and an appearance of a good deal of comfort about the room.

While the repairs were being made upon the Hall, the family lived in a cottage completely embowered among trees and shrubs, which we afterwards passed; and I had the honor of catching a glimpse, through the foliage, of a form in a gray coat which, I was assured, was the good Sir Watkins himself.

Soon after leaving the park, I crossed the Esk by a very high stone arch, built "by Sir Watkins," as some ragged boys and girls, who were employed in collecting for manure the horse-dung that dropped upon the road, informed me, and this was the last I heard of Sir Watkins.

CHAPTER XXVI

Stone Houses—Ivy—Virginia Creeper—A Visit to a Welsh
Horse-Fair—English   Vehicles—Agricultural   Notes—
Horses—Breeds of Cattle; Herefords, Welsh, and Smutty
    Pates—Character of the People—Dress—Powis Park

Shrewsbury, June 7th

I HAVE BEEN VISITING a gentleman to whom I was introduced
by Prof. Norton. His residence is on the east border of Wales,
amidst very beautiful scenery of round-topped hills, and deep,
verdant, genial dells. He has the superintendence of a large
number of mines of coal and metals, and of several agricultural estates, the extent of which   may be imagined from the
fact, that he is preparing to thorough-drain 5000 acres next
winter. He is building a tilery, and will employ seven draining-
engineers, each with two foremen to oversee the work. The
cost, it is estimated, will be from $23 to $25 an acre; drains,
seventeen feet apart and three feet deep.

The house is of stone, and is covered with ivy, which I
mention that I may contradict a common report, that ivy
upon the wall of a house makes it damp. The contrary, I have
no doubt, is the fact. The ivy-leaves fall one over another,
shedding off the rain like shingles; and it is well ascertained
that in a long storm, the inside walls of those rooms in a house
which are protected by the ivy, are much less damp than those

not so shielded. It is also generally supposed in America that stone houses are much damper than wood. This may be so with some kinds of porous stone, but I can testify from my own experience that it is not so with others. A slight *furring out* on the inside, and lath and plaster, will in all cases remove this objection to any stone. A good stone house is warmer in winter, cooler in summer,* equally dry and healthful, and, if built in convenient and appropriate style, every way much more satisfactory and comfortable than our common, slight-framed buildings. As for the ivy, I think it is one of the most beautiful things God has given us, and the man who can and does not let it beautify his habitation, is sinfully ungrateful. It grows luxuriantly on the north side of a house or wall in the climate of New York. (My experience is with the Irish ivy.) †

The day after I reached here, my host had occasion to go to a horse-fair at Welsh Pool, a place some twenty miles distant, and invited me to accompany him. We went in a dog-cart, a kind of heavy gig, which here takes the place of our light boat-wagon. It is a box (large enough to hold a dog or two in driving to sporting ground), hung low, between two small, heavy wheels, with a seat on the top of it for two, looking forward, and sometimes another in which two more can sit looking backward. On the back, to exempt it from the tax upon more luxurious vehicles, is painted the owner's name, business, and place of residence, thus: "John Brown, Farmer, Oswestry, Shrops." All the humbler class of carriages are thus marked here, including farm carts.

The landscapes were agreeable in the country we passed through, but the farming in much of it no better than in some parts of the Connecticut Valley. Coarse, rushy grass, indicating the need of draining, grew in much of the meadow land—as I think it does, to the exclusion of more valuable grasses, in

---

* In a late rapid change of weather, the thermometer on the outside of my house rose in 18 hours from 19 deg. to 35 deg., while that within the walls remained stationary at 20 deg., not rising even one degree, though there was no fire within two rooms of it.

† I am sorry to say it has been sadly cut down by the winters of 1856 and 1857.

land that is ordinarily dryer than such as would spontaneously produce it in America. The buildings along the road were such as I have previously described; but I saw one old shackling board barn which, but for its thatched roof, would have looked very home-like.

Welsh Pool is a small, compact town (population 5000), with a market-house, and a single small church, on the tower of which a union-jack was hoisted, and within which there is a peal of three bells, that continually, all day long, did ring most unmusically; there were booths in the main street, in which women sold dry goods, hosiery, pottery, etc. In another street horses were paraded, and in other places cows and swine.

There was present a considerable crowd of the country people, which I observed carefully. I verily believe, if five hundred of the common class of farmers and farm-laboring men, such as would have come together on similar business— say from all parts of Litchfield County, in Connecticut—had been introduced among them, I should not have known it, except from some peculiarities of dress. I think our farmers, and particularly our laborers, would have been dressed up a little nearer the town fashions, and would have seemed a little more wide awake, perhaps, and that's all. I not only saw no drunkenness, except a very few solitary cases late in the day; no rioting, though there were some policemen present, but no *gayety;* every body wore a sober business face, very New England-like.

The small farmers and laboring men all wore leggins, buttoning from the knee to the ankle; heavy hob-nailed shoes; little, low, narrow-brimmed, round-topped felt hats, and frocks of linen, blue or white in color, the skirts reaching below the knee, very short waists, a kind of broad epaulette, or cape, gathered in, boddice fashion, before and behind, loose shirt-like sleeves, and the whole profusely covered with needle-work. I suppose this is the original *smock-frock*. An uglier garment could not well be contrived, for it makes every man who wears it appear to have a spare, pinched-up, narrow-chested, hump-backed figure. The women generally wore printed calico jackets, gathered at the waist, with a few inches only of skirt, and blue or gray worsted stuff petticoats, falling to within a few inches of the ankle—a picturesque, comfortable, and serviceable habit, making them appear more as if they were accustomed to walk and to work, and were not ashamed of it, than women generally do. Most incongruously, as a topping off to this sensible costume, a number of women had crowded their heads into that *ultima thule* of absurd invention, a stiff, narrow-brimmed, high-crowned, cylindrical fur hat. What they did with their hair, and how they managed to keep the thing on their heads, I cannot explain. They did do it, notwithstanding something of a breeze, as well as the most practiced man, and without showing evidence of any particular suffering.

There were, perhaps, a hundred horses offered for sale; among them one pair only of fine carriage-horses, one large and fine thorough bred cart-horse, and a few pretty ponies. All the rest were very ordinary stout working-horses, much like our Pennsylvania horses. The average price of them was but a trifle over $100, about what they would bring at New York.

There were still fewer cattle, and they were all comprised in three breeds and their intermixtures: first, Hereford, which predominated; second, Welsh, small, low, black beasts, with large heads and white faces, black muzzles and long spreading horns; third, *Smutty Pates,* an old Welsh breed hardly to be found in purity now. They are longer and somewhat larger than Devons, a little lighter red in color, with invariably black or brindle faces. They were generally in fair condition, and would cut up particularly heavy in their hind quarters. A Smithfield man told me that he thought a cross of this breed with the Hereford made the best beef in England.

After dining with a number of gentlemen, most of whom had come from a distance to attend the fair, I took a walk out into the country, about the town. The only object of interest that I remember was "Powis Castle," the seat of a nobleman, nobly situated in a picturesque, mountain-side park. The castle itself is upon a spur of the mountain, and is hidden among fine evergreen trees. I had toiled up to within about ten feet of the edge of the plateau upon which it stands, when I heard a low, deep growl, and, looking up, saw above me a great dog asking me, with bristling back, curling fangs, and fierce grinning teeth, what business I had to be there. Considering that I had no right to be visiting the residence of a gentleman who was a stranger to me, unless I had some business with him, and concluding upon short reflection that indeed I had none I determined upon a retrogade movement; and taking care not to attempt even to apologize to his dogship for the intrusion until I had brought a few trees between us, I found that he *backed down* just about as fast as I did, so that at a distance of half a dozen rods he appeared a handsome, smooth, generous-natured mastiff, and I began to consider whether the earl would not probably be pleased to have an intelligent stranger see the beauty of his castle; but the moment I stopped, the dog's lips began to part and his back to rise again, and I concluded that whatever the earl's wishes might be, I could not make it convenient just then to accommodate him, and returned forthwith to the village.

The true mastiff is a somewhat rare dog in England, and I don't think that I ever saw one in America. He is very large and powerful, and smooth-haired.

CHAPTER XXVII

English Vehicles—A Feudal Castle and Modern Aristocratic Mansion—Aristocracy in 1850—Primogeniture—
Democratic Tendency of Political Sentiments—Disposition Towards the United States—Combativeness—Slavery

J. AND C., after a tramp among the mountains of Wales, which
they have much enjoyed, reached the village nearest to where
I was visiting last night. This morning a party was made with
us to visit——Castle. We were driven in a "Welsh car," which
is much the same kind of vehicle as the two-wheeled hackney
cabs that a few years ago filled the streets of New York, and
then suddenly and mysteriously disappeared. Two-wheeled
vehicles are "all the go" in England. They are excessively
heavy and cumbrous compared with ours, the wheels much less
in diameter, and they must run much harder, yet, over these
magnificent roads, they can load them much more heavily.

The castle is on high ground, in the midst of the finest
park and among the largest trees we have seen. The moat is
filled up, and there are a few large modern windows in the
upper part, otherwise it differs but little probably from what
it appeared in the time of the crusaders. The whole structure
is in the form of a square on the ground, with four low round
towers at the corners, and a spacious court-yard in the centre.
The entrance is by a great arched gateway, over which the old
portcullis still hangs.

We were kindly shown through all its parts, including much not usually exhibited to strangers, and I confess that I was not more interested in those parts which were its peculiar features as a feudal stronghold, than in those that displayed the sumptuous taste, luxury, and splendor of a modern aristocratic mansion. The state apartments were palatial, and their garniture of paintings, sculpture, bijoutry, furniture, and upholstery, magnificent and delightful to the eye beyond any conception I had previously had of such things. Let no one say it will be soon reproduced, if it is not already excelled, in the mansions of our merchant-princes in America. Excelled, in some respect, it may be, but no such effect can be reproduced, or furnished at once to the order of taste and wealth, for it is the result of generations of taste and wealth. There was, in all, never a marvelous thing, or one that demanded especial attention, or that proclaimed in itself great costliness; and while nothing seemed new, though much was modern, most of the old things were of such materials, and so fashioned, that age was of no account, and not a word was said by them of fleeting time. The tone of all—yes, the *tone*—musical to all who entered, was, Be quiet and comfortable, move slowly and enjoy what is nearest to you without straining your eyes or your admiration;—nothing to excite curiosity or astonishment, only quiet contemplation and calm satisfaction.

I liked it, liked to be in it, and thought that if I had come honestly to the inheritance of it, I could abandon myself to a few months living in the way of it with heartiness. But in the first breath of day-dreaming, I was interrupted by the question, Is it right and best that this should be for the few, the very few of us, when for many of the rest of us there must be but bare walls, tile floors, and every thing besides harshly screaming, scrabble for life? This question, again, was immediately shoved aside unanswered, by another: Whether, in this nineteenth century of the carpenter's son, and first of vulgar, whistling, snorting, rattling, roaring locomotives, new-world steamers, and submarine electric telegraphs; penny newspapers, free schools, and working-men's lyceums, this still, soft atmosphere of elegant age was exactly the most favorable for the production of thorough, sound, influential manhood, and especially for the growth of the right sort of legislators and lawgivers for the people.

It seems, certainly, that it would be hard for a man, whose mind has been mainly formed and habited in the midst of this abundance, of quiet, and beauty, and pleasantness, to rightly understand, and judiciously work for, the wants of those whose "native air" is as different from this as is that of another planet. Especially hard must it be to look with perfect honesty and appreciating candor upon principles, ideas, measures, that are utterly discordant with, and threaten to interrupt, this costly nursery song, to which his philosophy, religion and habits have been studiously harmonized.

I may as well here record my observation of the general disposition of the English people towards our nation, which I confess I did not find to be exactly what I had anticipated, and which I think must be generally much misconceived in the United States.

There is a certain class of the English—conservative whigs more than tories, as I met them—who look upon the United States as a nation of vulgar, blustering, rowdy radicals; very much as a certain set with us look upon the young mechanics and butcher-boys of the town—troublesome, dangerous, and very "low," but who are necessary to put out fires, and whose votes are of value at elections, with whom it is as well therefore to keep on civil terms. A considerable number of pretending, sub-aristocratic, super-sensible people, follow more or less in their wake. But the great mass of the educated classes regard us quite differently; not with unqualified respect and unalloyed admiration, but much as we of the Atlantic States regard our own California—a wild, dare-devil, younger brother, with some dangerous and reprehensible habits, and some noble qualities; a capital fellow, in fact, if he would but have done sowing his wild oats.

This may be well enough understood in the United States; but further, there is not in the English people, so far as I have seen them, rich or poor, learned or ignorant, high or low, the slightest soreness or rancorous feeling on account of our separation from them, or our war of separation. No doubt there are still a few "aged women of both sexes" who worship

the ghost of that old fool, "the good King George," who look
upon us with unaffected horror, as they do equally upon their
own dissenters and liberals. Yet it never happened to me,
though I met and conversed freely with all classes except the
noble, while I was in England, to encounter the first man who
did not think that we did exactly right, or who was sorry that
we succeeded as we did in declaring and maintaining our
independence.*

The truth is, I suspect, that, *at that time,* the great mass
of thinking men in England were much of that opinion. Our
war was with George and his cabinet, not with the people of
England, and if they did reluctantly sustain the foolish measures of the king, it was precisely as our Whigs, who were
opposed to the measures that led to the war with Mexico,
sustained, with money and with blood, that war when it was
inevitable. It is a remarkable thing, I have noticed, that there
are many men in England who were born at the time of, or
shortly subsequent to, our Revolutionary War, who are named
after the American heroes of that war—Washington, Jefferson,
and Franklin.

This and other circumstances, early in my visit to England, made me reflect that the hostile feeling of the people
had never been deeply engaged against us; while it soon became also evident, that very much less of so much hostility as
they once had towards us had descended to the present than
we are in the habit of calculating for.

The reason of the great difference in this respect of the
popular feeling in the two countries is evident, though it often
extremely puzzles and offends a liberal Englishman, who has
been in the habit of looking with a strong feeling of fraternity
towards the people of the United States, to find himself, when
he comes among them, expected in all his opinions and feelings to be either a traitor to his own country or an enemy of
ours. It is easily explained however.

There is a fondness for hostility in our nature that wants
some object towards which to direct itself. Seventy years ago,
and forty years ago, that object to us as a nation was the

---

* I have lived nine months in England since I wrote this sentence,
and it still remains literally true (1858).

kingdom of Great Britain. No other object, until within a few years, has been offered to us to weaken that traditional hostility. All our military and naval glory, the most blazing, though by no means the most valuable, jewels of our national pride, have been our victories in war with Great Britain. Almost our only national holidays have been in a great part exultations over our successful hostilities with Great Britain. "The enemy" and "the British," came to me from my fighting grandfather as synonymous terms. When I was a child I never saw an Englishman but I was on my guard against him as a spy, and would look behind the fences to see that there was no ambuscade of red-coats. I made secret coverts about the house, so that when they came to sack and burn it, and take our women and children into captivity, I could lay in wait to rescue them. In our school-boy games the beaten party was always called "British." If a law was odious it was termed a British law; if a man was odious he was called an "old Tory;" and it has been with us a common piece of political blackguardism till within a short time, if it is not now, to speak of those of an opposite party as under British influence.

The war had been with us a war of the people; not a woman, as she sipped her tea, but imbibed hatred to the taxing British, and suckled her offspring with its nourishment; not a man of spunk in the country but was hand to hand fighting with the British, and teaching his sons never to yield to them.

In England, on the other hand, comparatively few of the people knew or cared at all about the war; even the soldiers engaged in it were in considerable numbers mere hirelings from another people, whom the true English would have rather seen whipped than not, so far as they had any national feeling about it. Their hostile feeling was even then more directed towards France than towards America; and now, I do not believe there is one in a thousand of the people of England who has the slightest feeling of hostility towards us, descending or inherited, from that time.* It was much so again in the later war. England was at war with half the world in those days, and if a general disposition of enmity towards us

* Such a supposition is now to me utterly preposterous (1858).

had been at all aroused in the course of it, all recollection of it was lost in the fiercer wars with other nations that immediately followed. I doubt if one in a hundred of the voters of England could tell the name of a single ship engaged in the war of 1812; whether it was General Hull or Commodore Hull who was heroized in it; whether, in the assault upon New Orleans or Washington, it was that their forces were successful; or whether, finally, they carried or lost the diplomatic point for which their soldiers and sailors had been set to fighting.

Even if the people of England could remember us equally among other important nations as their enemy, it would be a very different feeling towards us that it would lead to, from the remembrance of us as their *old and only* enemy; so that not only was our original share of the hostile feeling of the people of England a very small one, being principally confined to the king and his sycophants, and the idolaters of the divine right, but the pugnacious element in the nature of an Englishman, of our day, is directed by much more vivid remembrances towards France, or Spain, or Germany, than towards us.

Altogether, considering the exceedingly queer company English travelers seem usually to keep when in the United States, and the atrocious caricatures in which, with few exceptions, they have represented our manners and customs to their countrymen, I was surprised at the general respect and the degree of correct appreciation of us that I commonly found. There is no country, not covered by a British flag, in the world that the British of 1850 have any thing like the degree of sympathy with, and affection for, that they have for the United States.

On the other hand, it is happily evident, that since our war with Mexico has given us a new military glory, it has also diverted our national combativeness, in a degree, from our old enemy; and since the general intercommunication between the countries has been made so much more frequent and speedy, and cheaper than it used to be, the disposition of our people towards the British has been much less suspicious, guarded, and quarrelsome than it very naturally, if not very reasonably, was, until within a few years.

Opinions differing with the views I have presented having been lately expressed by several persons in honorable positions, for one at least of whom I entertain the highest respect, I wish to repeat that, in the five months during which I traveled in Great Britain, in almost every day of which time I heard the United States talked about with every appearance of candor and honesty, I do not recollect to have heard any expression of hostile feeling (except from a few physical-force Chartists, with regard to slavery) towards our government or our people, and only from a few stanch Church-and-State men, against our principles of government. Perhaps the highest eulogy on Washington ever put in words was written by Lord Brougham. The Duke of Wellington lately took part in a banquet in honor of American independence. Having observed that Mr. Howard was threatened with a mob, for keeping an English ensign flying from a corner of the Irving House, I will add that I more than once saw the American ensign so displayed in England, without exciting remark; and I know one gentleman living in the country who regularly sets it over his house on the Fourth of July, and salutes it with gun-firing and festivities; so that the day is well known, and kindly regarded by all his neighbors, as "the American holiday."

The following paragraph is the commencement of a "leader" in the London Times, the organ not of the Government, as is supposed by many who do not see it in the United States, but of a power stronger than the Government. I quote it as confirmation of my view of the way in which the American Revolution is regarded in England:

"One hundred and fifty years after the formation of our principal plantations in North America, the sense of a common wrong and a common danger drove thirteen loyal English communities most reluctantly to form themselves into a Congress for mutual defense and protection. The hint was not taken, the same rash and overbearing policy was persisted in, the wisdom of Burke and the eloquence of Chatham were poured forth in vain, the star of our ascendancy gradually waned, and a dominion planted by our own hands, an empire boundless in extent, fertility, and natural resources, the proudest exploit of the nation, the noblest proof and offspring of our civilization, was violently rent from us for ever. One would have thought that so signal and disgraceful a calamity, so terrible an exception to that career of prosperity with which we have been blessed, would have made an indelible impression on the then present and all future generations, and that a dread of quarrels with our colonies, and an aversion to union between them, would be among the traditional instincts of the empire. It is now sixty years since we set ourselves to repair, in the great southeastern continent of Australia, the disgraces and reverses which our arms and policy had sustained on the shores of the Northwest."

CHAPTER XXVIII

Paintings—Cromwell—Pastoral Ships—Family Portraits
and Distant Relations—Family Apartments—Personal
Cleanliness—The Wrekin

THE PICTURES which most interested me were portraits of
Cromwell and Charles, one of Rubens, two of very beautiful
women of the family by Sir Peter Lely, a female face by Carlo
Dolci, and two or three little things by Rubens. The portrait
of Cromwell appears as if he might have sat for it, as, if I
remember rightly, is asserted. It looks like one's idea of him,
but not in the best light of his character—a deep melancholy,
stern, and somewhat sour face.

There is a large landscape representing a brook tumbling
over a rock into the sea, on which is a fleet of shipping. The
story is, that it was painted by a French artist on a visit here,
and when first exhibited had, in place of the sea, a broad
meadow through which the brook meandered. Lady——suggested that a few sheep on the broad, green ground of the
meadow would be a pleasing addition. "Sheeps! mi lady?" said
the chagrined artist, "suppose you better like it with sheeps, I
shall make de sheeps;" and so he painted a blue sea over the
green meadow, and abruptly embouched his brook into it,
that he might appropriately gratify Lady——'s maritime
penchant.

Among the family portraits one was shown having a title that sounded familiarly to us, and, after a moment's thought, we both remembered it to be that of the single nobleman, whom an antiquarian friend had informed us that our family had been, long before its emigration, connected with by marriage. If it had been a Scotch castle, we might perhaps have felt ourselves more at home in consequence. It was an odd coincidence, and made us realize the relationship of our democracy, even to aristocratic England, quite vividly.

In consideration of this, I think I may say a few words of the private apartments of the family, through nearly all which, apparently, we were shown. They were comparatively small, not larger or more numerous, and certainly not as expensively furnished as those of many of our New York merchants; but some of them were delightful, and would be most tempting of covetousness to a man of domestic tastes, or to a lover of art or of literary ease. Generally, there was exquisite taste evident in colors and arrangements, and forms of furniture, and there were proofs of high artistic skill in some members of the family, as well as a general love and appreciation of the beautiful and the excellent. Some of the rooms were painted in very high colors, deep blue and scarlet and gold, and in bizarre figures and lines. I hardly could tell how it would please me if I were accustomed to it, but I did not much admire it at first sight, and it did not seem English or home-like. It is just the thing for New York though, and I have no doubt you'll soon see the fashion introduced there, and dining-rooms, dressing-rooms, counting-rooms, and steamboat state-rooms, all equally flaring.

The bed-chambers and dressing-rooms were so furnished as to look exceedingly cosy and comfortable, but there was nothing very remarkable about them except, perhaps, the great preparation made for washing the person. I confess, if I had been quartered in one of them, I should have needed all my Yankee capabilities to guess in what way I could make a good use of it all.

There is a story told of two members of our Legislature, who came together from "the rural districts," and were fellow-lodgers. One of them was rather mortified by the rough appearance of his companion, who was of the "bone-and-sinew" sort, and by way of opening a conversation in which he could give him a few hints, complained of the necessity which a Repre-sentative was under to pay so much for "washing." "How often do you shift?" said the Hon. Simon Pure. "Of course I have to change my linen every day," he answered. "You do?" responded his unabashed friend. "Why, what an awful dirty man you must be! I can always make mine last a week."

The ball-room, or ancient banqueting-room, was a grand hall (120 feet long, I should think), with a good deal of inter-esting old furniture, armor, relics, etc. It also contained bil-liard-tables, and other conveniences for indoor exercise. A secret door, cut through the old oak wainscot which lined its wall, admitted us to the private apartments.

We peeped into a kind of broad well into which prisoners used to be lowered, like butter, for safe keeping, and ascended to the battlements of one of the towers, from which there is a very extensive and beautiful view, extending, it is said, into sixteen counties. A gauzy blue swelling on the horizon was pointed to as the *Wrekin,* a high mountain—the highest in midland England; hence the generous old toast, "To all around the Wrekin." We were let out through a narrow postern, which gave us an opportunity to see the thickness of the wall: it was ten feet—and in some parts it was said to be sixteen—of solid stone and mortar. The castle was a border fortress of Wales, on the dyke or ancient military wall between that country and England, remains of which can be seen run-ning each way from it. It has withstood many sieges, the last by Cromwell, the effect of whose artillery is largely manifest within the court. A decree of the Long Parliament is on record ordering it to be razed to the ground.

CHAPTER XXIX

Visit to a Farm—Farm-House and Farmery—Fatting
Cattle—Sheep—Vetches—Stack Yard—Steam Threshing—
Turnip Sowing—Excellent Work—Tram Road—Wages

IN THE AFTERNOON we were taken to visit a farmer who was
considered to be about the best in the district (Shropshire).
The house was in the middle of a farm of three hundred acres,
and was approached by a narrow lane; there were no
"grounds" but a little court-yard, with a few trees in it, in
front of the house, which was a snug, two-story, plain brick
building.

On entering, we found the farmer, a stout elderly man,
sitting alone at a dinner-table, on which were dishes of fruit
and decanters. He insisted on our joining him, and we were
obliged to sit some time with him over his wine, while he
talked of free trade, and questioned us how low we could
afford to send wheat from America, and how large the supply
was likely to be.

He then led us into the farmery, which was close by the
house, the rear door almost opening into a cattle-yard. I mention this, as it would be considered extraordinary for an American, who could afford wines at his dinner, to be content with
such an arrangement. There was not the least attempt at

ornament anywhere to be seen, beyond the few trees and rose-bushes in the enclosure of a rod or two, in front of the house: not the least regard had been had to beauty except the beauty of fitness; but every thing was neat, useful, well-ordered, and thoroughly made, of the best material—the barns, stables, and out-buildings of hewn stone, with slated roofs, grout floors, and iron fixtures. The cattle stables were roomy, well venti-lated and drained, their mangers of stone and iron; fastenings, sliding chains; food, fresh-cut vetches, and the cattle standing knee deep in straw.

The fatting cattle were the finest lot I ever saw, notwith-standing the forty finest cows that had been wintered, had been sold within a fortnight. These forty had been fattened on ruta-baga and oil-cake, and their average weight was over 10 cwt., some of them weighing over 12 cwt. They were mostly shorthorns. Those remaining were mostly Hereford bullocks.

Sheep were fattening on a field of heavy vetches: Cheviots and Leicester, and crosses of these breeds.

The VETCH is a plant in appearance something like a dwarf pea; it is sown in the autumn upon wheat stubble, grows very rapidly, and at this season gives a fine supply of green food, when it is very valuable. It requires a rich, clean soil, but grows well on clay lands. I think it has not been found to succeed well in the United States.

In the rear of the barns was a yard half filled with very large and beautifully made-up stacks of hay, wheat, oats and peas. The hay was of rye-grass, a much finer (smaller) sort than our timothy. The peas were thatched with wheat-straw. The grain stacks were very beautiful, several of them had stood three years, and could not be distinguished from those made last year. The butts of the straw had been all turned over at regular distances, those of one tier to the top of that below it, and driven in, so the stack appeared precisely as if it had been *served* with straw-rope, and I supposed that it had been, until I was told. The threshing of the farm is done by steam, the engine being in the stackyard, the furnace under ground, and the smoke and sparks being carried off by a sub-terranean flue to a tall chimney a hundred yards distant. (I have seen a hundred steam-engines in stack-yards since, without this precaution, and never heard of a fire occasioned by the practice.)

The grain on the farm had all been sowed in drills. The proprietor said that if he could be sure of having the seed perfectly distributed, he should prefer broad-cast sowing (i.e., as well as a first-rate sower could distribute it in a perfectly calm day). The wheat was the strongest we have yet seen, and of remarkably equal height, and uniform dark color. The ground was almost wholly free from weeds, and the wheat was not expected to be hoed.

We found fourteen men engaged in preparing a field for turnips; opening drills with plough, carting dung, which had been heaped up, turned and made fine; distributing it along the drills; plows covering it immediately, and forming ridges 27 inches apart over it; after all, a peculiar iron roller, formed so as to fit the ridges and furrows, followed; leaving the field precisely like a fluted collar. The ridges were as straight as the lines of a printed page; and any inequality to the height of half an inch, was removed by the equal pressing of the roller. A more perfect piece of work could not be conceived of. Seed (3 lbs. to the acre) will be sown immediately on the ridges, by a machine opening, seeding, closing and rolling six drills at once. The field is thorough drained (as is all the farm, three feet deep) and subsoil plowed.

I saw no farming that pleased me better than this, in all England. It was no gentleman or school farming, but was directed by an old man, all his life a farmer, on a leased farm, without the least thought of taste or fancy to be gratified, but with an eye single to quick profit; with a prejudice against "high farming," indeed, because it is advised by the free-traders as a remedy for low prices. He declared no money was to be made by farming: do his best, he could not pay his rent and leave himself a profit under the present prices. He had been holding on to his wheat for three years in hopes of a rise, but now despaired of it, except the protective policy was returned to.

There was a coal mine and lime-kiln within the boundary of the farm, and a tram-road from it to the railroad about two miles distant. A tram-road is a narrow track of wooden rails, on which cars are moved by stationary power or horses. On extensive farms they might be advantageously made use of. A road running through the barns and out-buildings of a farm-stead, on which straw, feed, dung, etc., could be easily moved by hand, would cost but little, and often afford a great saving of labor.

The fences were all of hawthorn, low and close-trimmed.

The farm servants had from $65 to $75 a year and their board. (The very next day a man told me he paid just half these sums.) Day-laborers from $2 to $2.50 a week (fair weather) and board themselves. A boy just over fourteen years old (under which age it is by law forbidden) told me he worked in the coal mines for sixteen cents a day.

CHAPTER XXX

Visit to Two English Common Schools

In COMPLIANCE WITH our desire to visit an English common school, we were driven from the castle to a village in the vicinity, in which was a school for boys, under the guidance of the British and Foreign Society, and one for girls under the control of the National or State Church Society. The schoolhouse of the former was a simple but tasteful stone building, standing a little to one side, but not fenced off, from the principal street, with a few large trees and a playground about it. The interior was all in one room, except a small vestibule. It was well lighted, the walls were plastered and whitewashed, and had mottoes, texts of Scripture, tables, charts, etc., hung upon them; there was no ceiling, but the rafters of the roof, which was high-peaked, were exposed; the floor was of stone. There were long desks and benches all around against the wall, and others, the form of which I do not remember, filling up the most of the body. The house and furniture was much too small and scanty for the number of scholars present, and the labor of the teacher must have been very arduous.

The boys all rose as we entered, and remained standing during our visit, a request from us that they might be seated not being regarded. Classes in arithmetic, geography and spelling were examined before us. The absence of all embarrassment, and the promptness and confidence of the scholars in replying to our questions, was remarkable. In mental arithmetic great proficiency was shown in complicate reductions of sterling money. In geography their knowledge of America was limited to the more important points of information, but so far as it went was very accurate and ready. With regard to Great Britain, their information was minute. The boys were bright, ready-witted and well-behaved, and surprisingly free from all excitement or embarrassment before strangers.

The schoolmaster was also parish-clerk, and his pay from the two offices was about $500 a year.* I judge that he had intended to make teaching his business for life, and had thoroughly prepared and accomplished himself for it. His manner to us, and two or three incidents which it would be impossible to relate, gave me the impression that his position in society was far from being a pleasant, or what we should deem a proper one for a teacher.

The "National School" for girls was a building of more highly finished architectural character, and had a dwelling for the schoolmistress attached to it. The whole school was engaged in sewing when we entered, the mistress, assisted by some of the older scholars, going from one to another, giving instructions and examining the work. It was not interrupted by our entrance, though the girls all rose, curtseyed, and continued standing. There were one hundred and thirty present in a room about twelve yards by six in area. The girls were neatly, though exceedingly plainly, dressed, and were generally very pleasing in their appearance. They seemed well instructed, and without the least want of desirable modesty, showed much more presence of mind, and answered our questions with more promptness and distinctness than any school of girls I ever visited before.

Both schools are conducted on the Lancasterian plan.

---

* Advertisements for common school teachers, "capable to instruct in reading, writing, arithmetic and the principles of the Christian religion," appear in the Times, offering salaries of from $150 to $300, with lodging and board.

CHAPTER XXXI

Shrewsbury—Angling in Curricles—Sheep-walks—Effect
of Thorough Draining on Dry Soils—Gorse—Church
Stretton—Churchyard Literature—Encounter with an Enthusiastic Free-Trader

Shrewsbury, June 7th

WE ARRIVED AT this fine old town by rail, this morning, and
have again had much delight in ancient domestic town architecture. The houses are of the same general style as those at
Chester, but with every conceivable variation of form, and
each with something peculiar to itself, so that we cannot tire
of rambling through the steep, narrow streets to study them.
There are a great many old churches, too: one remarkable for
a very light, tall, simply-tapering spire; another, the abbey
church, has a great mingling of styles, and in some parts is
very rich and elegant. Near it I noticed that some religious
house, once connected with it, had been built upon, roofed
over, and converted into a brewery. The roofs are universally
of flat tiles here; a few miles north we saw nothing but slates.

On one of the bridges over the Severn, which here divides
into two small streams, between which most of the town is
beautifully situated, we saw a number of anglers with *curricles,* a light portable boat made of hide, stretched out like an
umbrella-top by a wicker frame. It is easily carried on one

arm, and forms a usual part of a salmon-fisher's equipment in Wales.

In the afternoon J. and I walked on to Church Stretton, thirteen miles; our road, most of the way, through a level valley, with high, naked, bleak hills on each side. A man joined us who had been most of his life a miller, and had lately rented a sheep-walk of sixty-three acres on one of these hill-tops, or, rather, mountain-tops. They are to all appearance totally barren, except of *gorse,* and he said he could only stock at the rate of one and a half sheep to the acre.

Gorse (*furze* or *whins*) is an evergreen shrub, growing about three feet high, rough, thorny, prickly; flourishes in the poorest, dryest land, where, if it gets possession, it is extremely difficult to eradicate. It is sometimes used as a hedge plant, and for that purpose is planted thickly on high ridges. In some parts of England fuel is made of it, and when bruised by powerful machines made for the purpose, it forms palatable and nutricious food for horses and cattle. Hereabouts, however, we could not learn that it was made of any use, or regarded otherwise than as a weed. Half the surface of the hills was overgrown with it.

A strange story has been told me of the effect of draining on soils of this sort. A considerable estate, mainly on the tops of such hills, having come into possession of a friend of my informant, he immediately commenced under-draining it in the most thorough and expensive manner. The whole country thought him crazy. "Why! The hills were too dry already—the man was throwing away his money;" and his family interposed with expostulation and entreaty to check what they deemed a ruinous and disgraceful "folly." But he patiently carried it on, and waited the result; which was, that the increased rental in a very short time more than paid for the whole outlay, and the actual value of the land was trebled.

Church Stretton is a little village mostly made up of inns on the main street. We chose the Stag's Head, a picturesque, many-gabled cottage, part of it very old, and, as we were told, formerly a manor-house of the Earl of Derby, who spent one night (ever to be remembered!) in it. It was close by a curiously-carved church, and graveyard. From among a great many "improving" epitaphs, I select the following as worthy of more extended influence:

I

"A NON SEQUITUR"

> *"Farewell, my wife*
> *And children dear, in number seven,*
> *Therefore prepare yourself for Heaven."*

II

"AN HONEST MAN"

"Erected by the Curate of Church Stretton."

III

"Farewell, vain world, I have seen my last of thee;
Thy smiles I court not, frowns I fear,
My cares are past, my head lies quiet here,
My time was short in this world, my work is done,
My rest I hope is in another,
In a quiet grave I lie, near my beloved mother."

IV

> *"A Friend so true,*
> *There is but few,*
> *And difficult to find;*
> *A man more just,*
> *And true to trust,*
> *There is not left behind."*

V

> *"You that are young, behold and see*
> *How quickly death has conquered me;*
> *His fatal shaft it was so strong,*
> *And cut me off while I was young,*
> *But God above, He knew for why,*
> *That in my youth I was to die."*

The following, or something very like it, is to be found in almost every churchyard in England, often several times repeated:

VI

> "*Afflictions sore*
> *Long time I bore,*
> *Physicians' aid was vain;*
> *Till God did please*
> *To give me ease,*
> *And free me from my pain.*"

On the other side of the churchyard were two long rows of cottages built closely together, the street between them only nine feet wide.

After ordering supper, we were shown into a little room where there was a fire and newspapers, and two men sitting. One of them was a young, well-dressed farmer, stupid and boozy; the other a traveling mercantile agent, very wide awake. The latter almost immediately opened conversation.

"Did you notice the white nag in the stables, gents?"

"No."

"Ah, you should. It's not every day you'll see such a horse. It would be really worth your while, if I may be permitted to advise, to step out and see him. Why! if you'll believe me, sir, we gave the stage-coach twenty minutes start and beat her two and a half in eight, besides stopping—how many times?—a go of gin first and—two of brandy afterwards, wasn't it Brom? and now there he is—eating his oats just like a child!"

We showed no disposition to see this phenomenon, but putting our knapsacks on the table, had commenced reading the papers, when he again addressed us, suddenly exclaiming,

"Hem—wool's heavy!"

"What, sir?"

"Hops scarce?"

"What?"

"Sheffil line?"

"——!" (Stare of perplexity.)

"Tea?" glancing at our packs.

"Tea! oh no!"

"Oh, I thought it might be tea you were——Brummagem way?"

"We are—"

"Oh! ah! Good market at Le'm'ster?"

"We are from New York—traveling merely to see the country; our packs have—"

"From New York? why, that's in America."

"Yes, sir; we are Americans."

"What! Americans, are you? Hallo! why, this is interesting. Brom! I say, Brom!—look! do you see? from America; you see? furriners! If you will permit me, sir—your very good health, gentlemen. Brom! (damn it, man,) your *health—their* health. . . . Now look here! you'll allow me, sir (and he caught my leg); you brought this, I presume, from New York?"

"Yes."

"Made there?"

"Probably."

"And the wool?"

"Very likely from these hills."

"Exactly, sir; *exactly!* You see now, Brom—what was I telling you?—that's FREE TRADE, Brom. Most happy to meet you, sir; (intelligent persons, Brom! first-class furriners;) you are welcome here, sir; and, gentlemen— (your good health, sir)—and no one to molest or make you afraid— (won't you try the gin? I can recommend it)—wandering up and down, seeking what you may, eh?—see! Yes, sir, the sea is the highway of nations—else what is it mentioned in Scripture for? 'the great sea—to bring nations together—with ships thereon, stretching from Tiberia to Siberias, and from Jericher to,' eh? —hem—eh?—somewhere!"

"Your tea is ready, gentlemen," said the waiter; and we hastily took leave.

CHAPTER XXXII

Country Carrier's Cart—Independent Breakfast—Beauty
—Old Inn—Jack up the Chimney—Bacon and Bread;
Beer and Rum—Ludlow—An Apostolic Church—The
Poor-House—*Case* of a Broken Heart—Refreshment

WE ROSE the next morning at daybreak, and walked some
miles before we saw any body else awake. At the first public
house we found open, we stopped to breakfast. In front of it
was a carrier's cart—a large, heavy, hooped, canvas-topped
cart, drawn by one horse. As any body who reads Dickens
knows, this kind of rural package-express is a common thing
on the English roads, the carrier taking orders of country
people for what they need from the towns, and bringing them
any parcels they send for; taking live freight also when he is
not otherwise filled up: David Copperfield, for instance. The
representative of "Mr. Barkis" and "honest John Peerybingle"
was in the kitchen of the public house, and very glad to see us,
pressing us politely to drink from his glass, and recommending
the ale as the best on the road.

The house, however, was of a very humble character; the
"good woman" was gone to market, and the landlord, though
very amiable and desirous to please, was very stupid and ill-
provided. He could not even find us an egg, every thing having been swept off to market. There was some good bread,

however, which the carrier had just brought, and milk. We found a saucepan, cleaned it, and scalded the milk, and, stirring in the bread with pepper and salt, soon made a comfortable hot breakfast, greatly to the admiration of our host and the carrier.

Fine English weather today: gleams of warm, thick sunshine alternating with slight showers of rain. The country beautiful; the road running through a rich, well-watered vale, with the same high, steep hills as yesterday, but now regularly planted with wood to the summits. Before us they fall back, one over another, till they become blue under the thick mists that curl about the tops of the most distant, and then, again, blush red before the sun, when the breeze lifts this veil.

Seeing a singular ruin a little distance from the road, we went to visit it. It had been a castle, with a church or large Gothic chapel attached. Different parts of it, having received more modern, yet ruinously decayed, timber and *noggin* additions, were occupied as sheep-stables, granary, and workshop. A moat remained about it, enclosing also a court-yard; and on the opposite side of this from the main structure, was a high, four-gabled timber house, with a gateway through it, entered across the moat by a bridge, formerly a draw-bridge, and with some remains of a portcullis. The wood-work of the gables, and much of the timber, the heavy brackets and the doorways, were covered with quaint carvings. An interesting history it must have had, yet all we could learn of it was, that it was "farmer——'s barn."

At noon we stopped at a superannuated old stage-coaching house, going at once to the kitchen, which was a large room with heavy beams in the ceiling, from which depended flitches of bacon; a stone floor, a number of oak benches and tables, rows of pewter mugs hanging about the walls, and a great fireplace and chimney. A stout, driving landlady received our orders; a piece of meat was set to roasting before the fire on the old turn-spit, and we were left alone to dry ourselves. Soon we noticed that one end of the spit with the meat was being raised, and we attempted in vain to readjust it. It continued to rise, and I tried to disconnect the chain by which it was turned, and which was now drawing it up the chimney; I could not, and still it rose. I clung to it, and hallooed for assistance. In rushed the landlady, three maids, and a man-servant, and I yielded the spit to them; but the power was too strong—their united weight could not long detain it; up it rose—rose—rose, till the prettiest maid stood first on tiptoe, and then began to scream; then the landlady, disengaging the meat from it, and dropping it hastily on a plate, fell back exhausted on one of the oak benches and laughed—oh! ha, ha! oh! ha, ha! ha, ha! ho, ho! ha, ha, ha! —how the woman did laugh! As soon as she recovered, she sent the man and the maids up to the machinery, being too much out of breath to go herself; and in a few minutes the chain, which had fouled on the rusty crank at the chimney top, was unwound and the spit lowered to its place, the joint put on and set to turning again, all right.

While we were eating our dinner, five young men— laborers—came in for theirs; most of them ate nothing but bread and cheese, but some had thin slices of bacon cut from the flitch nearest the fire, which they themselves toasted with a fork and ate with bread which they had brought in their pockets, as soon as it was warmed through. All drank two pints of beer, and, after dining, smoked, except one, who took hot rum-and-water.

It appeared that while three of them preferred to spend their money for beer rather than bacon, none of them chose bacon at the expense of beer. The man who took rum drank two glasses of it, and the others two or more pints of beer; but no one who took beer took any rum at all, nor did he who took rum take any beer. A similar observation I have frequently made. The habit of beer-drinking seems to weaken the taste for more alcoholic stimulants.

We remained about the inn, looking at some pretty model cottages erected by Lord Clive, until C., who had made a quick walk of nearly thirty miles to overtake us, arrived, and then walked into Ludlow.

Ludlow is a pleasant town, beautifully planted in the bight of a broad, shallow, musical stream, amongst high, bluffy hills. It has a ruined castle, celebrated in Royal history, parts of which, half hidden by tall old trees among which it stands, and adorned with ivy, are very picturesque. There are fine avenues and public walks about it, and just over the river, which is crossed by two bridges, is a very large common, extending to the top of high and steep hills, which is used as a public pleasure-ground. In the middle of the town is a venerable old church, with richly painted windows and many curious monuments and effigies of Crusaders and learned doctors sleeping with their wives. In it I also first saw a beadle in the flesh, and very funny it was, in cocked hat, red nose and laced coat. There are many curious old houses, particularly one of the inns, ("The Feathers;") and over the Ludford bridge there is a pretty little rural church and a number of pretty cottages, both ancient and modern, the modern being built in the fashion of the timber houses that I described in Cheshire.

Our chess-playing friend on the ship had given us a note to a relative residing here, and having left it with our card at his house, he very soon called upon us, and was extremely kind in his attentions and offers of service. C. had asked with regard to the religious service which would be held in the town the coming day; after replying to his inquiries, he remarked that he belonged to a congregation of Christian brethren, whose worship he would be gratified if it would be agreeable for us to attend. They had no distinct organization, but simply met as a company of believers, to worship as they were prompted in the spirit. They liked to have any one join with them, who loved Jesus Christ, whatever his theoretical opinion might be.

The next morning I breakfasted with this gentleman, and afterwards attended the meeting of the brotherhood. It was held in a plain "upper room," apparently designed for a school-room, which was well filled with people, representing every class, except the aristocratic, in the community, females being slightly preponderant. The services were extremely simple—much like those of a Presbyterian prayer-meeting, with the addition of a rather lengthy exhortation from one who, I was told, was, like myself, a stranger to the most of those present, and concluded with the administration of the communion.

Nothing could be greater than the contrast of the place and its furniture, and the style of the exercises, with what I had seen and heard at the cathedral the previous Sunday; yet I could not but notice the marked resemblance between the simple solemnity of manner and sincere unendeavoring tone of the gentleman who conducted the ceremony of the communion, and that of his robed and titled brother who performed the same duty within those aweing walls.

In the afternoon I went with one of "the brethren" to the Union poor-house, which is a little out of the town. The inmates, so far as I saw them, were nearly all aged persons, cripples, or apparently half-witted, and it all appeared very much like a hospital. The chilling neatness, bareness, order and precision, reminded me of the berth-deck of a man-of-war. Among the sick was a young woman who had now for four days refused to take food or to speak; when broth was set before her in our presence, she merely moaned and shook her head, closed her eyes and sank back upon her bed. Her disease was a broken heart. A week ago her cottage was destroyed by fire, and her child (illegitimate) burned to death in it.

At sunset we found much such a company strolling on the common opposite the town as that we saw promenading the walls at Chester last Sunday night. The shaded walks about the castle were also thick with happy-looking, grateful-looking, orderly men and women, boys and girls, superabundantly attended by healthy, sturdily-tottering babies.

In the evening C. called on the Independent clergyman. He spoke highly of the spiritual character of the brethren, but he evidently regarded them as rather wild and untractable abstractionists. They had drawn away several of the leading members of his flock, and, in his observations upon them, he possibly showed a little soreness on this account. He continued on terms of friendly intercourse, however, with them.

CHAPTER XXXIII

Physical Education—A Rustic Village—Farm-House Kitchen—An Orchard—Stables—Leominster—A Trout Brook—Fruit Culture

Monday, June 10th

AFTER ANOTHER BREAKFAST with the Independent minister, (the term clergyman is never applied in England except to those of the established church,) he walked with us for six miles out of town upon our road. Three little boys and girls, the youngest six years old, also accompanied us. They were romping and rambling about all the while, and their morning's walk must have been as much as fifteen miles; but they thought nothing of it, and, when we parted, were apparently as fresh as when they started, and were very loth to return.

After looking at several objects of interest near the road, we were taken by a narrow, crooked lane to a small hamlet of picturesque old cottages, in one of which a farmer lived who was a parishioner of our guide's. It was a pretty, many-gabled, thatched-roofed timber-house, almost completely covered with vines and creepers. We were sorry to find the farmer not at home; his wife, an elderly, simple-minded dame, received us joyfully, however. In entering the house, as we have noticed to be usual in old buildings, whatever their purpose, we found that the stone floor of the narrow hall was a step below the street and general surface of the ground outside. The kitchen, to which we were at once conducted, was a large square room, lighted by a single broad window, and having a brilliant display of polished metal utensils upon and about a great chimney, all as neat and nice as a parlor. "The huge oak table's massy frame bestrode the kitchen floor;" a linen cloth was spread upon it, and coarse but excellent wheat bread, butter and cheese, brought from the pantry, and cider and perry from the cellar. The cider was "hard" enough; the perry, (fermented juice of pears,) a beautiful, bright, golden liquid, tasted much like weak vinegar and water. We had entered the district of cider and apple-trees, for these liquors were home-made, and the first extensive orchard that we have seen, adjoined the rear of the house: during the rest of our day's walk the road was frequently lined with them for long distances.

The trees, in a considerable part of this orchard, were of every age, and stood very irregularly at various distances from each other. It appeared as if when an old tree was blown down, or became worthless from age and decay, and an unshaded space was thus left, or likely to be, two young trees were planted at a little distance on each side of it, and thus perhaps the orchard had been renovated and continued on the same ground for several generations. Two hundred years ago it was considered that "the best way to plant an orchard is to set some kernels of the best and soundest apples and pears, a finger deep, and at a foot distance, and to leave the likeliest plants only in the natural place, removing the others only as time and occasion shall require." The orchards of the Rhine, at the present day, in which apple, pear, cherry and nut-trees are intermingled, seem to have been planted with as little regard to regularity of distance. The grafts were commonly inserted at from six to eight feet from the ground, and the limbs trimmed so as to allow free passage to cattle beneath them. The land was in an old weedy sward, and was pastured by horses and cows. It had not been in any way drained, and was in some parts boggy. In these, willows, and sallows or osiers, (basket willows,) were growing. The trees all appeared to be unhealthy, mossy and stunted. A few pear-trees grew here and there, indiscriminately, among the apples. The cider-mill was just like the old fashioned ones, with a stone wheel, common in New England.

After seeing the orchard in such condition, I was surprised to find excellent, neat and well-ordered stables. The horse-stalls were large, with iron racks and mangers, and a grating and drain to carry off the liquid. The manure in the yard was piled up in a large, oblong heap, covered with earth, to prevent evaporation, with a space of clean pavement, wide enough for a cart to pass all around it. The liquid overflow of the yard was conducted off by a drain, so as to flow over the orchard pasture.

We reached Leominster at noon, after a few miles further of walking through a pleasant country, remarkable for its pretty old cottages. At Leominster, (pronounced *Leminster*,) there are also a more than usually quaint sort of houses, grotesquely carved; and on the market-house, an odd old building, there are some singular inscriptions. I recollect only one, which runs in this way: *"As columnes do pprope up"* a house, so do a gentry support a state.

In the afternoon we walked for some distance on the banks of a trout brook, in which a good many ladies and gentlemen were angling, with but poor success. The trout were small, and if I recollect rightly, rather lighter colored than ours, and not so prettily mottled. Some of the anglers called the stream "the Arrow," and some "the Harrow."

The field-bean is a common crop here; it is now in blossom, and a peculiarly sweet scent from it, every now and then, comes in a full, delicious flood over the hedges.

The country over which we walked in the afternoon, between Leominster and Hereford, was in some parts extremely beautiful: considerable hills, always, when too steep or rocky or sterile for easy cultivation, covered with plantations of trees; the lesser hills and low lands shaded by frequent orchards. These were generally of apples, sometimes with pears intermixed—somewhat rarely entirely of pears. Many of them appeared much like the one I have described, and occasionally there was a regularly planted one of fine, thrifty trees. In the poorer orchards, where the trees were of all ages, they frequently were planted not more than fifteen feet apart, and when so, as far as I observed, were invariably small in size and unhealthy. In the better ones, the trees stood oftenest thirty feet apart one way, and twenty another; rarely at much greater distance than this, but sometimes as much as forty.

CHAPTER XXXIV

English Orchard Districts—The Most Favorable Soils and
Climate—Lime—Practical Deduction—Diseases—Preven-
tion and Remedies—Suggestions

THERE ARE BUT FEW orchards in England, except in certain
districts, and in these they abound, and are often very extensive. The inquiry naturally arises, What has given those districts their distinction in this respect? Have they any natural
advantages which makes orcharding more profitable in them
than in other parts of the country? In reply, I learn, that the
orchard districts are all distinguished for a comparatively mild
climate. They are nearly all in the south and southwestern
counties, while in the northern and eastern counties I know of
none. Hereford is a somewhat hilly county, and, as I have
remarked, where the hills are too steep for easy cultivation, it
is usual to plant orchards; but the south side of such hills is
preferred to the north, and, even here, a crop is sometimes
entirely lost by a late and severe spring frost. A southeast slope
is preferred, the southeast winds being the driest. I suspect
another reason why it is found better is, that the southwest
winds, coming off the ocean, are the stronger. My own observation has led me to think that the apple-tree is much affected
by an exposure to severe winds. Few trees thrive well upon the
seashore, and this is usually laid to the account of salt spray or

"salt in the air." It will be found, however, that trees grown inland upon very exposed sites, have the same peculiarities with those in the vicinity of the sea; that is, they are slow of growth and "scrubby."

Another important circumstance to be noticed, as distinguishing the apple districts, is in the nature of their soils. These are found, however varying otherwise, invariably to have a large proportion of lime, and generally of potash, in their chemical composition. With reference to this I quote the observations of Mr. Frederick Falkner.*

> Great light has been lately thrown upon the adaptation of soils to particular plants, and it is now easy to account for the predilection, so to speak, of the apple-tree for soils that abound in clays and marls. All deciduous trees require a considerable proportion of potash for the elaboration of their juices in the leaves, and are prosperous, or otherwise, in proportion to the plentiful or scanty supply of that substance in the soil. Liebig has shown, that the acids generated in plants are always in union with alkaline or earthy bases, and cannot be produced without their presence . . . Now the apple-tree, during its development, produces a great quantity of acid; and therefore, in a corresponding degree, requires alkaline, and, probably, earthy bases also, as an indispensable condition to the existence of the fruit.

Again, the same writer:

> It cannot be denied that ammonia, and also the humus of decaying dung, must have some influence on the growth of the tree in such soils, and also of the development of the fruit; but it is most certain, at the same time, that these alone would be perfectly inefficient for the production of the fruit without the coöperation of (the alkaline bases.) The size, and perhaps the flavor of the fruit, may be somewhat affected by the organic part of the manure, but its very existence depends upon the presence in the

---

* Journal of the Royal Agricultural Society, vol. iv, p. 381.

soil of a sufficient quantity of those inorganic or mineral substances which are indispensible to the formation of acids.

But it is also found by analysis that lime enters into the composition of the *wood* of the apple-tree in very large proportions. By the analysis of Fresenius, the ash of the wood of the apple contains 45.19 per cent. of lime, and 13.67 per cent. of potash. By the analysis of Dr. Emmons, of Albany, N. Y., the ash of the sap-wood of the apple contains of lime 18.63 per cent., and 17.50 per cent. of phosphate of lime.

But it is not wherever soils of the sort I have described (calcareous sandstones and marly clays) abound in a district, that you find that the farmers have discovered that it is to their interest to have orchards; nor are they common in all the milder latitudes of England; but I believe that wherever you find a favorable climate, conjoined with a strongly calcareous and moderately aluminous soil of a sufficient depth, there you will find that for centuries the apple-tree has been extensively cultivated. Evelyn speaks, 1676, of the apples of Herefordshire, and says there were then 50,000 hogsheads of cider produced in that county yearly. The ancient capital of modern Somersetshire, one of the present "Cider Counties," was known by the Romans as Avallonia, (the town of the apple orchards.) It would not be unlikely that the universal ceremony in Devonshire, of "shooting at the apple-tree," (hereafter described,) originated in some heathen rite of its ancient orchardists.

To obtain choice dessert fruit, the apple in England is everywhere trained on walls, and in the colder parts it is usual to screen a standard orchard on the north by a plantation of firs. There is no part of the United States where the natural summer is too short for most varieties of the apple to perfect their fruit. In Maine, and the north of New Hampshire and Vermont, the assortment of varieties is rather more limited than elsewhere, I believe; but I have eaten a better apple from an orchard at Burlington, Vermont, than was ever grown even in the south of England. We may congratulate ourselves then, that all that we need to raise the best apples in the world, anywhere in the northern United States, is fortunately to be procured much more cheaply than a long summer would be, if that were wanting. The other thing needful, judging from the experience of England for a length of time past record, in addition to the usual requisites for the cultivation of ordinary farm crops, is abundance of lime. This is experience; and science confirms it with two very satisfactory reasons: first, that apple-tree wood is made up in a large part of lime, which must be taken from the soil; and, second, that before the apple-tree can turn other materials which it may collect from the soil and atmosphere into fruit, it must be furnished with a considerable amount of some sort of alkali, which requisite may be supplied by lime.

There is but little else that we can learn from the English orchardists, except what to avoid of their practices. The cider orchards, in general, are in every way miserably managed, and the greater number of those that I saw in Herefordshire were, in almost every respect, worse than the worst I ever saw in New England. The apple in England is more subject to disease; and I should judge, from what was told me, that in a course of years it suffered more from the attacks of insects and worms than in America. The most deplorable disease is canker. This malady is attributed sometimes to a "cold, sour" soil, sometimes to the want of some ingredients in the soil that are necessary to enable the tree to carry on its healthy functions, sometimes to the general barrenness of the soil, and sometimes to the *"wearing out of varieties."* The precaution and remedies used by gardeners (rarely by orchardists) for it, are generally those that would secure or restore a vigorous growth to a tree. The first of these is deepening and drying the soil, or deep draining and trenching. The strongest and most fruitful orchards, it is well known, are those which have been planted upon old hop-grounds, where the soil has been deeply tilled and manured for a series of years with substances that contain a considerable amount of phosphorus, such as woolen rags and bones. The roots of the hop also descend far below the deepest tillage that can be given it; (in a calcareous gravelly subsoil they have been traced ten feet from the surface;) a kind of subsoiling is thus prepared for the apple by the decay of the hop roots. In some parts it is the custom to introduce the hop culture upon the planting of a young orchard, the hops occupying the intervals until the branches of the trees interfere with them. Nothing is more likely than this to insure a rapid and healthy growth of the trees.

I recommend to those who intend planting an orchard, to have the ground for it in a state of even, deep, fine tilth beforehand, and to plant in the intervals between apple or pear-trees, some crop which, like hops, will be likely to get for itself good feeding and culture for several years.

An impenetrable bottom of stone, at not more than three feet from the surface, is frequently made use of by gardeners, as a precaution against canker. I have been told that in the ancient orchards attached to monasteries, such a flagging of brick or stone is often found under the whole area of the orchard. This would seem at first sight to be directly opposed to the other precaution, of thorough draining and deepening the surface soil; but it may be considered that the injury which stagnant water would effect is in a degree counteracted when the roots do not descend below the influence of the atmosphere and the heat of the sun. It is not unlikely that these influences would extend to a depth of three feet from the surface, in a soil that had been so thoroughly trenched and lightened up as it necessarily must be to allow of a paving to be made under it. The paving does not probably much retard the natural descent of water from the surface, nor does it interfere with its capillary ascent; the trenching makes the descent of superabundant water from the surface more rapid, while the increased porosity of the trenched soil gives it increased power of absorption, both from the subsoil and the atmosphere, as well as of retention of a healthy supply of moisture. The paving also prevents the roots from descending below where this most favorable condition of the soil has been made to exist. The effect would doubtless be greatly better if thorough draining were given in addition; but so far as it goes, the under-paving and trenching is calculated to effect the same purpose as deep drainage: to secure a healthy supply of heat, light and moisture to all the roots.

It is evident that the precautions and remedies which have been found of service against canker, whether operations upon the roots or the foliage, are all such as are calculated to establish or replace the tree in circumstances favorable to its general thriving, healthy condition.

This suggests the idea that canker may be the result of a general constitutional debility of the tree, not occasioned by any one cause or set of causes, but resultant from all and any circumstances unfavorable to the healthy growth of a tree; and it is a question whether the same may not be thought of the peculiar diseases of other trees, the peach, the pear, the plum, the sycamore, and perhaps even of the rot of the potato.

CHAPTER XXXV

Decay of Varieties—Two Theories: Knight's, Downing's—
English Theory and Practice—Practical Deductions—
Causes of Decay—Remedies—Hints to Orchardists—
Special Manures—Pruning—Thorough Drainage—A Sa-
tirical Sketch—Shooting the Apple Tree

It is known that many varieties of apples, which fifty years
ago were held in high esteem as healthy, hardy sorts, bearing
abundantly very superior fruit, have now but a very poor
reputation, and varieties which a hundred years ago were very
highly valued and extensively cultivated, are now extinct. It is
believed, too, that the most celebrated old varieties that are
yet cultivated, are much more subject to canker than others;
or, in other words, that trees of these varieties are more easily
affected by unfavorable circumstances, or have a more delicate
constitution.

To account for this, there are two theories held by different scientific horticulturists. The first—which originated with
the late Mr. Knight, a distinguished vegetable physiologist of
England, who devoted much attention to the subject, and
made a long series of experiments upon it—may be stated as
follows:

Each seedling tree has a natural limit to its life, and
within that will have a period of vigor, succeeded by a natural

and inevitable decline, corresponding to the gradually increasing feebleness which attends the latter part of the natural life of a man. And all trees also which have been propagated from such a seedling by means of buds or grafts, or, in other words, all trees of the same variety, are to be considered as merely extensions of that seedling, and will have a contemporary vigor and decline and decease with it. The period of vigor or decline may be much extended by circumstances favorable to the general health of any particular tree, and by unfavorable influences it may be shortened: but however well situated, sooner or later it will manifest feebleness by the change in the quality of its fruit, the small quantity it is able to bear, by the decay of branches, and especially by its liability to be attacked by disease, such as the canker, which rapidly destroy its remaining vitality. These diseases may be guarded against, and may often be cured; but the longer the period since the origin of the variety from a seed, the greater the liability and the more difficult the cure.*

This theory is entirely discredited by other distinguished botanists and horticulturists, among whom are Dr. Lindley in England, Decandolle on the Continent, and Mr. Downing and H. W. Beecher in America.

These consider that there is no such similarity between the life of a tree and the life of an animal, and that a bud and a seed contain equally the germ of new life; that they are, in fact, the same thing, except that they are prepared to be developed under different circumstances. That each bud, twig, and branch, has a life of its own, and the trunk is but an association of roots, or of connections between each bud and its roots. It may be separated from this trunk as a seed is, and will continue to live if ingrafted upon another trunk, where it will connect itself again in the ground and grow, and through

* Professor Turner, of Illinois College, advocates the view that every time a seedling tree is divided, whether in root or top, its natural longevity and proportionate vital force are proportionally divided, abstracted and shortened; and believes that some of the worst forms of hereditary, and also of annual diseases, flow from a succession of such mutilations through a series of generations, or are produced by an effort of nature to resist and repair this interference with her natural process.

it other independent lives will be produced and sustained. Or it may be removed from its parent and placed upon the ground, where it will make roots and extend and reproduce again as independently, in all respects, as a seed. It is held that the death of trees does not rise from any natural period being assigned to their existence, but that the tissues of a tree, as they grow old, become dry and hard; no longer transmit sap, lose their vitality, and gradually decay; yet the process of growth may continually be renewed exteriorly to this death, so that large cavities will often exist in the interior of trees. As, however, the peculiar natural food of the tree, within the limits to which it can extend its roots, becomes exhausted, or, as other unhealthy circumstances affect it, its vital power and its re-vitalizing power will be diminished, and finally may become extinct.

If, however, a bud or germ of a new branch can be taken from the tree before its decay, or from any part of it that yet retains its vigor and health, and be transplanted by means of cuttings in the earth, or inoculations or grafts upon another healthy stock of the same species, it will have all the vital energy, and, in every respect, all the natural character, of a seedling.

In explanation of the general deterioration of certain favorite old varieties, according to the theory of Downing and Lindley, their state should be compared (taking care not to run the analogy too far into the ground) to what is popularly understood as a *scrofulous* condition of human beings, rather than to the decrepitude of old age. From various causes—want of proper food, unfavorable climate, propagation upon unhealthy stocks, high feeding, and any unnatural stimulus producing imperfect succulent growth, and from constant repropagation from trees that have in a greater or less degree so suffered—the trees of the variety have very generally lost their natural, strong, active, resisting, and recuperative vital energy, and have a general tendency to disease, which will be developed in different forms according to circumstances. A wound upon a scrofulous subject is more difficult to heal; exertion produces more fatigue, and rest brings less return of strength. Food, which in its natural state would be most nourishing and healthful, it can no longer digest, and it does it more harm than good; exposure to cold, to malaria, or contagion, is more dangerous, and if it escapes all acute disease, it gradually grows more and more feeble, until finally it has "died of a decline."

Sterility attends the decrepitude of age, but not the scrofulous debility in man, neither does it the degeneracy of the old trees. But the scrofulous habit is hereditary in man; so it is believed to be in the old varieties. If, however, the scrofulous inheritance is not very virulent, by a judicious course of regimen it may be gradually overcome, and a strong vigorous constitution once more reëstablished. So it is argued, and facts are cited that seem to sustain the position, may the old varieties be restored to their pristine excellence, by care to select scions from the most healthy trees, and from the most vigorous parts of them, and to propagate these under the most favorable circumstances for their healthy growth.

The predisposition to disease in these ill-treated trees *may* result in a contagious malady, and this may spread beyond them and attack trees of ordinarily good constitution, and in the most salubrious situations, though, of course, the liability of these to take the malady, and their recuperative power under its attack, will be proportionate to their strength and soundness. The disease known as the yellows, in peach-trees, seems to be of this nature.

There are many facts unfavorable to both these theories, and many phenomena which neither of them, in my opinion, satisfactorily explain. The popular judgment in England seemed to have accepted Knight's hypothesis. But while every body was mourning over the degeneracy of old favorites, the utter neglect or miserable mismanagement of their orchards seemed to me to bear strong testimony to the correctness of the contrary theory.

The practical deduction, it may be remarked, from either view, does not greatly differ. By judicious management, the health, vigor, and profit of a fruit-tree, which would otherwise, after a certain time, pine away and die, may be greatly extended, if not made permanent; and trees which are already failing from decrepitude or disease, may be restored. On the other hand, if trees are planted in unhealthy positions, insufficiently supplied with those materials that are necessary to the formation of strong, compact wood; if they are cruelly mutilated, crowded too close together, etc., they will not only be feeble and unproductive, but will be particularly liable to the attacks of vermin, disease, and parasites, and, in their weak condition, will soon yield their life to these enemies. Moreover, the insects which are bred in them will extend their ravages to surrounding trees, the seeds from their parasites will be scattered over the neighborhood, and the disease which is generated in them may be indefinitely extended among their species.

The most common causes of disease, decay, and decline of a fruit-tree, which it is in the power of the orchardist, in a great degree, to control, are these: the exhaustion from the soil of those materials which are its necessary food; the attacks of vermin, and the growth of moss or parasites; the loss of large limbs or other severe wounds; too great exposure of the trunks to the sun; too rapid and succulent growth from the stimulus of heat or exciting manures; and an impervious subsoil, which will allow water frequently to stagnate about its roots, producing what is commonly called by farmers "a cold, sour soil."

Some of my readers, who have not yet studied the subject, may be glad to have me concisely indicate the most approved means of avoiding or counteracting these dangers.

Manures should be applied to orchards frequently and in moderate quantities, rather than in heavy supplies at distant intervals; and, to avoid unhealthy stimulation, they should be well decomposed. The best ordinary manure in the United States has been found to be a mixture of dung with an equal quantity of peat or black swamp-earth, chip-dirt, or rotten wood or leaves; and it is better that this compost should be mixed some time (the longer the better) before it is applied.

But, in addition, I have shown from the English experience that the apple-tree requires a more than ordinary supply of lime, (say a peck of air-slaked stone or shell lime to each tree, every year.) In the same way the pear is known to require especially potash, iron, and phosphorus.

Iron is found in sufficient quantity in most clay soils;

where needed, it may be supplied by scattering bog-ore (found generally underlying swamps in America), or iron filings, or the sweepings and scoriæ from forges. One pound of crude potash dissolved in water and poured over the compost manure, or half a bushel of wood ashes, to a tree, will be a good yearly allowance of potash; and half a peck of bones to a tree will supply the phosphorus. For the plum and the quince, salt is found particularly useful, and ashes for the peach. But let it not be forgotten that the apple cannot live on lime alone, nor the peach on potash, only that it is a special supply of these that they more particularly require.*

The Hereford orchards suffer much more from moss, parasites, and insects, and less pains are taken to guard against them or to destroy them than is usual in New England. There is a fine moss that will not easily be detected, that often collects upon the branches, and, diverting the juices of the tree to its own nourishment, eventually, if not removed, destroys the bark; and limbs are seen frequently thus denuded of their natural defense, and the wood consequently decaying. This is doubtless a common cause of organic disease. The ordinary preventive and remedy for every thing of this sort is to wash the trunk and principal limbs of the tree every year with a weak lye—in which it is a good plan to put a little sulphur— all insects having a particular repugnance to it.† If there is much dead, scaly bark, it should be first rubbed or scraped off.

Trees should be allowed to branch low and naturally. The "trimming up" and unnatural exposure to the sun of the trunk of the pear-tree is known to particularly predispose it to a most fatal malady. Where trees are properly managed while young, it will never be necessary to prune their limbs in our climate; and there can scarcely ever be a case where the cutting off a limb larger than a man's arm will not be likely to

* Copperas (sulphate of iron) seems to act as a tonic upon trees. If applied to feeble, pale-leaved shrubs and trees, it will often wonderfully invigorate them. It may be dissolved in water. A mild solution of sulphate or muriate of ammonia has a similar effect, but must be used with care.

† 1 lb. of potash, *or* 1 quart soft soap, and 4 oz. sulphur, to 1 gallon of water.

do more harm than good. Wherever it is done, or wherever a large branch has been blown off, the stump should be squared off neatly, and a salve of clay and cow-dung spread over it and secured upon it by a cap of canvas or sheet-lead. Smaller stumps should be covered with paint, or with a coating of shellac dissolved in alcohol.

Too rapid and succulent growth, making imperfectly formed wood, through which the future processes of the growth of the tree or the fruit formation will be inefficiently performed, is occasioned either by too stimulating food in the soil, or by a forcing heat in the climate, which excites a growth unnatural to the original habit of the tree. There are also probably other yet unexplained causes for it. The preventive must be determined by the cause. The immediate remedy is shortening-in with a knife one-quarter or one-half of the growth of each year. This is absolutely necessary to the successful cultivation of the peach in many situations in the United States, and, as I have shown, is sometimes used as a remedy for canker in the apple-tree in England.*

Too retentive a subsoil, or a cold, sour, malarious bed for the roots of an orchard, is only to be remedied by underdraining. Mr. Thompson, of the London Horticultural Society, gives a striking instance of the profit which may attend this operation.

Having detailed several experiments, he remarks, that "want of drainage deprives the roots of proper nourishment, subjects them to a chilling temperature, and forces them to absorb a vitiated fluid." He then describes an orchard planted, in 1828, upon a retentive marly clay. He says, "the trees grew tolerably well for some time; but after seven years they began to exhibit symptoms of ill thriving, and were every year getting worse. I saw them in 1840, and instead of increasing in size they seemed to be decreasing." The trees grew worse, and the following year several died. It was then determined to

---

* The principal enemy of the peach-tree is the borer, a worm which works under the bark, near the surface of the ground. Its presence may be known by the exudation of gum. Trees should be examined for it every spring and fall; and it may be easily pricked out and killed with a sharp-pointed knife.

drain the land: 3000 feet of draining-tile were laid, 3 feet deep, in parallel lines, 48 feet apart. In the spring of 1843, and in the autumn of the same year, 3000 feet of drain pipes, 1¼ inch bore, were laid at 30 inches deep, so that the drains were then only 24 feet apart; the ground at the same time was dug over eight inches deep, and the trees pruned. The following year the proprietor writes; "I never housed *any thing like* 50 bushels before; now there are at least 75 bushels, while my summer fruit was at least double the usual quantity." Upon this, Mr. Thompson remarks:—"The lopping-in of the trees and digging the ground, as above described, were doubtless advantageous proceedings; but the draining of the ground was unquestionably the main cause of the extraordinary change in the condition of the trees; for stunted specimens, that previous to the draining were covered with moss, had made no shoots for years, and were in such a state of decrepitude that there was nothing to cut away but dead wood; these had produced vigorous shoots when I saw them in 1847, and have continued to do so up to the present time. Such vigor cannot be attributed to the cutting-in, for in these cases it was not practiced; nor to the digging of the ground, for although this was done before draining was thought of, yet the trees went backwards; the decay of their branches increased under all circumstances till 1843, when recourse was had to draining, and since then they have continued to do well, producing vigorous shoots—shoots upwards of three feet in length; and in the present season the fruit was abundant, large, and highly colored."

A case was mentioned before the Staten Island Farmers' Club, in 1850, of an under-drain having been run near two greengage plum-trees, which had previously been for many years entirely barren; the year after, without any other operation upon them, they bore *bushels* of fruit.

The following satirical sketch of the management of the Devonshire orchards, contains an amusing account of the ceremony of "shooting at the apple-tree," before alluded to.*

* From the London Gardeners' Chronicle.

The trees are planted, to a large extent, apparently without considering what sort of soil or situation is best, and without making any previous preparation; a situation is chosen, a pit is dug with a curious clumsy bit of iron, having a large socket-hole at one end of it, in which is driven a large, strong pole, which answers for a handle; it is worked with both hands over one knee; the depth that the roots are buried does not seem to be of any moment, provided the trees are firmly fixed, so as to prevent the wind from driving them down. I have never observed any pruning performed, except such as is done by bullocks, horses, donkeys, etc.; and as I have not observed any "horse-ladders" here in use, of course the pruning is not very effectively performed about the top part of the very lofty trees. The only digging or stirring the surface of the ground among the trees that I have observed is done by pigs, which are occasionally allowed to rove in some orchards, at certain seasons of the year, with the rings taken from their snouts. In a moist season these intelligent animals occasionally turn up the ground in a tolerable regular manner; and where this is the case the good effects of their industry are obvious. However, it is only on rare occasions that they are allowed to perform this surface operation. The animals that do the pruning are the principal business-performing creatures, as, in addition to that operation, they tread down the under crop of grass, weeds and other rubbish, take the fruit to the cider-mill, and the cider to the consumer; besides, on rare occurrences, a little manure is conveyed by them, and placed over the roots, close to the trunks of the trees; it is sometimes, although rarely, placed at the great distance of three or four feet from the trunk. Bipeds, notwithstanding, perform some of the most interesting and essential parts, such as planting, collecting the fruit, consuming it in part, and assisting in making the cider; together with shooting at trees annually on Old Twelfth-night. Let it rain, hail, blow or snow, this very essential and interesting ceremony is always commenced at 12 o'clock at night, a tremendous fire being kept up for several hours afterwards. They repeat or sing the following interesting song, with all the might which their lungs will permit. The juice of the fruit is generally made use of for many hours, pretty freely, previously to this interesting ceremony, so that a perfect ripeness of address and expertness in gunnery is the result. Guns and firelocks long laid by are on this remarkable occasion brought forward. The following is what I have heard sung on these occasions, although much more is added in some localities:

"Here's to thee, old apple-tree,
Whence thou mayest bud, and whence thou mayest blow;
And whence thou mayest bear apples enow;
Hats full, caps full!
Bushel, bushel-sacks full!
And my pockets full too!
If thee does not bear either apples or corn,
We'll down with thy top, and up with thy horn."
                    (Here the natives shoot at the tree.)

CHAPTER XXXVI

Roofs; Shingles; Tile; Thatch: The Advantages and Dis-
advantages of Each—The Use of Thatch in America—
Hereford—Christian Hospitality—A Milk Farm—The
Herefords—A Dangerous Man—Primitive Christianity

SOMEWHERE IN THIS REGION, we passed two small churches or
chapels with roofs of wooden shingles; in both cases the pitch
of the roof was very steep, and the shingles old, warped and
mossy. These were the only shingle roofs I recollect to have
seen in England; but I was told they were not very uncommon
upon old farm-buildings in Devonshire. The roofs hereabouts,
generally, are of flat tile. In moulding these tile, which are of
equal thickness at both ends, a hole is made in the upper part,
by which they are pegged to slats, which run horizontally
across the rafters; (about London a protuberance is moulded
upon the tile, by which it is hung.) This peg is covered, as the
nails of a shingle are, by the lower part of the tile of the next
tier above it. If no precaution to prevent it is taken, there will
sometimes be crevices in a tile roof, through which snow will
drive; in dwellings, a thin layer of straw is often laid under
the tile, and sometimes they are laid in mortar. *Pan-tiles*
(common on old houses in New York) are also made tight
with mortar. Roofs of this kind will last here about twice as
long as shingle roofs with us, without repairs, and are fire-

proof. Unless laid over straw, they give *less* protection than shingles against heat and cold.

The roofing material changes completely often in one day's walk; flat tiles giving place to slates, slates to pan-tiles, etc. In Monmouthshire, the roofs are generally made of a flat, shaly stone, called *tile-stone*, quarried not less than an inch thick. It is laid with mortar, or straw or moss, like tile, and requires strong timber to support it. The better class of houses and modern farm-buildings, almost every where, are slated; sometimes metal roofed; rarely covered with compositions or felt. Cottages, and old farm-houses and stables, every where, except in the vicinity of slate quarries, are thatched. Straw thatch is commonly laid about eight inches thick. Its permanence depends on the pitch of the roof. Ordinarily it may last twenty-five years; and when a new roof is required, the old thatch is not removed, but a new layer of the same thickness is laid over the old one. Frequently three and sometimes more layers of thatch may be seen on an old building, the roof thus often being two feet thick. It is a cheaper roof than any other, and is much the best protection against both cold and heat. The objection to it is that it harbors vermin, and is more liable to take fire from sparks than any other. The danger of the latter is not as great, however, as would be supposed. I saw and heard of no house on fire while I was in England, except in London. I frequently saw cottages in which coppice-wood was being burned, the top of the chimney not a foot above the dry straw thatch, and the smoke drifting right down upon it. The dangers from fire would be somewhat greater in America, where wood is more commonly used as fuel, and rain is much less frequent. There are some situations in which it might be safely employed, however, (if on dwellings, the chimney should be elevated more than usual,) and where it would form the cheapest and most comfortable, and much the most picturesque and appropriate, roof.

The cost of the thatched roof of a double cottage, fifty by fifteen feet, is estimated at one hundred and forty dollars, of which about forty dollars is for straw, forty dollars for thatcher's work, and the remainder for the frame, lath, etc.

The walls of laborer's cottages are of stone, or brick and

timber, or of clay. In making the latter, which travelers frequently describe as "mud walls," and which are very common, the clay, having been well forked over and cleaned of stones, is sprinkled with water, and has short straw mixed with it, and is then trodden with horses and worked over until it becomes a plastic mass. The more it is trodden the better. A foundation of stone is first made; one man forms the prepared clay into balls, or lumps as large as bricks, and passes these to another, who lays and packs them well and firmly together, dressing off smooth and straight with a trowel. After the height desired for the wall is attained, it is commonly plastered over inside and out with a thin coat of more carefully prepared clay, and whitewashed. This makes an excellent non-conducting wall, equal, in every respect, except in permanence, and almost in that, to stone or brick. Very respectable houses, as villas and parsonages, are sometimes built in this way. The cost is about 30 cts. a square yard.

I once or twice saw the walls of cottages made of or covered with thatch, and have no doubt, as long as vermin were kept out of them, that they were, as was asserted, exceedingly comfortable. These were gentlemen's country boxes, not laborers' cottages.

On reaching Hereford, a city of 10,000 inhabitants, we were met by a gentleman to whom it seemed that word had been sent by some of the "Brethren" at Ludlow, who begged us all to come to his house, and, upon reaching it, we found rooms prepared for us, and his family expecting us.

After tea he walked with us about the town, and even took us into the country, to see a small milk-dairy and orchard-farm. The cows were of the Hereford breed, but not full-blooded, nor have we seen many that were. Most of the cattle in this vicinity have more or less of the marks of the breed, and their quality is about in proportion to its purity. The poorest cattle I have seen in England were within two miles of Hereford, but there was no mark of Hereford blood in them, and they had probably been bought out of the county, and brought there to fatten. The best milkers on this farm were not the best-bred cows. The average value of the herd was about $35 a-head. They were kept in a long stable; mangers and floor of wood, a slope of half an inch in a foot to the latter, with a gutter in the rear. They were entirely house-fed, on green clover. They were milked by women, and the milk all sold in the town.

Late in the evening, our host called with us on the Rev. Mr.—, a right warm, manly, Christian gentleman, who, though in domestic affliction, on learning that we were Americans, received us cordially. We found him singularly familiar with American matters, both political and theological; a portrait of Dr. Bushnell, of Hartford, along with that of Dr. Arnold, and other worthies, was over his mantel, the last "New-Englander" on his table, and a fragrance peculiarly adapted to make an American feel at home, soon pervaded the atmosphere of his study. We had a most agreeable conversation, and it was long before we could return to our hospitable quarters for the night. Mr.——is an Independent, or, as he prefers to be called, a Congregationalist; but is accounted somewhat heterodox, and treated with a cold shoulder by some of the scribes and doctors of that persuasion, we were afterwards informed.

When we came into the parlor, at half past seven next morning, we found a breakfast party met to greet us. Our host had been to an early daylight prayer-meeting, and some business had detained him; but his friends introduced each other to us, and we went to breakfast without waiting for him. It was a good, warm, respectable breakfast—fit for a Christian. English breakfasts in general are quite absurd; not breakfasts at all, but just aggravations of fasts, and likely to put a man in anything but a Christian humor for his day's work. As for the better part of the meal, see C.'s letter, (from which I here extract):

"I shall not soon forget those earnest, simple-hearted men. In many circles one would be repelled by such constant use of religious phrases, but in them it did not seem like *cant* at all—rather the usual expression with them of true feeling. It was a company too well worth considering. Opposite me sat a middle-aged gentleman, who had been a major-general in the East India service, and who belonged to one of the first families in the kingdom. Yet he had given up his commission and his position in society for the sake of doing good as an humble Christian. His half-pay, too, he had refused, believing it inconsistent for a religious man to receive money for services of such a nature. He had been a scholar also, and had written a dictionary of the Mahratta tongue. Besides him, there was a lieutenant in the navy, who had thrown up his commission from similar religious scruples, and a prominent surgeon of the city, devoted, like the rest, to Christian efforts almost entirely. They had been to a prayer-meeting, and the conversation, with the Bible open on the table, commenced at once on a passage in John. It was beautiful, the simple, natural way they all conversed of religious topics—no straining for sanctity, but easily and earnestly, as men usually would speak of weighty political matters.

"But, free as is the plan of these brethren, I am sorry to say that in real liberality they do not go beyond most others. The conversation during breakfast turned on the Roman Catholics. Most of them went so far as to doubt whether a Papist ever could be a Christian. The major disagreed with them, and it was noble, the enthusiasm with which he spoke of the pure and earnest Pascal. Generally, however, their feeling toward men of different doctrinal opinions was much like that of any sectarians. The Independent clergyman at Hereford says that the most he has known are men of the Church of England, and that they have just grasped a few great ideas, which the Independents have been preaching since the time of Cromwell. And certainly, as compared with 'the Church,' their religious character is most simple and free."

In addition to the evidence of the sincere character of the "Brethren" instanced above, I may mention that another of our company had been an apothecary, and given up his business from a conviction that Homeopathy was a better way than the common drugging, and that we afterwards met one, a near relative of one of the most distinguished noblemen and statesmen of Great Britain, who had retired from a highly honorable and lucrative official position, from a desire to live more in accordance with his religious aspirations than his duties in it permitted. I shall omit to narrate what more we saw of them, as we proceeded further on our journey; but must say, to conclude, that if, in letting no man judge them in meat or in drink, or in respect of a holy day—if, in teaching and admonishing one another with psalms and hymns and spiritual songs—if, in bowels of mercy, kindness, humbleness of mind, meekness, self-sacrifice, and zealous readiness to every good work—if, especially, in real genuine hospitality to strangers, there be any thing of "primitive Christianity," our entertainers seemed to us to have had no ordinary degree of success in their purpose to return to it. They certainly were not without their share of bigotry and self-confidence in such matters of creed as they happened to hold in common; but this did not seem to have the effect upon them of destroying geniality and good fellowship, nor of cramping the spirit of practical, material, and unromantic benevolence. They were quite different, too, in their way of talking upon those subjects on which they conceived their minds to be "at rest," from the theological students at——, whom——describes as studying as if they had bought tickets for the night-train to heaven, and, having requested the conductor to call them when they got there, were trying to get into the most comfortable position to sleep it through.

CHAPTER XXXVII

The County Jail—English Prison Discipline—The Perfection of the Present—Education and Taxation—What Next?—Captain Machonochie—The Mark System—The Christian Idea of Punishment

AFTER BREAKFAST, we visited the county prison. It is on the plan of the celebrated Pentonville model prison, near London, which is supposed to be an improvement on what is called the Philadelphia plan. Any of my readers who are much interested in the great and puzzling problem of prison discipline, are probably familiar with the elements of the last experiment of the British Government upon the sad subject.

This specimen of it at Hereford was all that could be asked for in its way. Evidently, no skill in planning and no expense in execution had been wanting to make it as perfect as such a thing could be.

We were first conducted through several long, light, and airy corridors, upon which opened the well-ventilated sleeping-cells of the prisoners—each cell appearing the perfection of a cell, as if made to the order of some rich amateur rascal, in the most complete and finished style which would be appropriate to an apartment bearing that designation; the walls of plain hewn stone, but white as a bishop's linen; the floor damp-proof, of asphalte; the bedstead of iron, the bed of sufficiently appropriate coarseness, snugly and neatly made up as if by the joint labor of a tasteful upholsterer and a skillful laundress; warmed on the hot-water plan; furnished with a wash-bowl, and constant pure water by pipes; softly lighted by filtrated beams of sunshine by day, and a batswing burner at night; provided also with a bell or signal, by which the interesting inmate may at any time, in case of bodily ailment, summon a well-diplomaed physician to his relief, or a perfectly authenticated, veritable and legitimate "descendant of the apostles," in case he should be taken suddenly aback with repentance during the night: at every bed-head, too—regularly as the crucifix in the dormitories of monks, or the squat, yellow "Josh" in Chinese cabins—a bible. "The Bible! ah, how must his heart melt, and his dark mind be enlightened, as in his retirement from the wild temptations of the wicked world, the prisoner is left to be absorbed in its glorious tidings. What a feast, what a treasure, what a—" Nay, the shining leather and sticking leaves tell us that even Bible Societies may throw pearls before swine.

"Aye," says the turnkey: *"He can't read*—a young chap—in for two months; petty larceny."

We open and read:—"He that knew not, and did commit things worthy of stripes, shall be beaten with few stripes. For unto whomsoever much is given, of him shall much be required; and to whom men have committed much, of him they will ask the more."

It was given him to have a mind uneducated, except in ignorance and criminal contrivance, and it was required of him, he might tell us, either to starve or to steal; and then there is given him good, comfortable, clean, wholesome air, water, food, lodging, and exercise (not work). Moreover, there is added this sealed book.

But we are not allowed to moralize or criticise. We are expected only to admire, and are passed along to the culinary department.

Perfection again—of a kitchen with an admirable, stout, dignified *chef,* graduate of Paris doubtless, presiding. The diet-table, he explains to us, is scientifically ordered; the beef and bread and vegetables are of the best, and we are shown how the quantity for each man, in each particular, is accurately weighed out. The patients are also weighed periodically, and the allowance of food and of exercise is studiously adjusted to the condition of each.

Next we are taken to the day-cells, which are in several separate courts. Within each is an ingeniously-contrived crank, attached to a common shaft, revolving through all. This crank is the exerciser. The prisoner stands at a certain distance before it, takes hold of it with both hands, and, as it turns, a certain motion is given to his whole body—the most healthful sort of motion: expanding the chest, and moving every joint of his limbs. He remains in this cell ten hours each day, Sundays excepted; and the usual allowance of exercise is half an hour, with ten minutes rest after it, continued alternately during that time. There is a library in the prison, from which primers, picture-books, and tracts, are served out for the exercise of his mind during the ten minutes bodily rests.

For Sundays there is provided another sort of cells, which are so arranged that each prisoner can look at the same central point, but cannot see any other prisoner. At the central point is placed an humble vessel, (doubtless as perfect as can be made by ordinances, and duly clad in regulation vesture,) from which a stated dose of gospel privileges is scientifically exhibited, and systematically imbibed by every patient—prisoner I mean. There are two such rations given on Sunday, with a dinner between, and opportunity for reflection in private, before and after.

It is a first principle of the plan that labor should end where it begins. The exercising shaft is sometimes applied to a pump-brake, to fill the reservoir over the prison with water, but never in any other way saves labor. Pains are taken in every way, not with absolute success it is admitted, to secure utter silence, and to prevent all communication between the prisoners. Criminals are rarely sent here for more than twelve months; and it is said that, with all the science and care that can be devoted to them, their health, both bodily and mental, is endangered, if their confinement is protracted longer.

It may be, as its admirers have no doubt, the happiest idea of a prison most happily realized that the world yet knows; yet it is one of the most painful things to examine that I ever saw. It is hardly possible to speak well of it but in irony, or to describe it without sarcasm, so absurd seems all this scientific care for the well-being—physical, mental, and moral —of these miserable transgressors, contrasted with the studied neglect, justified and made praiseworthy by strictly economical and religious reasoning, of the unoffending poor. While no talent, painstaking, and complicated machinery is too expensive and cumbrous to be devoted to the keeping of the criminal, of the unfortunate, society, through the state, still says— *Am I my brother's keeper?*

Hold the hand! Dash not the book behind the grate, my conservative friend; I would hint at nothing more dangerous than *education*—a word one may yet speak in America without being finally condemned as an infidel and a socialist, and a man given to isms. Would you still call me to order, remind me that I am writing on the subject of prisons—English prisons—and that I may take up the subject of schools in another chapter. Yet there may be lessons learned from prisons, and English prisons teach lessons that all who do not care for the subject of education would do well to heed.

In the prisons of England, in 1841, it was found that out of every hundred criminals then supported by the state—

33 had never learned to read or write;

56 were able to read and write imperfectly;

7 were able to read and write well; and only

1 in two hundred and twenty-two had been favored with "instruction superior to reading and writing."*

Only 28 in every hundred were over 30 years of age.

The chaplain of the Brecon jail reports, that though the majority of the prisoners to whom he ministers are able to read imperfectly, yet their education has been so defective that they have no notion of the bearing and connection of one part of a sentence with another. Nine out of ten of them were ignorant of the merest rudiments of Christianity. The chaplain of the Bedford jail states, that the great majority of prisoners there confined are "Ignorant, stupid, and unconcerned."

* Parliamentary Document, 1842.

Another jail chaplain observes of those "children, or men still childish," under his care, who had been instructed in reading and writing, "they had not learned to think about or understand any thing that they had been taught; the ears had heard, the tongue had learned utterance, but the mind had received no idea, no impression." (The reader may be reminded of what I said of sailors' reading.*) From the Bucks county jail it is reported that about half the prisoners have never been taught to read and write, and about one quarter are ignorant of the alphabet; and that *"ignorance is uniformly accompanied with the greatest depravity."*†

To return to the Hereford jail: I intimated that every thing said in admiration of it seemed necessarily ironical and bitter; but I do recall one pleasant, and, I doubt not, true word, for it—"it is a palace compared with the old one."

Yes, to be sure, that is good. No one will ask us to go back to packing criminals, and all under surveillance of the law, promiscuously into stone pens, giving them rotten straw to rest upon, and supplying only the cheapest food that may answer the purpose of keeping body and soul together. Few will be inclined to think that the world's prisons—hell triumphant in Austria and Naples, excepted—are not better now than in the day of Howard. Progress there has been; progress there must be. This palace-prison is but a mile-stone on the road.

What next? There are some pamphlets before me in which an answer to this question is attempted to be given.‡ The matter is one of so much difficulty and so great importance, so nearly connected with the progress of Christianity and civilized law, and the plan of a new prison is so often to

* P. 21.

† Jail Returns to the House of Commons, 1848.

‡ "The Principles of Punishment," by Captain Machonochie, R. N., K. H.: J. Ollivier, Pall Mall, London. "Crime and Punishment," by Captain Machonochie: J. Hatchard & Son, London. An "Essay on Criminal Jurisprudence," by Marmaduke B. Sampson: Highley & Son, London. These works may all be obtained through the agency of the publishers, and will be found to contain (especially the last) most valuable hints and suggestions applicable to other matters besides prison discipline. Their cost is trifling.

be discussed and established among all our states and counties, that I must beg my readers to carefully examine the new system of punishment that they propose, and I urge it the more, because, so far as I know, it has, up to this time, entirely escaped the attention of the American press.

But first let us distinctly recall to mind what is most unsatisfactory and clearly defective in our present prisons and system of criminal punishment.

There are two general principles with regard to the punishment of crime that have been theoretically received and approved in the minds of all enlightened and Christian people, and yet to which there is much in our present system that is practically false and repugnant. We say "necessarily so," and that this necessity is one of the awful results of crime or sin. God knows if we are right. If not, we are terribly wrong.

The principles or rules with regard to punishment, to which I refer, are these: that it should not be vindictive or revengeful, for it is not the business of human jurisprudence to satisfy the abstract claims of justice, *"Vengeance is mine, saith the Lord."* That, on the other hand, it should be our purpose, in the treatment of criminals, so far as may be consistent with the good of society, to do them good, to make them better, stronger and happier. This also is a corollary of the second principle, which I would recall to mind, namely: That the great end of criminal law is to prevent, discourage and lessen crime.

Yet, practically, among the mass of our community, the punishment of criminals is engaged in as if it were the satisfaction of a vindictive feeling against an enemy of society, a satisfaction that the law makes him pay in the inconvenience and suffering of his confinement and hard labor, for the injury he has done society or some member of society. Practically, the criminal has the counterpart of this feeling, considering that society looks upon him as its enemy, and, when it catches him, vindictively makes him suffer for his crime, as if it were a match between him and the law, in which he was the loser; and the effect of looking upon it in this way is to aggravate and intensify the evil which we theoretically propose to cure by his imprisonment.

It is true, that in accordance with the purpose of improving the character of criminals during (I cannot say by) their imprisonment, we employ chaplains to preach and counsel them, and give them books, which, it is supposed, in the absence of any other employment of the mind, may engage their attention. And these are the only means employed at present for the purpose of training them to be active, efficient, industrious and well-disposed members of society, upon their release. Few will be inclined to deny that for this purpose these means constantly prove themselves entirely inadequate; that, in this respect, our system is a constant and complete failure. Why?

Let us see: The criminal is sentenced, we will suppose, for ten years, and finds himself locked into a narrow cell, where it is only at occasional and comparatively distant intervals that he can be communicated with, even by his keeper, chaplain or physician, the only human beings who have access to him. It may be for a certain time each day he is set to labor; hard labor being given him, not as a privilege, not as a relief, not as a means of bettering his condition, or in any way as to be loved and valued; but as an addition to the punishment of solitary confinement. He is mainly left to his own thoughts. His recollections are vicious; are his anticipations likely to be virtuous? With ten years to be spent under these circumstances, to what will his mind be most likely to direct itself? To relief from monotony, to anything which promises excitement, to dramatic action, to overcome or mislead the minds he finds acting upon him, or to self-forgetfulness, sleep, sloth, and to the avoidance of so much of the punishment imposed upon him as possible, that is to the hard labor part, in which his only success must be obtained by deception. Thus, with whatever preaching in words, his training is directly to hatred and contempt of labor as a means of no good, but only of fatigue to himself, to unwholesome mental excitement, to deception and to perfect indolence and uselessness.

And is this lame, inconsistent plan, so working at cross purposes, the end of all the philanthropic labors, private and associated, that have been given to the subject during the last fifty years? The result, friends, not the end. Then, in God's name, what next?

An answer from Captain Machonochie will be found in the Appendix B, and I again beg for it, with all earnestness, the thoughtful perusal of my countrymen. It is based on plain, distinct, uncontradictory principles, which are applicable to the punishment of all criminals, and to the construction of all criminal laws. It is the plan of no closet philosopher, but of a cool-headed, warm-hearted sailor, who was chosen by his government, for his manifest natural qualifications for undertaking the superintendence of criminals, to take charge of one of its most difficult penal establishments. It is a plan that has been well considered, and is ably defended to the minutest details, as the reader, who is willing to study it further, will find, on referring to the pamphlets I have mentioned in the note on a previous page.*

* For a refutation of objections, see, particularly, the Report of the Committee on Criminal Law of the "*Society for Promoting the Amendment of the Law.*"

CHAPTER XXXVIII

A Hit—The Debtor's Prison—Utter Cleanliness—"City"
and "Town"—"Down" and "Up"—Hereford Cathedral—
Church and State—The Public Promenade

I MUST NOT FORGET two incidents of our visit to the jail. Punishment is inflicted by withholding food; also, I imagine, for
slight offenses, in other ways. An officer with us noticed some
untidiness of dress upon one of the prisoners, and pointing to
it, said—"You are an Englishman: *I don't want to treat you as
an Irishman.*" As we entered a certain apartment, our conductor said, "This is the debtors' prison."

One of us remarked, "We have generally abolished imprisonment for debt in the United States."

The officer, quietly, "It's a pity that you have."

The quarters of the debtors were not cells, but decent
rooms, and there was a large hall common to them. Every
thing here, though, as every where else, was awfully clean,
dreary and mathematical; a housekeeper gone mad, such as I
know of, would have thought it heaven. I should suppose that
the prisoners would long, more than for anything else, to have
one good roll in the gutter, and an unmeasured mouthful of
some perfectly indigestible luxury. It was a relief, after being
but an hour within the walls, to step out once more into the
good old mud and clouds and smells of Nature again.

Among the debtors, one was pointed out to us as a well-educated lawyer, formerly having a large and respectable practice, and enjoying a considerable fortune. He had been confined for several years, but, it was thought, would soon be released. The placards of an association for taking the part of imprisoned debtors were posted in the hall.

The title *city* is applied, in England, only to a town which is the residence of a bishop, and is equivalent to "a cathedral town." Hereford is a city; Chester is a city; but Liverpool, with ten times the population of both of them, is not a city. The term *town,* again, in England, is never applied to the subdivisions of a county (a township), but is used to designate a place that is closely built, and with a considerable population—what we should give the title of *city* to. Thus London, the largest town, is every where called "the town." "The city" designates a small part of London, near the Cathedral of St. Paul. (All over Great Britain they speak of going "up to London," never "down." This use of "down" and "up," meaninglessly, in a sentence, I had supposed was a "down-east" idiom; but it is common in old England.)

The cathedral at Hereford, built in the time of William the Conqueror, is in a more ornamented style of Gothic than any ancient religious edifice we had seen. I did not greatly admire it. Considerable additions or repairs have been lately made. On one of the new gables I was surprised to see some fifty of those grotesque heads, freshly cut. They were not very ugly, or very droll—indeed, had no marked character, or any thing that showed a genius, even for the comical, in their designer or executer. They were not necessary to the harmony of the modern work with the old; were, I think, discordant, and what they were put there for I don't know. Extensive alterations had lately been made in the choir, and it was the most convenient hall for public exercises that I recollect to have seen in any English cathedral. The ceiling was painted (in encaustic) in the bright-colored bizarre style that I spoke of at the castle near Shrewsbury. As I entered, it seemed to me to be in bad taste for a place of meditation and worship. We attended the daily morning service, and heard some fine, gentle music—the organ sweetly played, and the singers all boys.

I noticed that our dissenting friends seemed to have a pride and sense of possession in the cathedral, as if they were not in the habit of thinking of it as belonging exclusively to those who occupied it, but as if it was intrusted to them, and as well to them as to any other division, as representative of the whole Catholic Church of all English Christians. This way of looking upon "the Church" usurpations is quite commonly observable among the dissenters. It is not so honorable to them when applied to other things than mere furniture; as, for instance, giving the exclusive teaching of religious doctrine to the children, or paupers, or soldiers, in whom they have a common interest, to the State Church, from a supposed necessity of giving it to some one in preference to all others; and if not to their particular church, then of best right to the church of the strongest. The idea that some State Church, separated from others by its doctrinal basis, is expedient, and almost necessary, to a Christian government, is quite common among dissenters. In my judgment, it cannot be expedient, because it is very evidently unjust. What is in the least degree unjust can never be expedient for a state, the very purpose of which should be to elevate and secure justice among the people who live under its laws.

Nor can I conceive of any thing so likely to strangle a church as to be hung with exclusive privileges from the state. For what are these? Bribes for the profession of doctrines and the acceptance of rules of debatable expediency; giving encouragement, so far as they have any influence (that they would not have if the church were independent of the power of the state), to insincerity and the unearnest formation of opinions—to unreality, which is deadness in a church.

That the constant practice of perjury and the most miserably jesuitical notions of truth and falsehood, and that weakness and imbecility of both Church and State, is the direct and inevitable result as the present day of such a connection as is attempted to be sustained between them in England, is as obvious and certain to me as any thing can be, that such great and good men as the divines and statesmen of England have different opinions with regard to.

There is a large green, close planted with trees, about the cathedral, and facing upon it are the official residences of the regiment of clergy, high priests and low, that under some form or other are provided with livings in connection with it. In front of one of the barracks was planted a bomb-mortar—with what signification?

There is another public promenade in Hereford, upon the site of an old castle which was demolished by Cromwell. The ramparts are grassed over, and there are fine trees, ponds, gravel-walks, an obelisk in honor of Nelson, some graceful irregularities of surface, and a broad, purling stream of clear water flowing by it all. Here, before noon, we found a considerable company, of varied character: ladies walking briskly and talking animatedly; invalids, wrapped up and supported, loitering in the sun; cripples, moving about in wheel-chairs; students or novel-readers in the deepest shades; and every where, many nursery-maids with children. Not a town have we seen in England but has had a better garden-republic than any town I know of in the United States.

CHAPTER XXXIX

Shady Lanes—Rural Sketches—Herefordshire and Monmouthshire Scenery—Points of Difference in English and American Landscapes—Visit to a Farm-House—The Mistress—The Farm-House Garden—A Stout Old English Farmer—The Stables and Stock—Turnip Culture—Sheep —Wheat—Hay—Rents—Prices—A Parting—Cider

TURNING OFF the main road soon after leaving Hereford, we pursued our way, guided by the gentleman who had so kindly entertained us, for several miles through narrow by-ways. It was a rarely clear, bright, sunshiny afternoon, and while on the broad highway we had found, for the first time in England, the temperature of the air more than comfortably warm. The more agreeable were the lanes;—narrow, deep, and shady, often not wider than the cart-track, and so deep, that the grassy banks on each side were higher than our heads; our friend could not explain how or why they were made so, but probably it was by the rain washing through them for centuries. On the banks were thickly scattered the flowers of heart's-ease, forget-me-not, and wild strawberries; above, and out of them, grew the hawthorn hedges in thick, but wild and wilsome verdure, and pushing out of this, and stretching over us, often the branches mingling over our heads and shutting out the sky clear beyond the next turn, so we seemed walking in a bower, thick old apple and pear trees with pliant twigs of hazel-wood, and occasionally the strong arms of great brooding elms. Then we came upon a low, thick-thatched cottage with many bends in the ridge-pole, with little windows, and thick walls; a cat asleep in the door, and pigs and chickens before it, and, lying on the ground, in the dust of the lane, playing with a puppy, two or three flaxen-haired, blue eyed children; a little further, a drowsy old she-ass standing in the shade, and a mouse-colored foal, as little as a lamb, but with a great head and large, plaintive dark eyes, and a meek and touching expression of infantile, embryo intellect.

Now and then the hedge is interrupted by the wall of a paddock or stack-yard; beyond it, a number of dilapidated hovels, sheds, and stables, clustering without any appearance of arrangement about a low farm-house with big chimneys, wide windows, and a little porch half hidden under roses, jessamine, and honeysuckle.

Sometimes a big dog would bay at us, and, a woman coming to the door, our friend would ask, "How is the master and the little ones?" and in turn be asked, "How is good mistress and young master?" and then we would be presented as strangers, who had come over the sea to view this goodly land, and would be asked, in pitying tones, about famine, and fever, and potatoes—the farm-wife, although she had an exceedingly sweet speech, apparently confounding New York with Connaught or Munster.

Again, broad fields, and stout horses, and busy laborers, and straight plow-furrows, or the bright metallic green of luxuriant young wheat and barley, in broad glades of glancing light; and a stout old man, who waddles towards us with a warm greeting, wiping the sweat from his brow, and mounting "a goodish bit of stuff, though she has seen twenty winters," rides for a little way along with us, breathing hard and speaking huskily; grumbling, grumbling at Free Trade and high rents, but answering all our questions about his draining, and boneing, and drilling, and dibbling, and very frankly acknowledging how much he has been able to increase his crops with new-fashioned ways and new-fangled implements.

Then leaving the lane, we take a foot-path, which, cross-

ing the hedges by stiles, leads through old orchards, in all of
which horses and cattle are pasturing; and there are beautiful
swells of the ground, and sometimes deep swales of richer
green, with rushes and willows growing at the bottom. Reaching a steeper hill-side, we enter a large plantation of young
forest trees, and soon pass all at once into an older growth of
larger and more thinly standing wood; and near the top of
this, find a clearing, where men are making faggots of the
brushwood, and stripping bark from the larger sticks, and
some little boys and girls are picking up chips and putting
them into sacks.

We reach another lane and cultivated fields, and, being
on elevated ground, at the gnarly feet of a gray, old beech-tree,
lay down, and, looking back upon the extensive landscape, tell
our friend in what differs from American scenery.

The chief peculiarity of the English landscape is found in
the frequent long, graceful lines of deep green hedges and
hedge-row timber, crossing hill, valley, and plain in every direction; and in the occasional large trees, dotting the broad
fields, either singly or in small groups, left to their natural
open growth, (for ship-timber, and, while they stand, for cattle shades,) therefore branching low and spreading wide, and
more beautiful, much more beautiful, than we allow our trees
to make themselves. The less frequent brilliancy of broad
streams or ponds of water, also distinguishes the prospect from
those to which we are most accustomed, though there are often
small brooks or pools, and much marshy land, and England
may be called a well-watered country. In the foreground you
will notice the quaint buildings, generally pleasing objects in
themselves, often supporting what is most agreeable of all, and
that you can never fail to admire, never see any thing ugly or
homely under, a drapery of ivy or other creepers; the ditches
and banks by their side, on which the hedges are planted; the
clean and careful cultivation, and general tidiness of the agriculture; and the deep, narrow, crooked, gulch-like lane, or the
smooth, clean, matchless highway.

There seems to me to be a certain peculiarity in English
foliage, which I can not satisfactorily describe. It is as if the
face of each leaf was more nearly parallel with all others near

it, and as if all were more equally lighted than in our foliage. It is perhaps only owing to a greater density, and better filling up, and more even growth of the outer twigs of the trees, than is common in our dryer climate.

There is a much smaller variety in the forest foliage, and usually a much milder light over an English landscape than an American, making the distances and shady parts more indistinct. The sublime or the picturesque in nature is much more rare in England, except on the sea-coast, than in America; but there is every where a great deal of quiet, peaceful, graceful beauty which the works of man have generally added to, and which I remember but little like at home. This Herefordshire reminds me of the valley of Connecticut, between Middletown and Springfield. The valley of the Mohawk, and the upper part of the Hudson, is also in some parts English-like.

After all here said, I feel that there is a fascination in the common-place scenery of this part of England, and generally of midland, rural England, which I do not fully comprehend. I have called it common-place, because there is nothing striking in it; no one point to be especially noted, or which can be remembered afterwards. Yet, though I have traveled far and wide, have visited scores of places greatly celebrated for the grandeur of their scenery, and have dwelt for months in the most beautiful, purely natural scenes of a pastoral character in the world (in Western Texas), I have been no where else so charmed as I was continually while walking through those parts of England least distinguished, and commonly least remarked upon by travelers as beautiful. The scenery is beautiful without intention or artifice for the purpose of man, and yet is full of the convenience of man's occupation; and it is picturesque without being ungentle or shabby. (1858.)

Descending into a broad, low tract of dale-land, we came at length to a farm occupied by a relative of our guide, and which was his destination. A branch of the lane in which we had been for some time walking, ran through the farm, and terminated at the farm-house. It was more picturesque and inconvenient, deeper, narrower, and muddier than any we had before been through. It was explained to us that it was a "parish road"—although leading to but one house—and, therefore, the farmer was not responsible for its bad repair.* Great trees grew up at its side, and these the farmer was not allowed to fell or trim—the landlord estimating the value of their increase as timber or for fuel, or their advantage as a nursery of game, higher than the injury they caused to the crops in the adjoining fields. Near the house the lane widened, and one side was flanked by a symmetrical yew-hedge; on the other side, however, the trees and high bank still continued, and two stout horses were straining every muscle to draw a cart-load of crushed bones through the mire, which reached close up to the gable-end of the house. Opposite the house was a cider-mill, cart-sheds, and some stacks; behind it, a large yard, surrounded by stables, sties, dairy-house, malt-house, granary, etc. Into this enclosure we passed by a great gate. A considerable part of it was occupied by a large heap of manure and a pool of green, stagnant liquid. The buildings were mostly old, some of them a good deal decayed, with cracks in the brick-work, timber bending and sustained by props and other patch-work, which spoke better for the tenant than his landlord.

By a wide open door, directly from this filthy yard, we passed without ceremony into the kitchen—a large, long room, with stone floor, black beams across the low ceiling, from which hung sides and hams of pork, a high settle, as usual, but not the ordinary kitchen display of bright metal and crockery. Old and well worn, every thing, but neat and nice as brand-new. On a table was a huge loaf with a large piece of cold fat bacon and a slice of cheese, and directly a maid came up from the cellar and added to these a pint of foaming beer—dinner or supper for the carter just returning from the town, whither he had gone early in the morning with a load of wool, and had now brought back bone-manure.

---

* In the proceedings of a Parliamentary Commission of the last century, the following questions and answers are recorded:

Q. What sort of roads have you in Monmouthshire?

A. None at all.

Q. How do you travel then?

A. In ditches.—*Survey of Monmouth.*

We are seated in a little parlor, and the "wench," as our friend addresses her (a buxom serving-maid), goes to call the mistress. The parlor is a small room neatly furnished; painted deal chairs, a printed-calico-covered lounge, the floor carpeted, and the walls papered; an oak writing-desk, a table and a sewing-stand; no newspapers or books, but a family-bible on the mantel and an almanac on the desk: a door and a window open from it upon the flower-garden.

In a few minutes the mistress enters, and, after kindly receiving us, rings a bell, and, when the maid comes, gives her a key and tells her to bring cider. Presently she takes us into the garden. A pleasant garden, with plenty of large and fine pansies, some roses, and great promise of more. It is extremely neat, clean and finely kept, and it is the pride of the mistress that she takes the entire care of it herself; as we walk, she has her scissors in her hand, and cuts flowers, and when we are seated in a curious little arbor of clipped yew, where she had left her "work" when she came in to see us, she arranges nosegays and presents them to us.

The house is small; the walls are of plain red brick; the roof of slate, with but moderate pitch; the chimneys and windows of the usual simple American country-house form and size. There is no porch, veranda, gable or dormer, upon the garden side, yet the house has a very pleasing and tasteful aspect, and does not at all disfigure the lovely landscape of distant woody hills, against which we see it. Five shillings' worth of material from a nursery, half-a-day's labor of a man, and some recreative work of our fair and healthy hostess' own hands, have done it vastly better than a carpenter or mason could at a thousand times the cost. Three large evergreen trees have grown near the end of the house, so that, instead of the plain, straight, ugly red corner, you see a beautiful, irregular, natural, tufty tower of verdure; myrtle and jessamine clamber gracefully upon a slight trellis of laths over the door; roses are trained up about one of the lower windows, honeysuckle about another, while all the others, above and below, are deeply draped and festooned with the ivy, which, starting from a few slips thrust one day into the soil by the mistress, near the corner opposite the evergreens, has already covered two-thirds of the bare brick wall on this side, found its way over the top of the tall yew-hedge, round the corner, climbed the gable-end, and is now creeping along the ridge-pole and up the kitchen chimney—which, before speaking only of boiled bacon and potatoes, now suggests happy holly-hangings of the fireside and grateful harvest's home, hides all the formal lines and angles, breaks all the stiff rules of art, dances lightly over the grave precision of human handiwork, softens, shades and shelters all under a gorgeous vesture of Heaven's own weaving.

Soon, while we are sitting in this leafy boudoir, comes "the master," as good a specimen of the stout, hearty, old English farmer as we shall find, and we go—lady and all—to look at the horses, cows and pigs. The stables are mostly small, inconveniently separated, and badly fitted up, and there is but little in them to boast of in the way of cattle; but there is one new building, incongruously neat among the rest, and in this there are some roomy stalls, with iron mangers, sliding neck-chains, and asphalte floor with grates and drain. Here is the best stock of the farm: among the rest, a fine, fat Hereford cow, which has just been sold to the butcher for $60, and a handsome heifer of the same blood, heavy with calf, which has been lately bought for $15, the farmer chuckling as he passes his hand over her square rump, as if it had been a shrewd purchase. He values his best dairy cow at $45.

We then go to the cider-mill and the sheds to look at some implements; next to the ground, at some distance, where the laborers are all at work ridging for turnips, (Swedes or *Rutabaga.*) The larger part of the field is already planted, and in some other fields the young plants are coming up. The turnip crop of the farm this year is to be grown on *one hundred acres,* the whole area of the farm being less than three hundred.

The soil of this field is a fine, light loam. It was last year in wheat; the stubble was turned under soon after harvest with a skin-coulter-plow, an instrument that pairs off the surface before the mould-board of the plow, and throws it first to the bottom of the furrow; cross-plowed and scarified again the same season with one of the instruments described at page 72; in the spring, plowed again, (eight inches deep,) harrowed fine and smooth, thrown into ridges with double mould-board plow, rolled, and finally drilled with a two horse machine that deposits and covers manure and seed together. The manure is ground bones, costing in Hereford 60½ cents a bushel, mixed with sifted coal-ashes. The expense of this application is about $12 an acre, but it must be remembered that the ground is already in high condition. The drills are thirty inches apart. The crop is principally used to fatten sheep, of which 500 are kept on the farm; the breed, Cotswold and Leicester.

We next went to a paddock in which were six Cotswold "tups" (bucks), as handsome sheep (of their kind) as I ever saw. One of them I caught and measured: girth behind the shoulders, exactly five feet; length from muzzle to tail, four feet and eleven inches.

Then to the wheat, of which there was also about one hundred acres, part after turnips and part after potatoes: the former, which had been boned, looked the best. A part of the land had been prepared by a presser (a corrugated roller used to give solidity to light soils), and this was decidedly superior to the remainder. Most of the wheat was put in with drilling machines, of which there were two used, one sowing at greater intervals than the other. Some of the wheat upon the pressed land, after turnips, was the finest we have seen. The farmer expected it to yield forty bushels of seventy pounds each, but would consider an average of thirty, from the hundred acres, a very good crop. He said the average crop of the county was thought to be but eighteen and a half bushels.

We afterwards walked through some pasture and a grass-field, and examined the hay in stacks; mostly rye-grass. The hay-fields yielded one to two and a quarter tons an acre, the average being under two tons. It took about four days to cure it after cutting, and the whole cost of hay-making was about four dollars an acre. Hay from the stack, of the best quality, would sell at this time in the city of Hereford for twelve dollars a ton.

The rent of this farm was seven dollars and a half an acre; tithes, one dollar and a quarter an acre; road-rates, seventy cents an acre; all paid by the farmer, together with poor-rates and other burdens.

A good pair of sound, well-broken, but rather light cart-

horses, cost here $185; horse-cart, $60; harness and gear for
each horse, $12. A smith will keep a horse shod for $5 a year.
Insurance of horses in the Royal Farmers' Company, 2½ per
cent. of value *per annum*.

After taking tea at the farm-house, our kind guide,
Brother——, made ready to depart by stuffing some tracts,
publications of the Brethren, mostly of a meditative character,
into our packs; we might learn more of their ideas from them,
he said, and if they did not interest us, or after we had read
them, it might do some one else good to leave them at the inns
where we stopped, or in the public conveyances. He begged us
if we got into any trouble or needed any assistance for any
purpose while in England, to let him know; and so we parted.
We had never heard of this man, nor he of us, till twenty-four
hours before. He had then merely received word that three
American Christians—wayfarers—would be passing through
his town that night, and so he came out into the highway
seeking for us, found us, and had so entertained us as I have
shown. He would now walk several miles alone and return
home by the night-coach.

The farmer afterwards had his favorite greyhound let out
for us to see, and after another short stroll, finding that we
were bent upon leaving him that night, insisted on our coming to the garden again and tasting some choice cider made
from the *Hagloe crab*—the pure juice he assured us it was—a
good wholesome English drink: a baby might fill its belly with
it and feel none the worse. So sitting on the door-steps, the
lady and the dog with us, we remained yet a long time, the
farmer talking first of sporting matters, and then getting into
the everlasting topics of Free Trade, and exorbitant rents,
taxes and tithes.

Walk with a Rustic—Family Meeting—A Recollection of the Rhine—Ignorance and Degraded Condition of the English Agricultural Laborer—How He Is Regarded by His Superiors—The Principles of Government—Duties of the Governing—Education—Slavery—The Diet of Labor-ers—Drink—Bread—Bacon—Fresh Meat

WE WERE BOUND for Monmouth that night, and soon after sunset, having one of the farm laborers for a guide, we struck across the fields into another lane. About a mile from the farm-house, there was a short turn, and at the angle—the lane narrow and deep as usual—was a small, steep-roofed, stone building, with a few square and arched windows here and there in it, and a perfectly plain cube of stone for a tower, rising scarcely above the roof-tree, with an iron staff and vane on one of its corners—"Saint Some-one's parish church." There was a small graveyard, enclosed by a hedge, and in a corner of this, but with three doors opening in front upon the lane, was a long, crooked, dilapidated old cottage. On one of the stone thresholds, a dirty, peevish-looking woman was lounging, and before her, lying on the ground in the middle of the lane, were several boys and girls playing or quarreling. They stopped as we came near, and rolling out of the way, stared at us silently, and without the least expression of recognition, while we passed among them. As we went on, the woman said something in a sharp voice, and our guide shouted in reply, without, however, turning his head, "Stop thy maw—am going to Ameriky, aw tell thee." It was his "missis," he said.

"Those were not your children that lay in the road?"

"Yaas they be—foive of 'em."

So we fell into a talk with him about his condition and prospects; but before I describe it, let me relieve my page with a glimpse of rustic character of another sort. It is one of the pleasant memories of our later ramble on the Rhine that writing of this incident recalls. A simple story, but illustrative in this connection of the difference which the traveler commonly finds between the English and the German poor people.

We had been walking for some miles, late in a dusky evening, upon a hilly road, with an old peasant woman, who was returning from market, carrying a heavy basket upon her head and two others in her hands. She had declined to let us assist her in carrying them, and though she had walked seven miles in the morning and now nearly that again at night, she had overtaken us, and was going on at a pace that for any great distance we should have found severe. At a turn of the road we saw the figure of a person standing still upon a little rising ground before us, indistinct in the dusk, but soon evidently a young woman. It is my child, said the woman, hastily setting down her baskets and running forward, so that they met and embraced each other half way up the hill. The young woman then came down to us, and, taking the great basket on her head, the two trudged on with rapid and animated conversation, in kind tones asking and telling of their experiences of the day, entirely absorbed with each other, and apparently forgetting that we were with them, until, a mile or two further on, we came near the village in which they lived.

Our guide was a man of about forty, having a wife and seven children; neither he nor any of his family (he thought) could read or write, and, except with regard to his occupation as agricultural laborer, I scarcely ever saw a man of so limited information. He could tell us, for instance, almost no more about the church which adjoined his residence than if he had

never seen it—not half so much as we could discover for ourselves by a single glance at it. He had nothing to say about the
clergyman who officiated in it, and could tell us nothing about
the parish, except its name, and that it allowed him and five
other laborers to occupy the "almshouse" we had seen, rent
free. He couldn't say how old he was (he appeared about
forty); but he could say, "like a book," that God was what
made the world, and that "Jesus Christ came into the world to
save sinners, of whom he was chief"—of the truth of which
latter clause I much doubted, suspecting the arch fiend would
rank higher, among his servants, the man whose idea of duty
and impulse of love had been satisfied with cramming this
poor soul with such shells of spiritual nourishment. He
thought two of his children knew the catechism and the creed;
did not think they could have learned it from a book; they
might, but he never heard them read; when he came home
and had gotten his supper, he had a smoke and then went to
bed. His wages were seven shillings—sometimes had been
eight—a week. None of his children earned any thing; his
wife, it might be, did somewhat in harvest-time. But take the
year through, *one dollar and sixty-eight cents* a week was all
they earned to support themselves and their large family. How
could they live? "Why indeed, it was hard," he said; "sometimes, if we'd believe him, it had been as much as he could do
to keep himself in tobacco!" He mentioned this as if it was a
vastly more memorable hardship than that, oft-times, he could
get nothing more than dry bread for his family to eat. It was a
common thing that they had nothing to eat but dry bread. He
got the flour—*fine, white wheaten flour*—from the master.
They kept a hog, and had so much bacon as it would make to
provide them with meat for the year. They also had a little
potato patch, and he got cheese sometimes from the master.
He had tea, too, to his supper. The parish gave him his rent,
and he never was called upon for tithes, taxes, or any such
thing. In addition to his wages, the master gave him, as he did
all the laborers, three quarts either of cider or beer a day,
sometimes one and sometimes the other. He liked cider best—
thought there was "more strength to it." Harvest-time they got

six quarts, and sometimes, when the work was very hard, he had had ten quarts.

He had heard of America and Australia as countries that poor folks went to—he did not well know why, but supposed wages were higher, and they could live cheaper. His master and other gentlemen had told him about those places, and the laboring people talked about them among themselves. They had talked to him about going there. (America and Australia were all one—two names for the same place, for all that he knew.) He thought his master or the parish would provide him the means of going, if he wanted. We advised him to emigrate then, by all means, not so much for himself as for his children; the idea of his bringing seven, or it might yet be a dozen, more beings into the world to live such dumb-beast lives, was horrible to us. I told him that in America his children could go to school, and learn to read and write and to enjoy the revelation of God; and as they grew up they would improve their position, and might be land-owners and farmers themselves, as well off as his master; and he would have nothing to pay, or at least but a trifle that he could gratefully spare, to have them as well educated as the master's son was being here; that where I came from the farmers would be glad to give a man like him, who could "plow and sow and reap and mow as well as any other in the parish," eighteen shillings a-week—

"And how much beer?"

"None at all!"

"None at all? ha, ha! he'd not go then—you'd not catch him workin' withouten his drink. No, no! a man 'ould die off soon that gait."

It was in vain that we offered fresh meat as an offset to the beer. There was "strength," he admitted, in beef, but it was wholly incredible that a man could work on it. A working-man must have zider or beer—there was no use to argue against that. That "Jesus Christ came into the world to save sinners," and that "work without beer is death," was the alpha and omega of his faith.

The laborers in this part of England (Hereford, Monmouth, Gloucester, and Wiltshire) were the most degraded, poor, stupid, brutal, and licentious that we saw in the kingdom. We were told that they were of the purest Saxon blood, as was indeed indicated by the frequency of blue eyes and light hair among them. But I did not see in Ireland, or in Germany or in France, nor did I ever see among our negroes or Indians, or among the Chinese or Malays, men whose tastes were such mere instincts, or whose purpose of life and whose mode of life was so low, so like that of domestic animals altogether, as these farm-laborers.

I was greatly pained, mortified, ashamed of old mother England, in acknowledging this; and the more so that I found so few Englishmen who realized it, or who, realizing it, seemed to feel that any one but God, with His laws of population and trade, was at all accountable for it. Even a most intelligent and distinguished Radical, when I alluded to this element as a part of the character of the country, in replying to certain very favorable comparisons he had been making of England with other countries, said—"We are not used to regard that class in forming a judgment of national character." And yet I suppose that class is larger in numbers than any other in the community of England. Many have even dared to think that, in the mysterious decrees of Providence, this balance of degradation and supine misery is essential to the continuance of the greatness, prosperity, and elevated character of the country— as if it were not indeed a part of the country.

A minister of the Gospel, of high repute in London, and whose sermons are reprinted and often repeated in America, from the words of Christ, "the poor ye have always among you," argued lately that all legislation or coöperative benevolence that had the tendency and hope of bringing about such a state of things that a large part of every nation should be independent of the charity of the other part, was heretical and blasphemous. Closely allied to such ideas are the too common notions of rulers and subjects.

In America we hold that a slave, a savage, a child, a maniac and a condemned criminal, are each and all born— equally with us, with our President, or with the Queen of England, free and self-governing; that they have the same natural rights with us; but that attached to those natural rights were certain duties, and when we find them, from whatever cause—no matter whether the original cause be with them, or our fathers, or us—unable to perform those duties, we dispossess them of their rights: we restrain, we confine, we master, we govern them. But in taking upon ourselves to govern them, we take other duties, and our first duty is that which is the first duty of every man for himself—improvement, restoration, regeneration. By every consideration of justice, by every noble instinct, we are bound to make it our highest and chiefest object to restore them, not the liberty first, but the capacity for the liberty—for exercising the duties of the liberty —which is their natural right. And so much of the liberty as they are able to use to their own as well as our advantage, we are bound constantly to allow them—nay, more than they show absolute evidence of their ability to use to advantage. We must not wait till a child can walk alone before we put it on its legs; we must not wait till it can swim before we let it go in the water. As faith is necessary to self-improvement, trust is necessary to education or restoration of another: as necessary with the slave, the savage, the maniac, the criminal, and the peasant—as necessary, and equally with all necessary—as with the child.

Is not this our American doctrine in its only consistent extension? We govern in trust only for another, and a part of our trust is the restoration of the rightful owner, by helping him towards that sound and well-informed mind and intelligent judgment that makes him truly free and independent. This is the only government that we of the free United States of America, whether as fathers or children, statesmen or jurymen, representatives or rabble, either claim or acknowledge. And it is of this that all true Americans believe—"that is the best government that governs the least." Using government in its properly restricted sense, as the authority and forcible direction of one over another, we hold this to be as self-evident as that the life of free love is better than the life of constrained legality, that the sentiment of mutual trust is nobler than that of suspicion or of fear, that the new dispensation of Christ is higher than the old one of Moses. What else there is, than this care over the weak and diseased in the public administration of our affairs, is no more than associated labor—the employ-

ment of certain common servants for the care of the common-
wealth.

Education, then, with certain systematic exercise or discipline of the governed, having reference to and connected with
a gradual elevation to equal freedom with the governing, we
hold to be a very necessary part of all rightful government.
Where it is not, we say this is no true and rightful government.

But we shall be at once asked, Is your fugitive law designed for such purposes? Do your slaveholders govern the
simple-minded Africans, whom they keep in restraint on these
principles?

So far as they do not, their claim is "heretical and blasphemous."

Let us never hesitate to acknowledge it—any where and
every where to acknowledge it—and before all people mourn
over it. Let us, who need not to bear the heavy burden and
live in the dark cloud of this responsibility, never, either in
brotherly love, national vanity, or subjection to insolence,
fear to declare that, in the misdirection of power by our slaveholders, they are false to the basis of our Union and blasphemous to the Father, who, equally and with equal freedom,
created all men. Would that they might see, too, that while
they continue to manifest before the world, in their legislation
upon it, no other than mean, sordid, short-sighted, and bar-
barian purposes, they must complain, threaten, expostulate,
and compromise in vain. If we drive back the truth of God, we
must expect ever-recurring, irrestrainable, irresistible reaction.
The law of God in our hearts binds us in fidelity to the principles of the Constitution. They are not to be found in "Abolitionism," nor are they to be found—remember it, brothers,
and forgive these few words—in hopeless, dawnless, unredeem-
ing slavery.

And so we hold that party in England, who regard their
laboring class as a permanent providential institution, not to
be improved in every way, educated, fitted to take an equal
share with all Englishmen in the government of the common-
wealth of England, to be tyrants, and insolent rebels to hu-

manity. (Many of them as good-souled men as the world contains, nevertheless.)

I have before said, and I repeat it with confidence, that I
believe this party to be the weaker one in England. I believe
that the love of justice, freedom, and consistency, is stronger
with Englishmen than the bonds of custom, self-conceit, and
blind idolatry of human arrangement, under however sacred
names it has come to them.

But our British friends will ask, Would it be practicable
to give these poor toiling semi-brutes any—the smallest—exercise of that governmental power, which, so far as they be not
wholly brutes is their right? Yes, we American farmers would
judge: yes, there are offices to be performed for the common-
wealth of each parish or neighborhood, of the requirement of
which they are, or soon would make themselves, fit judges. If
there are not, then make such offices. Who is a kind, firm, and
closely-scrutinizing master; who is a judicious and successful
farmer; who is an honest dealer with them; who is a skillful
plowman, a good thatcher, a good hedge-trimmer, in the mile
or two about them, they always have formed a judgment.

With regard to the habits of drinking, and the customary
diet of those by whose labor England is mainly supplied with
food, I fear my statements may be incredible to Americans; I
therefore quote from authority that should be better informed.

A correspondent of the Agricultural Gazette mentions
that, in Herefordshire and Worcestershire, the allowance of
cider given to laborers, in addition to wages, is "one to ten
gallons a-day." He observes that, of course, men can not work
without some drink, but that they often drink more than is
probably of any advantage to them, and suggests that an allowance of money be given instead of cider, and the laborers
be made to buy their drink. In this way, he thinks, they would
not be likely to drink more than they needed, and it would be
an economical operation for both parties. In Normandy, the
cider district of France, three gallons a-day is the usual allowance of laborers.

> The usual allowance given in Herefordshire by mas-
> ters, is three quarts a-day; and in harvest-time many labor-

ers drink in a day ten or twelve quarts of a liquor that, in a stranger's mouth, would be mistaken for vinegar. *Johnson and Errington on the Apple.*

Bacon, when they can get it, is the staff of the laborers' dinner." "The frugal housewife provides a large lot of potatoes, and while she indulges herself with her younger ones only with salt, cuts off the small rasher and toasts it over the plates of the father and elder sons, as being the *breadwinners;* and *this is all they want.—"A Rector and Conservative," in the Times.*

After doing up his horses he takes breakfast, which is made of flour, with a little butter, and water 'from the teakettle' poured over it. He takes with him to the field a piece of bread and (if he has not a young family and can afford it) cheese, to eat at midday. He returns home in the afternoon to a few potatoes, and possibly a little bacon, though only those who are better off can afford this. The supper very often consists of bread and water.—*"The Times Commissioner," in Wiltshire,* 1851.

It would be unjust not to add, that in a large part of England the laborers are much mor comfortable than these statements might indicate. I am also convinced that the condition of the laborer generally is improving, and that he is now in a much better condition than ten years ago. The main stay of the laborer's stomach is fine, white wheaten bread, of the best possible quality, such as it would be a luxury to get any where else in the world, and such as many a New England farmer never tasted, and, even if his wife were able to make it, would think an extravagance to be ordinarily upon his table. No doubt a coarser bread would be more wholesome, but it is one of the strongest prejudices of the English peasant, that brown bread is not fit for human beings. In Scotland and Ireland, and in some hilly districts of England, only, wheat bread is displaced by more wholesome and economical preparations of oatmeal.

With regard to fresh meat, a farmer once said to me, "They will hardly taste it all their lives, except, it may be, once a year, at a fair, when they'll go to the cook-shops and stuff themselves with all they'll hold of it; and if you could see them, you'd say they did not know what it was or what was to be done with it—cutting it into great mouthfuls and gobbling it down without any chewing, like as a fowl does barleycorns, till it chokes him."

CHAPTER XLI

Tintern Abbey and the Wye—English Screw Steamers
—Tide Deluge—St. Vincent's Rocks—Bristol-built Vessels
—The Vale of Gloucester—Whitfield "Example Farm"—
Hedge-Row Timber—Drainage—Buildings—Stock—Soil-
ing—Manure—Wheat—Beets and Turnips—Disgraceful
Agriculture—The Landed Gentry—Wages of Laborers

Chepstow

WE HAVE HAD a fierce storm of wind and rain today, notwithstanding which we have "done" (I am sorry to use the word)
Tintern Abbey and the celebrated scenery of the Wye.

The first every body has heard of, and many have dined
off it; for it is the subject of a common crockery picture. It is
"a grand exhibition of Gothic ruins, admittance twenty-five
cents; children half-price." It is indeed exceedingly beautiful
and interesting, and would be delightful to visit, if one could
stumble into it alone and contemplate it in silence; but to
have a vulgar, sycophantic, chattering showman, locking himself in with you, fastening himself to your elbow, holding an
umbrella over you, and insisting exactly when, where, what
and how much you shall admire—there was more poetry on
the dinner-plate.

The scenery of the Wye has, at some points, much grandeur. They say there is nothing else like it in England. There

is much with the same character, however, in America; and as we were familiar with scenes of greater sublimity, we found that we had been led to expect too much, and were rather disappointed with it.

We took passage from Chepstow to Bristol in a small iron screw-steamer. She was sharp and neatly modeled, and made very good speed—about fifteen knots. The captain said he could show his stern to any side-wheel steamer of her size in England. Near the junction of the Wye and the Severn there is a good breadth of water, and we found here a heavy swell and a reefing breeze. The little boat, with a small gaff-sail forward, "just to steady her," threw it off one side and the other, and made her way along handsomely and comfortably. It is my impression, that the English are a good deal ahead of us with screw-craft.

The tide-current in these rivers is a furious torrent. The rise and fall at Chepstow is fifty-three feet! (*Daniel's Shipmaster's Directory*.) At Bristol, I think it is even greater than this. The striking effects upon the banks, and the difficulty of navigation, may be imagined. Hence it is that Bristol ships have always been noted for strength, and so arose the term "Bristol-built," to describe any structure well put together.

St. Vincent's rocks, of which I had often heard sailors speak—immense banks of solid rock, that, for some miles below Bristol, the narrow, canal-like river flows between—are indeed very grand. It was most impressive to meet between them a merchant ship of the largest class—the tiny boy that we looked upright to see upon her royal yard not high enough by some hundred feet to look over them. And yet so perpendicular are they, and so narrow is the stream, that they are preparing to throw an arch over between them.

Passing with too little delay through the interesting towns of Clifton and Bristol, I parted with my friends, and went on the same day into the agricultural region known as the Vale of Gloucester.

The general aspect of this district is exceedingly beautiful; undulating, like Herefordshire, with more frequent extensive flat surfaces, very large hedges, and much timber; thickly peopled, the cottages and farm buildings old and picturesque, and the fields well stocked with cattle.

The agriculture of the district is similar to that of Cheshire, except that it is in general much behind it, neither draining nor boneing having been common improvements. The people I fell in with were usually lacking equally in courtesy and intelligence, and I learned nothing of value agriculturally, until I reached, at near nightfall, a farm conducted agreeably to the wishes of one of the landlords of the Vale, especially with the intention of giving his tenants an example of a better system of farming than they were accustomed to be content with.

For this purpose, an ordinary farm of 260 acres, in the midst of the estate, was, about ten years ago, put into the hands of an excellent Scotch Agriculturist, Mr. Morton. His first movement was to remove the superfluous fences and the enormous quantity of hedge-row timber that the farm, like all others in the district, was encumbered with. It gives us a great idea of the amount of this, as well of the value of timber in England, to learn that what was thus obtained merely from the fences of 260 acres was sold for over $17,000! There is now very little, if any, interior fencing upon the farm. The surface-water was drawn into one channel, and the whole farm under-drained with three-feet drains. Upon the steeper slopes the drains were laid with small stones, otherwise with tile. This was the only case in which I heard of stones being used by any good farmer of late years in England for drains. Even where stone is in the way upon the surface, it is found more economical to employ tile or pipes. After thorough drainage, every acre of the farm was subsoiled, and gradually the whole was limed, at the rate of one hundred and twenty bushels an acre, and divided into ten-acre lots, without fences.

Not the least unpractical labor or expense for show has been made. The walls, gates, farm-house, stables and outbuildings, are all of simple, even rude construction. As far as I could judge, every arrangement and every practice upon the farm was such as would commend itself to any farmer, and might be easily followed by any one who could command the capital which a similar extent of soil would seem to need for

its profitable cultivation. Almost every inch of the surface outside the buildings and the lane is tilled, there being no pasture. In the stables we found a stock of mongrel cows, mostly
of Hereford and Shorthorn blood, bought to be fattened. No
stock is raised. Each cow was in a separate loose box. They are
fed at this season with clover and trefoil, and supplied with a
great profusion of straw litter. The manure is allowed to ac-
cumulate under them until it becomes inconvenient. The cows
appeared to be in healthy and thriving condition; they were
generally lying down and quietly ruminating with an aspect
of entire satisfaction. The horse-stalls were of a form and size
most common in our cities; the horses rather lighter than the
ordinary English draught-horses. A steam-engine is employed
for threshing, cutting turnips, etc. All the crops but wheat, are
fed upon the farm, and all the straw is used as litter; of course
an immense stock of manure is manufactured, and little or
none needs to be bought to sustain a high fertility and large
crops of every kind.

Under this system, Mr. Morton is able to grow wheat
every second year; so that one-half the farm was covered with
magnificent crops of this grain, likely to yield full forty
bushels an acre, which would be worth at least $6,000. The
wheat is all drilled, and looked to me particularly clean and
even. The alternate crops are carrots, mangel-wurzel, ruta-
baga, potatoes and clover. Of the latter, forty acres; of the
roots, mangel-wurzel occupied the largest space. Mr. Morton
told me that he had, of late, much preferred it to turnips;
thought he could get thirty tons from an acre that would only
yield twenty of ruta-baga, with similar expense. A few acres
were devoted to vegetables and fruit for the family, and to the
raising of seeds for the root-crops. I do not recollect to have
seen a weed on the farm, except among the potatoes, which
were being hoed by laborers, with very large hoes made for the
purpose.

Of course the expense of such improvement as I have
described was very great; but the proprietor considers it to
have been a good investment. It is now leased by Mr. Morton
and his son.

It is called "Example Farm;" how appropriately, may be

judged by the following description of an ordinary farm of the county, by the "Times' Commissioner:"*

An inconvenient road conducted us to the entrance-gate of a dilapidated farm-yard, one side of which was occupied by a huge barn and wagon-shed, and the other by the farm-house dairy and piggeries. The farm-yard was divided by a wall, and two lots of milch-cows were accommodated in the separate divisions. On one side was a temporary shed, covered with bushes and straw. Beneath this shed there was a comparatively dry lair for the stock; the yard itself was wet, dirty and uncomfortable. The other yard was exactly the counterpart of this, except that it wanted even the shelter-shed. In these two yards are confined the dairy-stock of the farm during the winter months; they are supplied with hay in antique, square hayracks, ingeniously capped over, to protect the hay, with a thatched roof, very much resembling the pictures of Robinson Crusoe's hut. In each yard two of them are placed, round which the shivering animals station themselves as soon as the feeder gives them their diurnal ration, and then patiently ruminate the scanty contents. A dripping rain fell as we looked at them, from which their heads were sheltered by the thatched roof of the hayrack, only to have it poured in a heavier stream on their necks and shoulders. In the other yard the cows had finished their provender, and showed their dissatisfaction with its meagre character by butting each other round the rack. The largest and greediest having finished her own share, immediately dislodges her neighbor, while she, in her turn, repeats the blow upon the next, and so the chase begins, the cows digging their horns into each other's sides, and discontentedly pursuing one another through the wet and miry yard. Leaving the yard we passed into the fields, sinking at every step in the sour, wet grass-lands. Here, little heaps of dung, the exhausted relics of the hay, from which the

---

* Mr. Caird, a special traveling correspondent upon agriculture, of the Times.

cows derive their only support in winter, were being scattered thinly over the ground, to aid in the production of another crop of hay.

I have shown how much good a wealthy landlord may find it his profit to do in the way of improving agriculture. Mr. Caird intimates that for such a state of things as is exhibited in the last picture, we are also to hold the landlord accountable. Mr. Caird likewise says, "On all hands the farmer suffers: he pays rent for space occupied by his landlord's trees; he provides harbor for his landlord's game, which, in return, feed upon his crops; [it is for this reason many landlords will not allow the fences to be touched;] if he attempts to plough out inferior pasture, his crop becomes an additional feeding-ground for the game; whilst the small fields and crooked fences prevent all efforts at economy of labor, and compel him neither to restrict his cultivation, or execute it negligently and unprofitably."

God keep us evermore free from a "powerful conservative landed gentry," a curse not unmixed with good though it be.

Wages of laborers were mentioned to me at 8*s.* Caird says 7*s.* and 8*s.*, and sometimes 6*s.;* but it was added, significantly, that 6*s.* worth of work is only given in such a case.

CHAPTER XLII

Bath—Warminster—Surly Postmaster—A Doubtful Character—Polite Innkeeper and Pretty Chambermaid—The Tap-Room Fireside—Rustic Civility—Rainy Morning in a Country Inn—Coming to Market—The Road in a Storm —Scudding

IT WAS RAINING HARD when I again reached Bristol, and I at once jumped on board a train ready to leave for Bath. Here I found that my friends had walked on, and after looking at the "pump-room" and a grimy old cathedral, and getting a dinner, I determined to follow them. There was no public conveyance that evening, and I started on foot, thinking to overtake them at Warminster.

At the top of a high hill I stopped under a tree during a temporary torrent of rain, and looked back at what I could not help thinking would be a grand view if there were but a gleam of sunshine upon it; perhaps it was grander by help of the imagination in the obscurity of the rain and drifting scud and murky cloud of smoke that was swept fragrant towards me from the city. Bath is situated among and up the sides of extensive hills, and the country about it is much of it well wooded and studded with numerous villas. The town is remarkably well built, with numerous stately terrace-houses, of the same fine, soft-tinted sandstone (Bath-stone) that I de-

scribed at Liverpool. It is a famous old watering-place, you
know; "a mort of merry-making" there has been in it in days
past, but now, though by no means a decayed town, I believe
its glory in this respect has departed. I should judge it still to
be a place of great wealth and elegance, but less distinguished
for gayety and folly than formerly. All I can say of the inhabitants really, from personal observation, is, that they
"know enough to stay in when it rains," for I hardly saw one
in the streets, except the men who were waiting by the little
covered "chairs," such as Mrs. Skewton is represented by
Cruikshanks to be wheeled about in by her lanky page. I saw
hundreds of these, ranged in the streets as hackney-coaches are
in our towns, but no carriage of any kind, public or private;
perhaps the Bath coachmen had again "met to a cold swarry."

After a walk of two miles into the country, I found I had
been misdirected, and had a good deal of difficulty in finding
the right road. I once asked the way of two laborers, and their
replies were in such language, and they were so stupid, that I
could not get the least idea of what they meant. My guess was,
that they either could not understand what I wanted, or that
they did not know themselves whether or not it was the
Warminster road that they were at work upon. It was after
four o'clock when I at length got upon the straight road, with
seventeen miles before me—a hilly road, with a thin, slimy
chalk-mud under foot. I stopped once again during another
tremendous torrent, taking the opportunity to bait at a neat
little inn, and reached Warminster, after a hard pull, at nine
o'clock. The first building in the town, as you come from
Bath, is a fine old church, going round the yard of which you
enter abruptly upon a close-built street of old thatched two-
story houses.

The postmaster had no letters for me, and seemed to be
very angry that I should have expected him to have. I looked
from one inn to another, not finding my friends, and finally,
muddy, wet, and tired enough, stopped at what seemed the last
in the street, a house of humble appearance.

I desired to be showed to my room. Master, mistress,
maid, and Boots immediately surrounded and eyed me closely,
and I could not but remember that I might, probably, bear a

suspicious appearance to them. As I take off my cape, maid—a nice, kind-looking, black-eyed little girl—catches it up, and runs off to hang it by the kitchen fire (an absurd operation, as it is made of oiled silk); she is back in a moment with a light, and, lifting my knapsack, shows me up to a pleasant room, with a deep, dark-curtained bed—slides out, and is again back in a moment with slippers, and asks to take my shoes to be dried, and what would I wish for supper? I decline supper, and intend to go to bed at once. Down she goes, and, after a moment more, in pops the landlord. "Was you understood aright, sir?—no supper, sir?—not coming down, sir?—going to bed, sir?—directly, sir, without supper, sir?" and while saying this, he bustles about the room, locks the closet doors, puts the keys in his pocket, and then turns towards me with a suspicious look at my knapsack. "Yes," I answer, quietly; and, drawing out shirt, socks, and tooth-brush, "I took supper upon the road, and I thought I had best get my clothes off, and at once to bed." "Ah! I see, sir; quite right, sir; ah! yes, sir; dry stockings too, sir; yes, sir; indeed, sir, I was not aware; beg pardon, sir: but, indeed, would you step downstairs a moment, sir—fine fire in the tap, sir—dry yourself, if you would please, for a moment, I would have the room put in better order for you, sir; indeed, the bed is hardly—if you would, sir—thank you, sir."

In the tap-room were three fellows with smock-frocks. As I approached, one called to another, who was nearer the fire, to give me his seat, and offered me, with truly rustic grace, his half-emptied pot of beer. I dislike to repulse what is meant for kindness; so I tasted it, and tried to enter into conversation with them. I soon found it was impossible; for I could make nothing of two-thirds of their replies, and I doubted if they could understand me much better. So I contented myself with listening, while they continued to talk or mumble with each other. The subjects of their conversation were beer and "the girls:" of the latter topic they said nothing to be repeated; of the former, they wished the farmers never gave worse drink than that they were now enjoying—"it was most good for nothing, some of it, what they gave out." And one told how he had had to drink so much of it once, it had made him clear sick; and then another told how, on the other hand, he had made himself sick one day, when somebody wouldn't give him as much beer as he wanted, by taking a draught of cold water.

When the little maid came in to say that my bed was now "quite ready," and I rose to withdraw from the circle, they all gave a singular jerk forward of their heads and touched their foreheads with their right hand, as a parting salutation.

"Would you let me take something else down to be dried now, sir, your coat, sir, or any thing—the socks, sir; thank you, sir. Hope you'll sleep well, sir."

Well, I did sleep. It was nine in the morning when I awoke, and there was a steady roar upon the tiles—the rain still continued. I drew the window-curtain, and there was Geoffrey Crayon's picture almost to the life: a sleepy old gray mare "letting it rain;" a draggle-tailed cock on a smoking dunghill, eyeing with the air of a miserable sick saint the riotous orgies of a company of mad ducks, deep in their favorite liquor; half a dozen doves huddled moping together on the thatch of the stable—a sombre tone over every thing, and rain, rain, rain.

"Hope you rested well, sir," said the landlord, as I reached the foot of the crooked stairs; "a dirty day, sir. Have your shoes, sir? What'll you please to have for breakfast, sir? Steak, sir? O yes, sir—or chop, sir; give you very nice chop, sir; yes, sir, thank you, sir. Walk in here, sir? Ready shortly, sir."

To get to the breakfast I was led through the kitchen, a large room with saddles and box-coats and whips and straps hung up with the bacon on the ceiling and walls. The breakfast-room (dining-room) was much larger than any room you would have supposed, from the front of the house, it was likely to contain. Its plan was octagonal, with a single great red-curtained bow-window and stately, high-backed chairs, suggesting a corporation banquet.

"Going on, sir—yes, sir." All my things are brought, dry and warm, and nicely folded; and now I have curiosity to know what value is placed upon so much suavity. The landlord meets my request with deprecating gesture and grimace, as if it was a pity that the custom of society made such a form necessary between a host and his guest—as if he were about to say, "I am grieved that you should mention it; really, it is I that am indebted to you for this honor; but if you insist, why"—ending the *aside,* but still low, hurried, and indistinct—"sixpence for bed and a shilling for breakfast, and (shall I say thre'pence?) for Boots, sir." "Yes, and the rest to that excellent little chambermaid, if you please." "Oh, my little girl, sir; oh, thank ye, sir, you are very good, sir—yes, sir, you can't miss it, sir; straight road after you pass the gate, sir. *Good*-morning, sir; should be glad to see you if you are this way again, sir, or any of your friends. *Good*-morning, sir. Hope you'll have a fine day yet, sir! It's slacking up e'en now, I think. Indeed it is, sir! Ah, you'll have a fine day for a walk, sir. *Good*-morning, sir."

If it slackens at all, it is only for a moment, and then the rain pours down again densly and with renewed vehemence; and the wind, coming from behind, fairly twists me about, and hurries me along in its strong, fitful gusts. It is market-day in Warminster, and, as I go out, every body and every thing else seems to be coming in. Men, women, and children, in all sorts of English vehicles—spring-carts, taxed-carts, great broad-wheeled carts, or long wagons, with bodies of a curious curved form flaring out over the wheels, canvas tops, stretched over all, upon hoops; sometimes two horses abreast, drawing them in a double set of shafts; oftener two or three, and frequently four, five, or six, all in a line (tandem), great, intelligent beasts, keeping well to the left, where none will interfere with them, and they can legally harm no one. ("Keep the left," is the rule of the road in England; not the right, as with us.) They are driven without reins; and more than once this morning I saw the driver, well dosed with beer, I suppose, and fatigued with night-work, fast asleep on the top of his load. Once I saw a gentleman, who had nearly run against one of these sleeping fellows, strike him smartly with his whip as he passed—"You had best wake up, sir; who's your master?" "Mr.——, of——, sir," answered the man, rubbing himself. "Very well; I shall let him know what sort of a carter he has." A Yankee driver, so waked up, would have replied to the whip first, perhaps. Gentlemen come at a spanking pace, in dog-carts, or in the saddle, screwing their heads as deep as they can into their drab coats, bending low, and their hats pulled down tight upon their brows, hardly ever with an umbrella, but with a groom with gold hat-band by their side sometimes. They look scowlingly, as they approach, at me; with my hat-brim turned up before and down behind to shed the water from my face, my water-proof cape tightly fastened at my waist behind, and swelling and fluttering before, my arms folded under it, I return their inquiring stare complacently; some, as they come up, draw their lips resolutely tighter, and give me about quarter of a nod, as if they understood and approved my arrangement. Men on foot, and women, too, with clogs and pattens and old green and blue umbrellas, and bundles and bags and baskets and hampers and cages and parcels in handkerchiefs; old and young, lasses and lads, generally three or four couples together, coming to town for a holiday, loudly laughing and coarsely joking; bound to enjoy themselves spite of the shameful indelicacy of the wind, and the chill drenching of the rain, and the misplaced attachment to their finery of the spattering mud.

CHAPTER XLIII

The South-Downs—Wiltshire Landscape—Chalk and Flint
—Irrigation—The Cost and Profit of Water-Meadows—
Sewerage Water—Irrigation in Old Times

SOON AFTER LEAVING Warminster, began a quite different style
of landscape from any I have before seen: long ranges and
large groups of high hills with gentle and gracefully undulating slopes; broad and deep dells between and within them,
through which flow in tortuous channels streamlets of exceedingly pure, sparkling water. These hills are bare of trees, except rarely a close body of them, covering a space of perhaps
an acre, and evidently planted by man. Within the shelter of
these you will sometimes see that there is a large farm-house
with small stables. The valleys are cultivated, but the hills in
greater part are covered, without the slightest variety, except
what arises from the changing contour of the ground, with
short, fine grass, standing thinly, but sufficiently close to give
the appearance, at a little distance from the eye, of a smooth,
velvety, green surface. Among the first of the hills I observed,
at a high elevation, long angular ramparts and earth-works, all
greened over. Within them, and at the summit of the hill,
were several extensive tumuli, evidently artificial (though I
find nothing about it in the books), and on the top of one of
these was a shepherd and dog and a large flock of sheep,

appearing of gigantic size against the leaden clouds behind. In
the course of the day I met with many of these flocks, and
nearly all the hill-land seemed given up to them. I was upon
the border, in fact, of the great *South-down* district, and, during the next week, the greater part of the country through
which we were traveling, was of the same general character of
landscape, though not always as green, varied, and pleasing as
in these outskirts.

Geologically, it is a chalk district, the whole earth, high
and low, and to any depth that I saw it exposed, being more
or less white, generally gray, but sometimes white as snow.
The only stone is flint, which occurs in small boulders or
pebbles, cased in a hardened crust of carbonate of lime mingled irregularly with the chalk, more thickly on the hill-tops,
and often gathered in beds. The road is made of these flint
pebbles, broken fine, and their chalk-crust, powdered by the
attrition of wheels, is worked up into a slippery paste during
such heavy rains as I was experiencing, and makes the walking
peculiarly fatiguing. The soil upon the hills is very dry and
thin. In the valleys it is deeper and richer, being composed, in
a considerable part, of the wash of the higher country, and the
wheat and forage crops are often very luxuriant. Advantage
is sometimes taken of the streams to form water-meadows, and
the effect of irrigation can often be seen at a considerable
distance in the deeper green and greater density of the grass
upon them. As these meadows are of great agricultural value, I
will describe the method of construction and management of
them.

An artificial channel is made, into which the water of a
brook may be turned at will. This is carried along for as great
a distance as practicable, so as to skirt the upper sides of fields
of a convenient surface for irrigation. At suitable intervals
there are gates and smaller channels, and eventually a great
number of minor ducts, through which the water is distributed. The fields are divided by low walls, so that the water
can be retained upon them as long as is desired, and then
drawn off to a lower level. Commonly, a series of meadows,
held by different farmers, are flooded from one source, and old
custom or agreement fixes the date of commencing the irriga-

tion and the period of time at which the water shall be moved from one to another.

The main flooding is usually given in October, after the grass has been closely eaten off by neat stock. It is then allowed to remain resting or quietly flowing over the land for two or three weeks; or for two weeks, and, after an interval of a day or two, for two weeks more. This consolidates the grassy surface, and encourages the growth of roots. The grass springs and grows luxuriantly after it, and, as soon as it is observed to flag, the water is again let in for two or three weeks; it may be twice during the winter. Whenever a scum is observed to form, indicating that decomposition is commencing below, the water is immediately drawn. In warm weather this will occur very soon, perhaps in a day or two. I believe it is intended not to allow the water ever to freeze upon the meadows. In the spring, by the middle of March, sometimes, sheep and lambs are turned on to the grass. After being fed pretty closely, they are removed, and the meadows are left for a crop of hay. They are ready for mowing in less than two months, and are then, after a short interval, pastured again with horned cattle and horses. Some meadows are never pastured, and yield three heavy crops of hay. Mr. Pusey (a member of Parliament) declares, that he keeps sheep upon his water-meadows, in Berkshire, at the rate of thirty-six an acre, well fed, and intimates his belief that the produce of grass-land is doubled by irrigation. Grass and hay, however, from irrigated meadows, are of slightly less nourishing quality. It is generally said, that a single winter's flooding will increase the growth of grass equal to a top-dressing of thirty (thirty bushel) loads of dung.

We may judge somewhat from these facts and opinions of practical men, whether, in any given circumstances, we can afford to construct the dam, channels, gates, sluices, etc., by which we may use this method of fertilizing our meadows. There are millions of acres in the United States that could be most readily made subject to the system. The outlay for permanent works might often be very inconsiderable, and the labor of making use of them, after construction, would be almost nothing. The cost of conveying manure, and its distribution by carts and manual labor, is a very important item in the expenditure of most of our eastern farms; and, though this is felt less here, where labor is cheaper, we may obtain many economical hints with regard to it from British practice. Fields distant from the farmstead, and hill-lands not easily accessible, should nearly always be enriched by bone, guano and other concentrated manures; of which a man may carry more on his back than will be of equal value with many cart-loads of dung, or by some other means which will dispense with long and heavy transportation. I have obtained increased crops, with a saving of some hundred dollars a-year of expenditure, in this way.

Different streams vary in their value for irrigation. The muddiest streams are the best, as they generally carry suspended a great deal of the fertile matter of the land through which they have flowed; often, too, road-washings, and other valuable drainings, have been taken along with them, and these are caused to be deposited upon the meadow. A perfectly transparent fluid will often, however, have most valuable salts in solution; and I noticed that most of the Wiltshire streams were peculiarly clear, reminding me of the White Mountain trout-brooks. It is said that streams abounding in fish, and which have abundance of aquatic plants and luxuriant vegetation upon their borders, are to be relied upon as the most enriching in their deposit. Streams into which the sewerage of large towns is emptied, are often of the greatest value for agricultural purposes. A stream thus enriched is turned to important account near Edinburg: certain lands, which were formerly barren wastes, being merely the clean, dry sands thrown up by the sea in former times, having been arranged so that they may be flowed. The expense of the operation was great—about one hundred dollars an acre—and the annual cost of flooding is very much greater than usual—four or five dollars an acre; but the crops of hay are so frequent and enormous (ten cuttings being made in a season), that some parts of the meadow rent for one hundred dollars a-year for one acre, and none for less than seventy-five dollars!

It is estimated by the distinguished agriculturist, Smith of Deanston, that the sewerage-water of a town may be contracted for, to be delivered, (sent by subterranean pipes and branches, so that it may be distributed over any required surface,) eleven miles out of town, for four cents a ton. Mr. Hawksley, a prudent engineer, offers to convey it five miles, and raise it two hundred feet, for five cents a ton; the expense of carting it to the same distance and elevation being estimated at about $1. Another estimate makes the expense of conveying and distributing manure, in the solid form, as compared with liquid, at fifteen dollars to seventy-five cents, for equal fertilizing values. Professor Johnston estimates the annual fertilizing value of the sewerage of a town of one thousand inhabitants, as equal to a quantity of guano which, at present American prices, would be worth $13,000. Smith of Deanston estimates the cost of manuring an acre by sewerage, conveyed in aqueducts and distributed by jet-pipes, at three dollars an acre, and that of fertilizing it to an equal degree, in the usual way, by farm-yard manure, at fifteen dollars. Considering that the expense of conveyance and distribution of solid manure is much greater in America than in England, these figures are not without personal interest to us.

The use of manure-drainings and the urine of the cattle of a farm, very much diluted with spring water, has been found to have such astonishing immediate effects, when distributed over young herbage, that several English agricultural pioneers are making extensive and costly permanent arrangements for its distribution, from their stables, over large surface. It is first collected in tanks, where it is retained until putrefied, and mixed with the water of irrigation. This is then driven by forcing-pumps into the pipes which convey it, so that it can be distributed, (in one case, over one hundred and seventy acres.) The pipes are hard-burnt clay-pipes, an inch thick, joined with cement, costing here about twelve and a-half cents a-yard. The pipe is laid under ground, and at convenient intervals there are heads coming to the surface with stop-cocks, where a hose can be attached and the water further guided in any direction. For greater distances, a cart like those used for sprinkling the dusty streets of our cities is used. It is conjectured that, eventually, all manure will be furnished to land in a state of solution.

I believe irrigation is only used for grass in England; but

it probably would be found of great advantage to other valuable crops. I have seen large fields of roots, apparently of the character of turnips, irrigated in China: rice, though it grows very well on dry land, is so much benefited by irrigation that it is hardly anywhere made a staple crop, unless there are facilities for irrigation. I suspect that irrigation, and even that expensive form of it that I have last described, might be profitably used, for certain plants, by our market-gardeners; for celery and asparagus for instance; and it is well known that enormous strawberries, and unusually large and long-continuing crops of them, have resulted from an inefficient and unsystematic kind of irrigation. A small experiment, made by myself, with Indian corn, resulted in a great growth of stalk and in unhealthy malformed grain.*

Irrigation is of the least advantage upon heavy clay soils, and of the greatest upon light sandy loams with gravelly subsoils. It is very desirable that the construction of the soil should be such that the water may gradually and somewhat rapidly filter through it; and it is considered of great importance, when the water is drawn off after the flooding (*drowning* is the local term), that it should be very completely removed, leaving no small pools upon the surface. Stagnating water, either above or below the surface, is poisonous to most plants.

I may remind those who have a prejudice against new practices in agriculture, that irrigation was practiced as long ago as the days of the patriarchs. In this part of England it has been in use since about the beginning of the seventeenth century, at which time an agreeably-written book on the subject was published by one Rowland Vaughan, Esq. The account of the way that he was first led to make systematic trial of irrigation, and the manner in which he proceeded, is amusing and instructive:

> In the month of March I happened to find a mole or wont's nest raised on the brim of a brook in my meade, like a great hillock; and from it there issued a little

---

* I have seen extensive fields of maize irrigated, on the Rio Grande, and scarcely any is grown except by irrigation in the valley of that river.

streame of water (drawn by the working of the mole), down a shelving ground, one pace broad, and some twenty in length. The running of this little streame did at that time wonderfully content me, seeing it pleasing greene, and that other land on both sides was full of moss, and hide-bound for want of water. This was the first cause I undertook the drowning of grounds.

Now to proceed to the execution of my worke: being perswaded of the excellency of the water, I examined how many foote fall the brooke yielded from my mill to the uppermost part of my grounds, being in length a measured mile. There laye of meadow land thirty acres overworn with age, and heavily laden with moss, cowlips and much other imperfect grass, betwixt my mill stream and the mane river, which (with two shillings cost) my grandfather and his grandsire, with the rest, might have drowned at their pleasure; but from the beginning never anything was done, that either tradition or record could witness, or any other testimonie.

Having viewed the convenientest place, which the uppermost part of my ground would afford for placing a commanding weare or sluce, I espied divers water falls on my neighbours' grounds, higher than mine by seven or eight foote: which gave me great advantage of drowning more ground, than I was of mine own power able to do.

I acquainted them with my purpose; the one being a gentleman of worth and good nature, gave me leave to plant the one end of my weare on his side the river: the other, my tenant, being very aged and simple, by no perswasion I could use, would yield his consent, alledging it would marre his grounds, yea, sometimes his apple trees; and men told him water would raise the rush, and kill his cowslips, which was the chiefest flower his daughters had to tricke the May-pole withal.

After I had wrought thus far, I caused my servant, a joiner, to make a levell to discover what quantity of ground I might obtaine from the entry of the water; allowing his doubling course, compassing hills to carry it plym or even, which fell out to be some three hundred acres.

After I had plymned it upon a true levell, I betooke
myself to the favour of my tenants, friends and neighbours, in running my maine trench, which I call my
trench-royal. I call it so, because I have within the contents of my worke, counter-trenches, defending-trenches,
topping-trenches, winter and summer-trenches, double
and treble-trenches, a traversing-trench with a point, and
an everlasting-trench, with other troublesome trenches,
which in a map I will more lively expresse. When the inhabitants of the country wherein I inhabit (namely the
Golden Valley) saw I had begun some part of my worke,
they summoned a consultation against me and my man
John, the leveller, saying our wits were in our hands, not
in our heads; so we both, for three or four years lay levell
to the whole country's censure for such engineers as their
fore-fathers heard not of, nor they well able to endure
without merryments.

In the running and casting of my trench-royal,
though it was levelled from the beginning to the end,
upon the face of the ground, yet in the bottom I did likewise levell it to avoyde error.

For the breadth and depth, my proportion is ten foote
broad, and four foote deep; unless in the beginning, to
fetch the water to my drowning grounds, I ran it some
half mile eight foote deep, and in some places sixteen foote
broad. All the rest of the course, for two miles and a half
in length, according to my former proportion. When my
worke began in the eye of the country to carry a shew of
profit, it pleased many out of their courtesie to give it
commendations, and applaud the invention.

The author then makes a considerable digression, to account for a delay in his proceedings, which was occasioned by
processes issued against him from the courts of Star Chamber,
Chancery, and Wardes, to compel him to deliver his niece and
ward into their custody.

These courts, he observes, bred more white haires
in my head in one year than all my wet-shod water-works
did in sixteen. So leaving my wanton ward in London, in

the custody of a precisian or puritan taylor, who would not endure to heare one of his journeymen sweare by the cross of his shears; so full was he of sanctity in deceipt. But the first news I heard was, that he had married my Welch niece to his Englis nephew; and at my return, I was driven to take his word, that he was neither privy to the contract, nor the marriage.

Mr. Vaughan next gives the following directions for carrying this plan into effect:

> Having prepared your drowning course, be very careful that all the ground subject to the same, whether meadow, pasture, or arable, be as plain as any gardenplotte, and without furrows. Then follows your attendance in flood-times: see that you suffer not your flood water by negligence to pass away into the brooke, river, and sea, but by your sluice command it to your grounds, and continue it playing thereon so long as it appears muddy. In the beginning of March clear your ground of cold water, and keep it as dry as a child under the hands of a dainty nurse; observing generally that sandy ground will endure ten times more water than the clay. A day or two before you mow, if sufficient showers have not qualified the drought of your ground, let down your sluice into your trench-royal, that thereby you may command so much water to serve your turn as you desire. Suffer it to descend where you mean first to mow, and you shall find this manner of drowning in the morning before you mow so profitable and good, that commonly you gain ten or twelve days' advantage in growing. For drowning before mowing, a day, or even two or three, so supplies the ground, that it doth most sweetly release the root of every particular grasse, although the sun be never so extream hot. This practice will often make a good second mowing, and in walking over grounds, I will tread as on velvet, or a Turkey carpet.

CHAPTER XLIV

Flocks, Dogs, and Shepherds of Salisbury Plain—Village
Almshouses—Ostentation in Alms-Giving—A Forced March
—At Home in Salisbury—The Street Brooks—The Cathe-
dral—Architectural Remarks and Advice—Village Churches

THE CHALK-HILLS, or downs (locally called beak-land), are unenclosed, and rarely separated from the cultivated land by
more than a low turf-wall, often not at all. Once, in the course
of the morning, I came near a flock of about two hundred
sheep, feeding close to the road, and stopped a few moments to
look at them. They were thorough-bred South-downs; the
shepherd sat at a little distance, upon a knoll, and the dog was
nearer the flock. Growing close up to the edge of the road,
opposite the sheep, was a heavy piece of wheat; one of them
strayed over to it. The dog cocked his ears and turned quickly
several times towards his master, as if knowing there was business for him, and waiting for orders. But the shepherd was
looking another way, and others of the flock, lifting
their heads as I approached them, and seeing their com-
rade on the other side of the road, began to rush after him, as
is the manner of sheep; and directly there were a dozen eagerly nipping the wheat, and more following. The dog, sitting
erect, still waited for orders, till the shepherd, turning, spoke
quickly in a low monosyllable. Right over the heads of the

flock, bounding from head to head, sprang the dog, yelping sharply as he reached the road; the truants returned, and the whole flock broke at once into a hard run—the dog dashing first one way, then the other, closing them rapidly up, and keeping them in a dense mass, until, at another shout from the shepherd, who had not risen, all at once halted, and, turning heads out, went to feeding, soon closing about the dog, leaving only a space of a few feet vacant around him. The dogs used by most of the shepherds seem to be mongrels, generally low in the legs, with great heads, short necks, and rather shaggy. One that was said to be very sagacious and well-trained, and for which I was asked thirty dollars, appeared as if a cross of a spaniel with a terrier. Generally, the dogs were valued at only from two to five dollars.

It cleared about noon; and after the rain ceased the air was calm, hot, and steamy. I recollect but one village, two rows of ugly, glaring, red brick houses, relieved by a church, rectory, and two other buildings, cool and pleasing, under shade of ivy; and a large, old establishment, with cupalo and clock, and a square, green, shady court in front of it—devoted, as appeared by an inscription on its front, by somebody's bequest two hundred years ago, to the maintenance, in comfort, of a certain number of aged widowers and bachelors of the parish. Such retreats, for various denominations of the poor and unfortunate, called almshouses and hospitals (vulgarly, " 'spittals"), are to be seen in almost every town in England. They are of all degrees of comfort—some stately and luxurious—others, and these quite common, mere cottages—hovels sometimes—generally very old, and nearly always of ancient foundation. With more or less ostentation, the name of the founder is displayed on the front—sometimes with his bust, statue, arms, or a ridiculous allegorical sculpture. This plan for sending a dying sinner's name down to future generations, with the grateful embalmment of charity, seems latterly out of fashion. What improved type of character does it indicate, that the rich oftener prefer now to make their tribute to public opinion, by having their gift-money used while they yet live, and the amount of it paraded with their

names in the newspapers? Their "left hands," probably, do
not read the newspapers.

I was disappointed in not finding my friends at this village, but soon after leaving it met two Germans traveling on
foot, who said they had met, at three hours back, two gentlemen, who wore hats and knapsacks like mine. I feared that,
not hearing from me at Salisbury, they would conclude I had
gone on by Cirencester, to the Isle of Wight, and would go by
the five-o'clock train to overtake me. It was therefore necessary
that I should hasten in to arrest them. I yet made two or three
stoppages, once to converse with a shepherd, and once to
sketch the outlines of a group of cottages, intending to take
the coach, which I was told would be passing in a few minutes.
But when coming up a hill, I rose the fine spire of the cathedral, some three miles distant, and the coach still not in
sight, I strapped tight my knapsack and went the rest of the
way at "double quick." Teamsters stopped their wagons as I
met them, children at the cottage-doors called their mothers to
help look at me, and at the office of the "Wilts Game Law
Reporter," as I entered the town, taking the middle of the
street, a fat old gentleman in top-boots eagerly took out his
watch and timed me, evidently supposing it was some interesting affair on a wager. Finding the post-office, but not finding
any note for me, I hastened on still to the station, which was
well out of the town on the other side, and which I reached at
the same moment with the delaying stage-coach. The train
started a moment afterwards. The policeman in attendance
was certain that no persons such as I described had entered the
station-house, and I returned to the town, and going first to
the cathedral, there found J. and C. lying under the trees in
delighted contemplation of its beauty.

We spent Sunday at Salisbury. We were fortunate in finding a comfortable, quiet, old inn, in which we were the only
lodgers. After once getting acquainted with the crooked, elaborate stairways and passages, and learning the relative position
of our chambers and the common rooms, we were as much at
home, as quiet, and as able to command whatever we had
occasion for, as if we had leased the house, furnished, and
manned it. The landlady was our housekeeper, the servants

our domestics. We saw no one but them, (till night, when we happened to discover, in a remote subterranean corner, a warm, smoky, stone-cavern, in which a soldier, a stage-coachman, and others, were making merry with ladies, beer and song,) and them we saw only as we chose to. We had a large, comfortable parlor, with dark-colored furniture, of an age in which ease was not sacrificed to decoration; a dais and bow-window, old prints of Nelson's victories, and Garrick and Siddons in Shakespearian characters, a smouldering sea-coal fire, several country newspapers, and a second-hand last week's Times. Preposterous orders were listened to without a smile, receipts for Yankee dishes distinctly understood in all their elaboration without impatience, and to the extent of the resources of the establishment faithfully executed. Only once was the mild business-manner of our hostess disturbed by an appearance of surprise; when we told her that we were Americans, she raised her eyes in blank incredulity, and asked, "You don't mean you were born in America, sir?"—meaning, unquestionably, "how could you be so white?" The servants kept out of sight; our room was "put to rights," our clothes arranged in a bureau, while we were at breakfast; and when we were seated, and had got fairly under way with an excellent home-like dinner, the girl who acted for waiter, seeming to understand our humor, put a handbell on the table and withdrew, saying that we would please to call her when we wanted any thing.

Along the sides of many of the streets of Salisbury there flows, in little canals some six feet wide by two or three deep, with frequent bridges to the houses, a beautifully clear, rapid stream of water. Otherwise, the general appearance of the town is of meagre interest compared with others we have been in. But it has one crowning glory—the cathedral.

The cathedral, in many of its parts, and from certain positions, as a whole, is very beautiful; the symmetrical spire, especially against an evening sky, is very fine. It is taller by several feet than any other in England, though overtopped by several of the Continental churches.

We have more pleasure in contemplating it, and enjoy more to wander around and through it, than any we have seen

before. It is more satisfactory to us. This, I believe, is partly
because of its greater size, partly because of its completeness,
its unity: though six hundred years old, you would not readily
perceive in approaching it that it was not entirely a new edifice; no repairs, no additions, especially no meddlesome restor-
ations. Its history is worthy of note with respect to this: it was
only thirty-eight years in construction, except the spire, which
was added rather later, and is more florid, which is only to be
regretted.

We admire and enjoy it, and yet not nearly so much as we
should have expected to from an imagination of what such a
great, expensive, and artistic pile would be. You will wonder
why. I don't know that I can tell you. It fails in massiveness
and grandeur. From some quarters it appears a mere clutter of
wall, windows, buttresses, and pinnacles, each of which may be
fine enough in itself, but which gain nothing from their combination. There is nowhere a sufficient breadth and mass of
wall, I suspect, for the grandeur we demand. Once or twice
only did it awaken any thing like a sense of sublimity, and
then it did not appear to me to be due to any architectural
intention.

Once, late in the day, and alone, I was walking from the
end of one transept towards the other, when an emotion came
over me partaking of awe. Afterwards, in trying to analyze
what had occasioned it, I found that my face was turned towards two great, dark windows, a considerable space of unbroken wall about them, and a square, massive buttress, all in
the deep shade between the two transepts. From the simple,
solitary grandeur and solemnity of the dark recess, there had
come a sermon on humility and endurance, to me more eloquent than all else of the great cathedral.

The wall over and behind this, in an equal space, was
broken up by three of the triple windows, which, look at the
cathedral from any direction you will, you see every where
repeated, until the form becomes ugly. Not ugly in itself, but
ugly and paltry, by so much repetition, in an edifice of such
grandeur. If all these windows, with all their forms, proportion, color, and fashion of carving, had been the work of one
man, they were evidently that man's *one idea;* if of many men,

then they were servile imitations. One would be, perhaps, a worthy and beautiful design—a hundred are paltry, ignominious, mechanical copies; they might be iron-castings, for all the value the chisel has given them. Should there not be, with sufficient regard to symmetrical uniformity, evidence of independent design in the details of every part of an edifice of such magnitude?

From the little study that I was able to give Old-World architecture, my advice to all building-committee gentlemen of no more cultivated taste than my own (that to such these crude thoughts may give hints of value, is my apology for printing them), would be, Stick to simplicity. The grand effect of architecture must be from form and proportion. Favor designs, therefore, which, in their grand outlines, are at once satisfactory; then beware of enfeebling their strong features by childish ornaments and baby-house appendages. Simplicity of outline is especially necessary to any thing like dignity in an edifice of moderate size. The smallest parish churches of the old Saxon architecture, with thick, rude, unchiseled walls, strong enough to have needed no buttresses, and therefore having none—a low square tower or belfry, with flat, lead roof, and a very few irregularly-placed, deep, round-arched windows and portals, I have found far more inspiring of the solemnity of humility which should accompany the formal worship of the Almighty, than most of the very large churches that have been built with the greater wealth and more finical taste of later generations.

CHAPTER XLV

Salisbury Plain—Strange Desert Character of the Scenery
—The Agriculture—Sainfoin and Lucerne—Large Farms
—Effect on Laborers—Paring and Burning—When Expedient—Expense—Sheep-Folding—Moveable Railways
and Sheds

June 17th

STANDING ACROSS THE DOWNS: course E. by N., muggy weather
and light airs,"—regularly at sea, without chart or compass. A
strange, weary waste of elevated land, undulating like a
prairie, sparsely greened over its gray surface with short grass;
uninhabited and treeless; only, at some miles asunder, broken
by charming vales of rich meadows and clusters of farm-houses
and shepherds' cottages, darkly bowered about with the concentrated foliage of the whole country.

For long intervals we were entirely out of sight of tree or
house or man, or even sign of man, more than an indistinct
cart-track or trail. Had you any idea there was such a desert in
England?

The trails run crookedly, divide and cross frequently, and
but rarely is there a rude guide-post. Twice or thrice we were
as completely lost as Oregon emigrants might be in the wil-
derness, and walked for miles with only the dim, yellowish
spot that stood for the sun in the misty firmament, to be
guided by. Large flocks, with shepherds and dogs, we some-

times saw, and here and there a square clump of beech or fir trees, intended probably as an occasional retreat for the sheep. More rarely a great farm-house, with stacks and stables and great sheep-yards, always so sheltered about by steep slopes and trees, close planted upon some artificially-elevated soil, that we came by chance and unexpectedly in near proximity before we saw them. Occasionally, even on the downs, and entirely unenclosed, there is cultivated land and very large breadths of some single crop, much of good promise, too, but the wheat universally infested with charlock.

But the valleys are finely cultivated, and the crops, especially of sainfoin and lucerne, which is extensively grown here, very heavy.

Sainfoin and lucerne are both forage crops, somewhat of the character of clover. Sainfoin only succeeds well, I believe, on chalky soils or where there is much lime, and has not been found of value in the United States. Lucerne has been extensively cultivated in some parts, but not generally with us. I have heard of its doing well in a cold, bleak exposure upon the Massachusetts coast, but it should have a warm, rich soil, deeply cultivated, and be started well clean of weeds, when it may be depended upon to yield three to five heavy cuttings of green fodder, equal in value to clover, or three to seven tons of hay, of the value of which I am not well informed.

The valley lands are sometimes miles wide, and cultivation is extended often far up the hills. The farms are all very large, often including a thousand acres of tillage land, and two, three or four thousand of down. A farm of less than a thousand acres is spoken of as small, and it often appears that one farmer, renting all the land in the vicinity, gives employment to all the people of a village. Whether it is owing to this (to me) most repugnant state of things, or not, it is certainly just what I had expected to find in connection with it, that laborers' wages are lower probably than anywhere else in England—seven, and sometimes six, shillings ($1.68 and $1.44) being all that a man usually receives for a week's labor.

We saw seven plows at work together, and thirteen swarths of lucerne falling together before thirteen mowers, thirteen women following and shaking it out. It is not un-

common to have four or five hundred acres of wheat or two or
three hundred of turnips growing on one farm. One down
farmer has eight hundred in wheat annually. The prairie
farmer would not despise such crops.

As there is no chalk soil in America, I will not dwell
long upon its peculiarities or the system of agriculture
adopted upon it. The manner in which the downs are brought
into cultivation may, however, afford some hints of value for
the improvement of other poor, thin soils. "The sheepfold and
artificial manures are looked upon as the mainstay of the
Wiltshire down farmer. When the downs are first broken up,
the land is invariably pared and burnt, and then sown with
wheat. Barley is usually taken after wheat, and this is followed
by turnips eaten upon the ground, and succeeded by wheat. It
then falls into the usual four or five-field course, a piece being
laid out annually in sainfoin, to rest for several years before
being broken up again. The sheepfold is shifted daily until
the whole space required to be covered [*i. e.* manured] is gone
over. Turnips and other green crops are consumed where they
grow, which saves the labor of taking home the crop and fetch-
ing back the manure. The sheep are made the manure carriers
for any portion of the land on which it is thought desirable to
apply it. Much of the corn crop is stacked in the distant fields,
as it would be almost impossible to carry it home so far, with
the despatch necessary in harvest operations. In many cases it
is thrashed where stacked, a traveling steam-thrashing machine being hired for the purpose. The straw is carried out
and spread on the grass-lands from which clover hay had been
cut the previous year. Only a small proportion of the root crop
is carried home for consumption by the cattle, the number of
which, in these large farms, is quite inconsiderable."*

Sheep-folding, and paring and burning, are both processes nearly unknown in America, and which will probably
be advantageously employed in some situations among us.

Paring and burning.—"All soils," says Sir Humphrey
Davy, "that contain too much dead vegetable fibre," (such as
the sour black soils of our reclaimed swamps,) "and all such as
contain their earthy constituents in an impalpable state of

* CAIRD.

division, such as stiff clays and marls, are improved by *burning.*" It is therefore a common practice in the stiff-clay districts as well as upon the downs of England, the effect being to render a heavy soil light, friable, porous and highly absorbent. It increases the efficiency of drains (by letting water more rapidly into them), and, being more friable, the land works better and at less expense. It further promotes vegetation by converting into soluble matters available to plants, vegetable remains; which, in consequence of the usually wet, impervious nature of the soil, have become, as it were, indigestible, and therefore inert and useless. It is also advocated as being destructive of the roots and seeds of weeds; of insects, their larvæ and eggs; and, as is pretty clearly demonstrated, it enables land to bear the same crop in quicker succession, by its supposed effect upon the exudations left by former crops.* In executing the process, the surface, generally to the depth of three inches, is plowed or pared up (there are instruments made on purpose for it) and allowed to dry. It is then thoroughly harrowed and made fine; and in the downs the vegetable matter is racked out so far as practicable, and thrown into small heaps; a little earth is thrown over these and they are fired, the grass forming the fuel. The remainder of the earth which has been plowed up is shoveled on as soon, and to as great a depth, as it can be without danger of extinguishing the fire.

In the clay districts, and where there is much timber growing, brushwood is laid in rows, and the pared soil heaped over it, the sod being thrown as far as possible nearest the fuel, and the fine earth thrown over all to prevent too quick a fire.

The burnt soil is spread again over the field and plowed in. The first crop following is usually turnips. The cost of the operation is reckoned, in Suffolk (where it is called *denturing*), to be only about four dollars an acre, of which one-third is for fuel. Supposing the expense of labor to be doubled and that of fuel halved for the United States, it may be expected to cost us six dollars an acre. The effect, probably, is never lost to the land; but in those parts of England where it is most practiced,

---

* Report by practical farmers in Suffolk, 1846.

I believe it is usual to repeat the operation once in about
seven years. By feeding turnips upon the ground the autumn
following the burning, it is sufficiently stocked with manure to
require no further application during the course. Caird mentions crossing a field in which this had been repeated, burning
every seven years, and no other applications of manure than
what arose from the consumption of its own produce on the
ground being made, without any diminution of crops for fifty
years.

On the downs, however, paring and burning is not usually resorted to, except at the first breaking up of the original
soil, fertility being afterwards sustained by bones and guano,
or by feeding off the crops of herbage at the end of every
rotation by sheep; of which operation, common in all parts of
Great Britain, I shall presently speak.

In land greatly infested with weeds, or grubs or wire-
worm, in black, peaty soils, and in many stiff-clay soils, particularly where they are to be prepared for gardens or orchards, I
have no doubt paring and burning often might be profitably
performed in the United States. In thin, sandy soils it is likely
to be injurious. If the soil has not a pretty thick old sward, it
will be best to sow some grain crop upon it the year before
burning, that the roots and stubble may afford fuel. Old pasture will be most readily burnt. In England, clay is sometimes
charred in pits, and, after being mashed fine, applied broad-
cast or drilled with seeds, as a manure. It is sometimes found
surprisingly effective, probably owing to its absorbent quality;
but it is an expensive operation, and has not generally proved
profitable.

Sheep-folding is the practice of enriching a portion of
ground by confining sheep upon it. Thus, in Wiltshire, the
flocks are pastured during the day upon the "beak-land," and
kept at night upon the comparatively small portion of ground
which it is desired to manure, and which thus receives the
benefit of the fertilizing waste of the food obtained from the
pasture ground; or a portion of a field of sainfoin, or clover, or
turnips, is enclosed by a moveable fence (either iron or wooden
hurdles or strong hempen nets fastened to stakes), and the
sheep confined to it until they have eaten the crop clean (they

will eat the turnip in the ground), and left upon it a large amount of excrement; the fence is then moved on to a fresh spot, where the process is repeated, and so on day after day until the required space has been traveled over.

Sometimes naked ground or stubble-land is thus served; turnips or sainfoin being brought from where they grow and fed within the hurdles, which are daily moved on a bit. Latterly, moveable sheds with slatted floors, running upon plank railroads, which are easily taken up and relayed across the turnip fields, have been tried. The object is to avoid driving carts to take the crop off, or the treading of the sheep to feed it, on the ground, upon heavy clay soils, in which the pressure of these operations must be very objectionable. Twelve sheep are kept in each shed-car, and the turnips pulled and thrown into them. The expense of drawing off the crop and returning the manure is avoided, and the sheep have shelter and a dry bed, while the ordinary custom subjects them to danger of foot-rot and other diseases, and also must be attended with some waste of the crop.

CHAPTER XLVI

An Arcadian Hamlet—Out of the World, but not Beyond
the Reach of the Yankee Peddler—The Cottages of the
Downs—Grout and Cobble-stones—Character of the Laboring Class of the Downs—Want of Curiosity—Old Stockbridge, Winchester, William of Wykeham—His Legacy to
Wayfarers—The Cathedral—Some Remarks on Architectural Situation—Search for Lodgings—Motherly Kindness
—Railroad Mismanagement—Waterloo Day at Portsmouth

WALLOP, where we spend the night, is a most poetical hamlet,
so hidden by trees that, as we came over the downs, even when
within a few moments' walk of it, we had to inquire where it
was. It consists of a double row of cottages some miles long, on
the bank of a cool, silvery brook, at which, when we first saw it,
we rushed to drink like camels in the desert; and the water
was indeed delicious. It is exceedingly quiet. As we sit in our
window at the "Lower George," we can hear nothing but the
rippling of the brook, which threads its way through the trees
and among the cottages across the street, the rustling of the
trees in the gentle air, the peeping of chickens, and the chirp-
ing of small birds. There is a blacksmith's shop, but no smoke
ascends from it, and the anvil is silent. There is a grist-mill
further down; there is a little, square, heavy-roofed school-
house, and there is a church and graveyard. But there is no

stage-coach, no public conveyance, not even a carrier's cart by which we might send on our packs, runs through or from the hamlet. Yet this is a good inn, clean, and well provided; we have a large room, comfortably furnished; the landlord seems to understand what a tired traveler wants; and down stairs, in the parlor, there is—what do you think?

"IMPROVED BRASS CLOCK,
MANUFACTURED BY
H. WELTON, TERRYVILLE, CONNECTICUT.
(*Warranted, if well used.*")

It cost twelve shillings, and was a capital time-piece, only lately it had got a-going too fast, and the landlord wished Mr. Welton would send his man and have it fixed according to contract. It marked the hour rather behind our watches, but as it was the liveliest thing in the village, we have set it back to the landlord's notion, lengthened the pendulum, and oiled the "pallet," all to save the reputation of Mr. Welton and the universal Yankee nation.

The cottages here are generally built of a chalk grout, sometimes with lines of flint stones for ornament. In others, flint pebbles are laid regularly in courses set in grout, like the "cobble-stone houses" in western New York; in others, grout, and stones set in grout, alternately; or brick and stone in grout, in alternate tiers a foot thick. The village fences and the stockyard walls about here are also made of white grout, very thick, and with a coping of thatch. The thatch on the cottages is very heavy, sometimes two feet deep.

The laboring class upon the downs have generally a quiet, sleepy, stupid expression, with less evident viciousness and licentious coarseness of character, and with more simplicity, frankness, and good-nature than those we have previously been among. The utter want of curiosity and intelligent observation, among a people living so retired from the busy world, is remarkable. We have met but two today whose minds showed any inclination to move of their own accord: one of them was a pensioned soldier who had served at Halifax, and who made inquiries about several old comrades who had deserted and escaped to "the States," and whom he seemed to suppose we must have seen, as we were Yankees; the other, an old woman in Newtown-Tawney, at whose cottage we stopped to get water; she had at first taken us, as we came one after the other over the stile, for a "detachment of the Rifles," and on discovering her error was quite anxious to know what we were after, what we carried in our knapsacks, etc.

June 18th

In the morning we walked from Wallop through Stockbridge to Winchester. A down-land district still, as yesterday, but a well-traveled road, with houses, inns, and guide-boards; more frequent plantations of trees and more cultivated land, yet but little of it fenced, and the sheep restrained from crops by shepherds and dogs. Since we left Salisbury we have seen but three cows, each of which was tethered or led by a woman or child. We have seen no donkeys for the last hundred miles.

Stockbridge is a small village of one wide street, with two clear streams and a canal crossing it, the surface of the ground a dead flat; all as unlike its Massachusetts namesake as it is to a Pawnee village. We saw some fine horses near here.

Winchester—a name we remember as that of the school-place of many a good man—is an interesting old town in a cleft of the downs. Those who have heard Mr. Emerson's lecture upon England will remember it also as the town of *"William of Wykeham."*

We visited the cathedral, the college, and other notable institutions and monuments, and demanded and received our share of the legacy bequeathed by William of Wykeham, five hundred years ago, to all wayfarers passing by—a generous slice of good bread, and a draught of ale, served in an ancient horn. There is certainly no humbug about it, and the good bishop's hospitable will, in this particular, is yet as sincerely executed as if by servants under his own eye. Mr. Emerson was, nevertheless, unfortunate in his eloquent use of this circumstance to illustrate the simple honesty of English character, and the permanence and trustworthiness of English institutions; for it appears that, notwithstanding substantial bread and unadulterated beer, this is but the cleanliness of the cup and platter, and that in the real and worthy legacy which the far-reaching piety of the good prelate left to the future of England, there is much rottenness. Generally, the means which the piety of Englishmen of former generations bequeathed, for furnishing to the poor aliment of mind, have been notoriously diverted to the emolument and support, in luxurious sinecures, of a few individuals, whom, but for the association of their titles with religion, loyalty, law, and order, and the poor conscience-salve that it is the system and not they who are wrong, every man would know for hypocrites, liars, swindlers; more detestable than American repudiators, French sycophants, or Irish demagogues.

The cathedral is low and heavy, covering much ground; and exhibits, curiously interworked, the styles of Saxon, Norman, and early and later English architects. I again wrote in my notebook, "unimpressive;" but now, after two years, I find that my mind was strongly impressed by it; for there returns to me, as I very vividly remember its appearance, a feeling of quiet, wholly uncritical veneration, of which I believe a part must be due to the breadth of green turf of the graveyard, and deep shade of the old trees in which it is upreared. There were scarcely any edifices that I saw in Europe which produced in me the slightest thrill of such emotion from sublimity as I have often had in contemplation of the ocean, or of mountains, that it was not plainly due less to the architectural style, than to the connection and harmony of the mass with the ground upon which it was placed. The only church that stopped me suddenly with a sensation of deep solemnity, as I came unexpectedly under it, as it were, in turning the corner of a street, was one that stood upon a bold, natural terrace, and in which the lines of the angles of a heavy tower were continuous and unbroken from base to summit.

At half-past six we took seats in the second-class cars for Portsmouth, and were favored with a specimen of a corporation's disregard for the convenience of the public, and the accomplishment of their own promises, that a New Jerseyman would almost have growled at. There was a full hour's unnecessary detention at the way-stations, and after having arrived near the terminus that much behind the time-tables, the tickets were collected and the doors locked upon us, and we were kept waiting a long time within a few rods of the station-house. Some one at length got out at the windows, but was sent back by the guard. When we requested to know what was the objection to our leaving, we were answered it was against the rules of the company for any passengers to be allowed upon the ground without the station. After waiting some time longer, we rose in numbers too strong for the guards, who, however, promised that we should be prosecuted for trespass, and made our escape. I may say, in passing, that the speed upon the English roads is, *on an average,* not better than on ours. It is commonly only from fifteen to twenty miles an hour. The express trains, however, upon the main lines, run usually as fast as fifty miles an hour, sometimes sixty. For the accommodation, comfort, and advantage of all but those who choose and can afford to pay well, their railroad system is inferior to ours.

It was "Waterloo Day," and there had been a review of the forces at Portsmouth, before the Duke of Wellington and Prince Albert; the Queen had been off the harbor in her yacht, and received a salute; there had been a balloon ascension, and a carousal with long speeches. There was to be an illumination yet, and the town was full—some of the streets packed with soldiers and sailors and women. We spent several hours trying to get lodgings; every hotel, inn, tavern, and lodging-house, high and low, was full. The best thing that kindness or covetousness could be induced to offer, was room to lay upon a carpet on the floor, and this nowhere that we thought it likely we should be allowed to sleep. We got supper at a small inn, and the landlady informed us frankly that she charged us twice as much for it as she usually would, because it was "holiday."

It was late at night when, by advice of policemen and favor of sentinels, we had passed out through a series of ramparts, and were going up a broad street of the adjoining town of Portsea. "Good-night, my dear," we heard a kindly-toned voice; and a woman closed a door, and, after walking on a moment, ascended the steps to another. "Could you be good enough, madam," one of us took the liberty of inquiring, "to tell us of any house in this vicinity where we should be likely to obtain lodging for the night?"

"No—dear me!—who are you?"

"We are strangers in the town; travelers, who reached here this evening, and we have been looking for several hours to find some place where we could sleep, but all the inns are full."

"Come here; let me look at you. You are *young* men, are you not? come up to me, you need not be afraid—yes, I see; youths" (we had caps on, which is unusual in England except for school-boys). "Why, poor youths, I am sorry for you—strangers—you wait here, and I will call my servant and see if she does not think she can find where you can get a bed."

She then went in, and in a few minutes returned with a maid whom she called Susan, to whom she repeated what we had said; and then inquired further what was our business, were we "traveling with the consent of our parents," etc., and remarked—"Your parents are reputable people, I think:—yes—yes—dear me!—yes—poor youths. Yes, I will find beds for you. You are good youths, and Susan shall—but come in: you will sit in the parlor, and my servant, Susan, shall sit with you a few minutes, and I will see. Come in, come in, good youths."

While we remained in the parlor, it was infinitely droll to hear the kind old woman talking with another in the next room about the safety and propriety of lodging us. "I have known the world, and I cannot be deceived: these are good youths."

It was at length concluded that if we would each of us pay a shilling ("and then we could give whatever we liked besides to Susan"), and if we would be willing to have our doors locked on the outside, we should be provided then and there with beds. The old woman then came in again to see us, and with great severity reëxamined us, and finally informed us that we were to spend the night in her house. She then became exceedingly kind again, asked much about our parents and America, and at length asked us, with a whimpering laugh, as if she feared how we would take it, but begged that it might be considered a joke—"We wouldn't be offended if our doors should be locked on the outside?"

CHAPTER XLVII

The Deceit of Descriptions of Scenery—The Soul of a Landscape—The Isle of Wight, its Characteristics—Appropriate Domestic Architecture—Genial Climate—Tropical Verdure—The Cliffs of Albion—Osborne—The Royal Villa—Country Life of the Royal Family—Agricultural Inclination and Rural Tastes—The Royal Tenantry

THERE IS ALWAYS a strong temptation upon the traveler to endeavor to so describe fine scenery, and the feelings which it has occasioned him, that they may be reproduced to the imagination of his friends. Judging from my own experience, this purpose always fails. I have never yet seen anything celebrated in scenery, of which I had previously obtained a correct conception. Certain striking, prominent points, that the power of language has been most directed to the painting of, almost invariably disappoint, and seem little and commonplace, after the exaggerated forms which have been brought before the mind's eye. Beauty, grandeur, impressiveness in any way, from scenery, is not often to be found in a few prominent, distinguishable features, but in the manner and the unobserved materials with which these are connected and combined. Clouds, lights, states of the atmosphere, and circumstances that we cannot always detect, affect all landscapes, and especially landscapes in which the vicinity of a body of water is an

element, much more than we are often aware. So it is that the
impatient first glance of the young traveler, or the impertinent
critical stare of the old tourist, is almost never satisfied, if the
honest truth be admitted, in what it has been led to previously
imagine. I have heard "Niagra is a mill-dam," "Rome is a
humbug."

The deep sentiments of Nature that we sometimes seem to
have been made confident of, when among the mountains, or
on the moors or the ocean—even those of man wrought out in
architecture and sculpture and painting, or of man working in
unison with Nature, as sometimes in the English parks, on the
Rhine, and here on the Isle of Wight—such revealings are
beyond words; they never could be transcribed into note-books
and diaries, and so descriptions of them become caricatures,
and when we see them, we at first say we are disappointed
that we find not the monsters we were told of.

The greater part of the Isle of Wight is more dreary,
desolate, bare and monotonous, than any equal extent of land
you probably ever saw in America—would be, rather, if it
were not that you are rarely out of sight of the sea; and no
landscape, of which that is a part, ever can be without variety
and ever-changing interest. It is, in fact, down-land, in the
interior, exactly like that I described in Wiltshire, and sometimes breaking down into such bright dells as I there told of.
But on the south shore it is rocky, craggy; and after you have
walked through a rather dull country, though pleasing on the
whole, for hours after landing, you come gradually to where
the majesty of vastness, peculiar to the downs and the ocean,
alternates or mingles with dark, picturesque, rugged ravines,
chasms and water-gaps, grand rocks, and soft, warm, smiling,
inviting dells and dingles; and, withal, there is a strange and
fascinating enrichment of foliage, more deep, graceful and
luxuriant, than I ever saw before. All this district is thickly
inhabited, and yet so well covered with verdure, or often so
tastefully appropriate—quiet, cosy, ungenteel, yet elegant—
are the cottages, that they often add to, rather than insult and
destroy, the natural charm of their neighborhood. I am sorry
to say, that among the later erections there are a number of
strong exceptions to this remark.

In this paradise the climate, by favor of its shelter of hills on the north, and the equalizing influence of the ocean on the south, is, perhaps, the most equable and genial in the northern temperate zone. The mercury does not fall as low in winter as at Rome; deciduous trees lose their verdure but for a brief interval; greensward is evergreen; tender-roses, fuschias, and the dark, glossy shrubs of Canaan and of Florida, feel themselves at home, and flourish through the winter.

Where the chalky downs reach the shore without an intervening barrier of rock, or a gradual sloping descent, they are broken off abruptly and precipitously; and thus are formed the "white cliffs of Albion," and a coast scenery with which, for grandeur, there is nothing on our Atlantic shore that will in the least compare: notwithstanding which, and although they really are often higher than our church-steeples and monuments—the familiar standards with which we compare their number of feet—they have not the stupendous effect upon the mind that I had always imagined that they must have.

We were rambling for the greater part of two days upon the island, spending a night near Black-Gang-Chine. Returning, we passed near Osborne, a private estate purchased some years since by the Queen, upon which she has had erected a villa, said to be an adaptation of the Grecian style to modern tastes and habits, but of which nothing is to be seen from without the grounds but the top of a lofty campanile, from which is now displayed the banner with the royal arms, which always indicates the presence of the reigning sovereign of Great Britain. It is the custom of the royal family, when here, to live in as retired and unstately a way as they can ever be permitted to. The Prince himself turns farmer, and engages with much ardor in improving the agricultural capabilities of the soil, much of which was not originally of a fertile character, but by thorough drainage, and judicious tillage and manuring, is now producing greatly enlarged crops. The Prince is well known as a successful breeder and stock-farmer, having taken several prizes for fat cattle, etc., at the great annual shows. Her Majesty personally interests herself in the embellishment of the grounds and the extensive oak planta-

tions which are being made, and is in the habit of driving
herself a pair of ponies, unattended, through the estate, studying the comfort of her little cottage tenantry, and in every way
she can trying to seem to herself the good-wife of a respectable
country gentleman.

CHAPTER XLVIII

The Queen's Yacht—Yachts of the R. Y. Club, their Build
and Rig—Comparison with American Yachts and Pilot-
Boats—Seamanship—Cut of Sails—The Navy-Yard at
Portsmouth—Gun-Boats—Steamers—Evening at Portsea
—Curiosity—About Boasting and Some English Character-
istics—Conversation with a Shopkeeper on the "Glory of
England"

IN CROSSING THE SOLENT, on our return to Portsmouth, we saw
the Queen's yacht, and passed through a squadron of the
Royal Yacht-Club yachts. The former was a large, heavily
hampered, brig-rigged steamer, with great plate-glass ports,
and a large oak-colored house on deck, less seaman-like in
appearance and more in the American style than most English
steam-vessels. The yachts were as sweet craft as I can imagine,
most of them over two hundred tons in burden and schooner-
rigged; but, whether one or two-masted, spreading more canvas for the length of their hulls than I ever saw before. They
were all painted black, and their ornaments and deck-arrange-
ments struck me as being more simple, snug and seaman-like
than those of most of our Union Clubs' yachts. The reverse is
the case aloft. My *guess* was that they would be more than a
match for anything on our side in light winds, but that in bad
weather, particularly if working to windward, they would do

nothing against a New York pilot-boat. Like all the English small craft, when going before the wind, the cutters and schooners always hauled up the tack of the mainsail, that the wind might draw under it to fill the foresail and jib. Another reason given for it is, that the wind, drawing downward from the belly of the sail, tends to make the vessel bury, and by lifting the tack she is made more buoyant. It is never done in America.

This was before the race in which the "America" beat the English yachts. I suspect that her superior sailing qualities were more owing to her peculiarities of rig, the cut and material of her sails, and to seamanship, than to the model of her hull. I have no doubt we can still build and rig a vessel that will be her superior. While the English stick to flax canvas, long gaffs, heavy top-sails and graceful curves, I do not think there is any danger that they will. When the Englishman is close-hauled with his boom as near amidships as he can get it, his long gaff will swing off so far that there must always be a considerable part of his canvas in the peak that actually retards more than it assists him. The Englishman thinks much of beauty of form in his sails, but his standard of beauty is arbitrary—a fashion. To my eye, without regard to the primary beauty of utility, the simplicity of the cut of our sails is much more agreeable.

On the deck of the flag-schooner, we saw the commodore of the Club (an Earl), a grey-haired old gentleman, who sat in an armchair, reading from a newspaper to some ladies.

On reaching Portsmouth we took a boat to visit the navy-yard, within the walls of which, being foreigners, not having a pass, we could not enter. Our boatmen told us that if we chose to enter we should not be challenged, as no one would suspect us as being other than Englishmen, and that the prohibition was a silly old form that prevented no one from seeing the yard who wished to enough to lie for it.

The number of vessels (of the navy) in port was much less than I had anticipated seeing, and most of these were hulks, or "advance ships" (with guns and water-tanks on board.) Those we went on board of (one of them ready for sea), seemed to me, compared with ours of the same class, inferior in all respects, except it might be in some novelties in their rigging, of the efficiency of which I could not judge. The extent to which wire-rigging was employed in some surprised me. We saw four gunboats (large barges with a swivel-gun in the bow), manned by the workmen of the yard, whose awkward evolutions were very amusing. The landsmen working in the yard are divided into two squads, one of which alternately with the other, is drilled in the Jefferson plan of harbor defense two evenings in each week. They are dressed in a simple uniform, and armed as boarders.

There were more steamers in the harbor than in all our navy.

In the evening we called at the old lady's in Portsea, and received from Susan some clothes, which she had undertaken to get washed for us, and a watch which my brother had accidentally left in his bed-room. The kind old woman received us cordially, apologized again for the prudence which had led her to lock us in, and introduced us to some friends. Of their simplicity and curiosity, as shown in their questioning of us, I might, if I chose to report our conversations, give as amusing a picture as English travelers enjoy to do, of that of those they meet in American boarding-houses. Of fidgety anxiety lest we should not discover that everybody and everything in the country is superior to anybody and anything anywhere else in the world, which so annoys visitors to the United States, I must confess that we have seen but little in England. With the poorer class of Englishmen, patriotism seems to have been starved out. If they ever speak of their country's greatness and prosperity, it is as a servant speaks of his master's wealth; they would see it become a dependency of France or Russia with entire indifference, certainly with exultation if it were promised them that wages should be higher and bread cheaper for it. Again, the Radicals and men of earnest religious faith, with the strongest affection to their country, are in the habit of looking much at what is wrong and shameful in her institutions and qualities, and of comparing them with what is better in other lands.

Cultivated and large-minded people of all classes, of course, in England as everywhere else, rise above prejudice and vanity, and think and speak fairly and frankly equally of their own or foreign states; of such eminently, we recognize the Earl of Carlisle and Sir Charles Lyell, and of such are, I believe, a great number of the higher rank of commercial men. The traditional self-complacency of an Englishman, as an Englishman, is more often to be detected, at the present day, by some unnecessary pains he will take to point out to you deficiencies and defects of a trivial character in the article or institution or custom you are considering, he having entire confidence that in contrast with that of any other country it will but be exalted by any such faint disparagement of it as is possible. Among the lower class in towns, or in the country, those who have been servants, or in some way connected with or dependent on wealthy old families, there is sometimes to be found the most ludicrously absurd old Tory ideas and prejudices, quite in character with John Bull of the farce; but the best specimens of it that I have seen were among the smaller sort of shopkeepers, particularly those who advertise themselves to be under the patronage of some noble lady. I remember one that we encountered, soon after we resumed our walks in England after we had been on the Continent, that amused us very much—a little, fat, florid, bald-headed John Gilpin of a man. He was wrapping the article we had purchased in a paper, and, while we waited, asked,

"Travelers, gentlemen?"

"Yes, sir."

"On foot it appears?"

"Yes, sir."

"Traveled far so, might I ask?"

"Oh, yes—a number of hundred miles."

"Indeed—you must have seen a good bit of Old England. Ever was on the Continent, gentlemen?"

"Yes."

"In France, it might be?"

"Yes."

"Anywhere else but France?"

"Yes—in Holland, Germany and Belgium."

"Ah! Gentlemen, I should like to ask you now, if I might

be so bold, I should like to ask you a question, just one question. I haven't been myself, you see, to France nor to Holland
nor to those other countries, but I have read of them, and
according to the best sources of information I could reach, I
have informed my mind about them and formed my own independent opinion, you see, in which I may be right, of
course, and I may be wrong, but I think I'm right. And I have
had a coming in here a many of traveling gentlemen like you,
who had seen all those foreign countries, and had also in
course seen England. Well, I always asks these gentlemen one
question when they does me the honor, and they have always
been so good as to answer me, and now I should be pleased
to ask you the same question, if I may be so bold. Though, to
be sure, I can imagine what you'll answer, but then to confirm
the independent conclusion which I had arrived at from my
own reflections, you see, and for edification—thank you. Now
then, gentlemen."

He laid the parcel on the counter, and, holding it firmly
with his left hand, continued to tap it lightly with the fore-
finger of the other:

"So it appears, gentlemen (if I might be so bold), that
you have wandered far and near over the face of the inhabited
world, and have seen many foreign parts and lands, and cast
your lot among other peoples and nations, that all thought as
their inheritances was very fine, doubtless: but now, gentlemen! can you say on candid reflection—now have you ever
seen any where's else, for instance, any castle as was comparable compared to Windsor Castle?"

"No, sir."

"Or any park like unto Windsor Park, in foreign parts?"

"No, sir."

"Nor any country of them all, what, on the whole, take
her altogether, taking her castle and parks, also her towns and
her rail'ays and station-houses, her forests and her manufac-
tures, and her coal and iron; her church and her constitution,
her people and her horses, and such like—did you ever, in all
your wanderings—taking her altogether so—did you ever now,
gentlemen—ever see any place exactly like your own country
after all?"

"No, indeed, sir."

" 'No, indeed, sir!' I know you didn't—you hear that?
'No, indeed, sir'—and so say you all, gentlemen? and so say
you all. Well, then, I am satisfied, and much obliged to you,
gentlemen. There isn't none of the foreign principalities that
is like this blessed land; and that's what I am always telling
them, and only goes to confirm the independent conviction
which I had previously arrived to of my own preliminaries.
Thank you, gentlemen;" (handing us the parcel;) "good-
morning. I wish you a pleasant continuance of your promenade in our glorious old land."

CHAPTER XLIX

Rural Police—The "Anchor" Inn—The Garden—"Old Coaching Times"—Heath Land—A Dreary Landscape—Murder and a Highway Adventure—Human Vanity

Liphook, June 20th

WALKED HITHER from Portsmouth today. For twenty miles the road is through a hilly chalk country, much of it unenclosed downs, generally interesting, and the walk at this season agreeable.

We had, for a short distance, the company of a rural policeman. He had his quarters, with several others, in a small cottage in a village, was paid $4.70 a week, and furnished with three suits of clothes every year—one for winter, one for summer and one for Sundays, besides gloves, etc. The uniform is of blue cloth, of a simple, semi-military fashion. He said no one was employed in the force who was less than six feet high, and that they were exercised in the use of small-arms. Of duties he seemed to have no definite idea himself, but was ready to do anything he could in the way of fighting roguery, when he should be called upon by his officers. The only crime which he seemed to apprehend in the neighborhood was *rick-burning*—laborers who were discontented and envious, or who had for any reason become angry with the farmers who employed them, setting fire to their stacks of grain. This was common.

We spent the night at the *"Anchor,"* a good, large, old inn, with a finely-shaven plot of turf and well-kept graveled walks, and a good vegetable and fruit garden, with famous gooseberry and apple bushes (apples on dwarf stocks), in the rear. The landlord, a bluff, stout, old man, a little while ago brought us in samples of five different sorts of malt liquor that he had in his cellar. They vary in strength in the proportions from 8 to 32, and somewhat more in price.

Before the railways, thirty-two four-horse coaches stopped at this house daily, besides post-coaches, which, when the fleet was about to sail from Portsmouth, passed through the village "like a procession." He then kept one hundred horses, and had usually ten postboys to breakfast, who had been left during the night. Now, but one coach and one van passed through the town.

June 21st

Near Liphook, instead of the broad, bleak chalk-downs, with their even surface of spare green grass, we find extensive tracts of a most sterile, brown, dry, sandy land, sometimes boggy (moory), producing even more scanty pasturage than the downs, but with scattered tufts of heath or ling. Most of this is in commons, and a few lean sheep, donkeys, and starveling ponies are earnestly occupied in seeking for something to eat upon it. Very little of it, for miles that we have passed over, is enclosed or improved, except that there are extensive planations of trees. Timber grows slowly upon it; but the shade of the foliage and the decay of leaves so improves the soil that it is worth cultivating after its removal. It is also improved so as to bear tolerable crops, by paring-and-burning and sheep-folding—as described on the downs of Wiltshire.

We had walked half-a-dozen miles this morning, when I discovered I had lost my watch, and turned back. When about three miles from Liphook, I met our landlord of *"The Anchor."* He had found the watch in my room, and immediately mounted a horse, and rode hard to overtake us. He refused any compensation, unless it were "a glass of grog to drink my health." I had happened to show him one of those villainous Spanish quarters that so successfully hold their place against our legitimate currency, which I had had left in my pocket on leaving New York, and he said, if I didn't value it, he would be glad to take it as a keepsake of us. I have no doubt he will always remember us as the three gentlemen who had the good taste not to go from Portsmouth to London by "the infernal railways."

It was a day of thick, rapidly passing clouds, and in a part of my walk, which was through a well-wooded, rolling country, with very steep hill-sides and deep, narrow valleys, I saw some most charming effects of broad shadows, chasing over waving foliage, with angel-flights of sunshine, often disclosing long, narrow vistas of distant, deep glens, or glances of still water, becalmed and warm under high, dark, quivering, leafy bluffs. But the greater part of this country (but a day's walk from London) is the most dreary, desolate, God-forsaken-looking land that I ever saw or imagined. Hills and dales, picturesque enough in form, high, deep, and broad; all brown, gray, and black; sterile, parched, uninhabited—dead: the only sign of life or vegetation a little crisp moss, or singed, prostrate, despairing ling—seeming exactly as if an intense fire had not long since swept over it.

Such was the whole dreary landscape, far and near—only "blasted heath." A great black squall-cloud had for some time thrown additional gloom—a new intensity of gloom—over it; and I was walking slowly, in bereavement of all sympathizing life in this sepulchral ground of Nature, when my eye fell upon a block of stone, bearing inscription—"In detestation of the murder of a sailor on this spot, by [three persons whose names are given], who were hung near here. 'Whoso sheddeth man's blood, by man shall his blood be shed.' *Look on the other side.*"

I was still half kneeling and musing before this monument, when I heard myself gruffly addressed, "Wull tell me what's the time o' day?"

Without rising, I turned my head and saw over my shoulder a tall, heavily whiskered, ruffianly faced fellow, half sportsman, half sailor in dress, carrying a stout stick and a bundle in a handkerchief. How did he get there? I must have seen him before if he had come either way by the road; he must have approached from over the hill behind me, and that cautiously; apparently he had been concealed there. I confess that I wished for a moment that I had in "my interior reservoirs a sufficient Birmingham horse-pistol," wherewith to make myself alike tall with him if he should give me need; but, still bending over the memorial of murder, I drew my watch and answered him civily, whereupon, without even a "growl," he "sidled off," and soon passed from my sight. My friends had seen the same man, in company with another, near the same place, an hour and a-half before.

On "the other side"—oh, human vanity!—was the name of the man who had caused the stone to be placed there. Posterity is requested to remember the murderers and the murdered, and especially not to forget the *detester*.

CHAPTER L

London Lads—Railway Ride—Observations in Natural
History

AT HALF-PAST FIVE, having overtaken my friends and dined at
Godalming, I took seat with them in the third-class carriages
of a train bound to London, intending, however, only to take
a lift so that we might walk in before dark.

The carriages were nearly empty, till, stopping at a way-
station, they were suddenly and with boisterous merry haste
taken possession of, filled full and over-filled with a class of
people differing in their countenances, manners, language,
and tone of voice from any we had before seen in England.
They were more like New York *b'hoys,* a little less rowdy and
a shade more vulgar. "London lads," one of them very civilly
told me they were, employed in a factory out here in the
country, and having just received their week's wages were
going in to spend them. They were pale, and many effeminate
in features, rather oily and grimy, probably from their employment; talked loudly and rapidly, using many cant words,
and often addressing those at a distance by familiar, abbrevi-
ated names; lively, keen, quick-eyed, with a peculiarly fearless,
straightforward, uneducated way of making original remarks,
that showed considerable wit and powers of observation;
rough, turbulent, and profane, yet using a good many polite
forms, and courteous enough in action.

Two or three men, as soon as the train was in motion, held up each a brace or two of rabbits, at which there was cheering and laughter from the rest. All, indeed, were in the greatest possible good humor, joking and bantering and making engagements, or telling of their plans for dining together, or meeting for some degrading excitement on Sunday. Of us and others in the car, when they entered, they took little notice, though treating us with respect in not jostling or crowding us; but as soon as they were well settled in their places they began to make game of one another; to tell stories, evidently inventing comic anecdotes of their employers and other common acquaintances, both absent and present. A dignified person, who stood upon the platform, was made very uncomfortable, and reduced considerably in height and stiffness, by urgent invitations to join them. The "guard," too, as he passed, was an especial butt, and several illustrations were given of the ignorant character of railway-people in general. "There vas von o' them Mefodis wisitin-coves, you know, wot 'awks tracs and suchlike, in here a Vensdy wen we come up; and ven the guard come along he arks him did he know the Lord's prayer? 'Lorspraer?' says he, 'vot is he?' says he; 'is he a *stoker* or a *driver?*' says he, ha! ha! ha! I'm blowed 'f'e didn't."

"I saw one of them same fellows other night," continued another, "wot 'ad 'old of another on 'em. He treats 'im to a go o' gin first, you see, to make him sharp like, and then he axes him did he know any think about the eternal world. ' 'Turnulwool?' says he—' 'Turnulwool?—no such place in the Farnham branch, sir—hadn't you best enkvire of the station-master, sir?' says he."

" 'Ternal world's the place where they hadn't got the rails down to yet—last adwices; aren't it?—and they carries the nobs on there with lays o' busses wot runs erry day in the year oney Sunneys and her Majestee's birth-day."

"No, no; I'll tell you where 'tis—it's the kentry what the coves in Astraly cuts to wen the kangarwoos gets short and the gin-trees gives out and they's 'ard up."

"Kangurerhoos—what's them?"

"Kind of fish as is covered with feathers 'stead o' scales."

"I know it—I see a sailor as 'ad a vestcoat made on 't;

short vethers like spangled welwet, black and goold—stunnenest thing you ever see."

"What's a gin-tree?"

"I know—there is—a big tree wot runs gin wen yer tap her—and there's a bread-tree, too—"

"What bears fresh kortern loavs erry morning."

"Hurray for Polytechny! Ain't they all sliced and buttered?"

"In course they is, and ven you shakes 'em off, the skin cracks open, and they all valls buttered side up—coz vy? Vy the trees is werry 'igh and the buttered side's the lightest to be sure."

"That's the place for this chile—I'm bound to go there— only waitin' for an act of Parliament; and wen I get there— Buffalo gals!"—

"When he gets there you know what he'll do? When he comes to the gin-trees he'll treat all 'round. First time in his life. Ha! ha!"

And with such constantly-combining streams a flood of original information and entertainment was poured out to us until we reached the little station about nine miles out of London, to which we had taken tickets.

CHAPTER LI

Rural Laborers near London—Our Mother Tongue—
Cockneys—Provincialists—On the Naturalization of For-
eign Words—Authorities—Suburban London—London—
The Thames—"Saint Paul's from Blackfriar's Bridge"

UPON OUR ASKING DIRECTIONS, a gentleman who left the first-
class carriage offered to be our guide for a little way. He led us
between fields in which men were hay-making. We spoke of
the "London lads" we had been riding with, and the gentleman agreed with us that, bad as they might appear, they were
less degraded than the mass of agricultural laborers.

"We could not stop to rest here on the stile," said he,
"but that every single man in that field, in the course of five
minutes, would come to us to ask something for drink; and the
worst of it is, it is not an excuse to obtain money by indirect
begging for the support of their families, but they would actually spend it immediately at the public-house."

We told him that we had never been in London, and
after a little conversation he said that he had been trying to
discover where we came from, as from our accent he should
have thought us Londoners. He had thought that he could
always tell from what part of England any stranger in London
came, but he could not detect any of the provincial accents or
idioms in our language. We told him that we had supposed

the cockney dialect was quite distinct, but certainly never imagined it at all like our own. On the contrary, he said, except among the vulgar classes, the Londoner alone has no dialect, but, much more than the native of any other part of England, speaks our language from infancy in its purity, and with the accent generally approved by our most elegant orators and generally-acknowledged authorities.

"But a liberal education must remove provincialisms, both of idiom and accent."

"In a degree only. A boy will generally retain a good deal of his provincial accent through the public school and university. At least, I have paid considerable attention to the matter, and I think I am always able to detect it, and say with confidence in which quarter of the kingdom a man spent his youth. You would yourself probably have no difficulty in detecting a Scotchman."

"I have noticed that Scotchmen who have resided long in England, and who had in a considerable degree lost their original peculiarities, usually spoke in a disagreeably high key and with great exactness and distinctness of utterance."

"That is the result of the original effort which it was necessary for them to use to speak correctly. They speak from the book, as it were, and the same is more or less noticeable in all provincialists who do not habitually speak with the accent of their youth."

We then informed him that we were Americans, which surprised him. I somewhat doubt myself the correctness of his observation. I am aware of habitually using many Yankeeisms myself, and have no desire to avoid them. The New England accent of words, except such as are not very commonly used, I should think might be generally agreeable to the most approved standards in England. The educated English certainly speak with much greater distinctness and more elegance than we commonly do; perhaps they generally err in being too precise and methodical, and it may be that the Londoners converse with more rapidity and ease, or carelessness, than others. That what are shown to us as peculiarities of cockney dialect, are mere vulgarisms and slang, not altogether peculiar to the metropolis, is very true.

Agreeably to Walker, the educated English often give the sound of *a* to *e,* pronouncing Derby, *Darby;* clerk, *clark,* etc. This at first seemed very odd; but when I returned home, our own way had become foreign to me. With us, except in society which has a more than ordinary European element, foreign words in common use, are more generally Anglicized than in England; and though when one is accustomed to the more polite sound there may seem an affectation of simplicity in this, I cannot but wish that our custom was more general. The French almost universally adapt foreign words of which they have need for common use to the requirements of their habitual tongue changing not only the pronunciation but the orthography: they write *rosbif,* for English roast beef; *biftek,* for beefsteak. So we write and pronounce *cotelette,* cutlet; why need we say "angtremay," for *entremets?* or if we choose that sound, and like it also better than *"side-dishes,"* why not print it "angtremay?" We write Cologne, for Köln; why not Leeong, for Lyons? or if Lyons, let us also speak it Lyons, and consider Leeong an affectation except when we speak it in connection with other plainly French words. The rule with regard to such matters is, to follow custom. Singularity is impertinent where it can be gracefully avoided; but as there is more tendency to Anglicize foreign words that are in general use in America than in England, and this is a good and sensible tendency, let us not look for our rules to English custom. Let us read *Venus de Medicis,* Venus de Medicis, rather than stammer and blush over it because we are not perfect in Italian. I once heard a clergyman call it "Venu-de-Medisy:" two-thirds of his congregation understood what he meant as well as if he had given it the true Italian pronunciation; but if he had read it with the sound they would naturally attach in English reading to that connection of letters, nearly all would have known what he meant, and no one would have had a reasonable occasion to laugh at him. But why is not our own language fit to speak of it in—the Medicean Venus? Why should the French word *envelope* be used by us when we have the English envelop? Why the Italian *chiaro-oscuro,* when there is the English clare-obscure expressing the same? I am glad to see some of our railroad companies accepting the word *station,* which is good old English, in place of the word *depot,* which, as we pronounce it, is neither French nor English.* In England, the designation *station* is invariable. *Depot* is only used as a military technicality, with the French pronunciation, *dapo.* If we really want a foreign word or phrase to express ourselves, it shows a deficiency in our language. Supply this by making your foreigner English: we in America must not be chary of admitting strangers. Naturalize it as soon as possible.

Neither let us think it of great consequence whether we say *Rush-an* or *Ru-shan,* for Russian; *trawf* or *truf* (as usual in England), for trough; *def* or *deef,* for deaf; or whether we spell according to Johnson, or Walker, or Webster, (or Webster modified); the custom varies, not only between England and America, but between elegant scholars of each country in itself.

Half-a-mile's walk brought us to a village of plain, low, detached, paltry shops, where our guide, having given us a very simple direction, took leave of us. We followed up the broad street; the shops, a large number of which were alehouses, soon were displaced in a great measure by plain, small villas of stone, or stuccoed brick, standing two or three rods back from the street, with dense shrubbery, enclosed by high brick walls before them. Gradually the houses ran together and became blocks; omnibuses, market-carts, heavy "vans" (covered luggage wagons), and pleasure-carriages, constantly met and passed, and when we had walked about three miles, the village had become a compact, busy town—strangely interrupted once by a large, wild, wholly rustic common. Then the town again: the sidewalk encroached upon by the grocers and hucksters; monster signs of "entire" ales and ready-made coffins, and "great sacrifices" of haberdashery and ladies' goods; the street wide and admirably paved, and crossed at short but irregular intervals by other narrower streets, and growing more busy every moment. Still it is nothing remarkable; a wide street, plain brick houses, a smell of gas now and then, and a crowd. I would hardly have known, from any

---

* Station is the word now used in the laws of New York.

thing to be seen, that I was not entering some large town in our own country, which I had never visited before. Indeed, it's quite like coming down the Bowery.

People were looking up; following the direction of their eyes, we saw a balloon ascending. The air was calm, and it rose to a great height—greater, says the Times this morning, than any ever reached before.

A shrill cry in the distance, rising faintly above the rumble of the wheels and hum and patter of the sidewalks, grows rapidly more distinct, until we distinguish, sung in a high key, *"Strawberrie—Sixpenny-pottle. Who'll buy?"* The first of "London cries."

We have been walking steadily, in a nearly straight line, for two hours, and now the crowd thickens rapidly until it is for a moment at the fullest Broadway density. There is a long break in the brick-house fronts, and we turn aside out of the crowd and halt to take an observation. We are leaning over the parapet of Blackfriar's Bridge. The Thames looks much as I had supposed; something wider than our travelers usually represent it, hardly an "insignificant stream" even to an eye accustomed to American rivers, but wide enough and deep enough and strong enough to make bridges of magnificence necessary to cross it, and answering all the requirements needed in a ship-canal passing through the midst of a vast town. A strong current setting upward from the sea gurgles under the arches; heavy coal-barges slowly sweep along with it; dancing, needle-like wherries shoot lightly across it, and numerous small, narrow steamboats, crowded with passengers, plow white furrows up and down its dark surface.

Upon the bank opposite—almost upon the bank, and not distant in an artist's haze—stand blackened walls and a noble old dome, familiar to us from childhood. It is only nearer, blacker, and smaller—wofully smaller—than it has always been. We do not even think of telling each other it is SAINT PAUL'S.

There is a low darkness, and the houses and all are sooty in streaks, but there is a pure—so far as our lungs and noses know—pure, fresh, cool breeze sweeping up the river, and overhead a cloudless sky; and in the clear ether, clear as Cin-

cinnati's, there is a new satellite—beautiful as the moon's daughter. It is the balloon, now so high that the car is invisible; and without any perceptible motion it blushes in golden sunlight, while we have been some time since left to evening's dusk.

The crowd tramps behind us. We turn and are sucked into the channel, which soon throws us out from the bridge upon a very broad street; up this, in a slackening tide, we are still unresistingly carried, for it is London, and that was what we were looking for; and for awhile we allow ourselves to be absorbed in it without asking what is to become of us next.

CHAPTER LII

A Pilgrimage

WHILE IN LONDON, I was one day visiting a library, when the friend who conducted me called my attention to a series of shelves, saying, "here are topographical and genealogical records, arranged under the head of counties—is yours an English name? I have never seen it in England."

"Yes, I believe it is—at least our family came to America from England."

"From what part—do you know?"

"Essex, I've heard it said."

"When," said he, taking down a book.

"1630 to '40."

"Yes, here it is—Manor of Olmsted, in Bumpstead Helens, Thaxstead; passed out of the family near the end of sixteenth century. Maurice de, married, and-so-forth. A moated grange, now belongs to —— College, Cambridge. Where's the Ordnance map of Essex? Here. Let's see—Thaxstead—Olmsted Hall; yes, here it is—only about six miles from a station. Better go out there and see it, hadn't you? You can do it in half a day easily enough."

The next day I went; traveling half an hour by rail, and then taking a chaise, by which a drive of six miles brought me to a small hamlet with a small and ruinous church in a very ancient graveyard. I inquired for the parish clerk and found him, a cobbler, at his work. The records were locked up at the curate's and the curate was away. Did any one live hereabouts of the name of Olmsted? No. Did he ever know any one of that name? No; no man—there was the old hall farm. What hall? Olmsted Hall they called it. Why? He did not know.

I asked to be directed to it and found it difficult of access, by narrow parish roads and farm lanes.

It proved to be a large, low and very common-place sort of farm-house of stone, in the midst of a level wheat farm of 200 acres. It belonged to one of the Cambridge colleges, and the family of the present tenant had occupied it for several generations. They received me kindly, and when I told them my name, was some little excitement and manifestation of respect, as if I had rights in the house. "Come into the old hall, sir," they said, taking me to the largest room—a low room, about 20 feet by 20, with a single low window nearly occupying one side, and a monstrous old fire-place, now bricked up for a coal grate, another.

"This is the old hall."

"Why do you call it the hall?"

"It always was called so. I suppose it's because they used to hold courts here, sir. The house used to be moated all around, but they filled up the moat in front when that lane was built; that was in my father's time."

The moat still remained around the garden, a deep ditch with a low earth wall, on which grew an old hedge. At one corner of the house was a yew tree, certainly several hundred years old. This house, as is a matter of record, was occupied by the Olmsteds for more than two hundred years before the Puritan emigration. After that period I could find nothing of them in England.

I have given this account, because the incident is so characteristic of an American's visit to England, as well as because it shows what an historic interest may attach to any old farmhouse in England. I once afterwards entered a cottage in Lincolnshire where a child was playing with what appeared to be an old iron pot, but which proved, upon examination, to be a helmet. The father, a clod-hopping yeoman, said it had been worn in France by some one of his forefathers. He had a horse-rug that came down to him with it. This he brought upon my asking to see it—a quilted horse cover, once elaborately embroidered. Since these things came back from some war in France, hundreds of years ago, they had always remained in this house, which, with some forty acres of land around it, he had inherited. He did not live very well, but his land was yet unincumbered, and he hoped his son might be a "yeoman-farmer" after him.

But it is a melancholy thing that there are so few yeoman now in England; that is, farmers owning the land they till, and independent of landlords.

APPENDIX A

Information and Advice for those wishing to make a Pedestrian Tour in England, at the least practicable expense

A young man with small means, and who is willing to "rough it," wishes to know with how little money it would be practicable for him to undertake a trip to England. I have no doubt there are many such who would visit the Old World if they were aware how cheaply and pleasantly they could do so. I have heretofore expressed my own obligation to Bayard Taylor, and it is probable that what I shall have to say will be, to some extent, a repetition of the instructions given in a chapter upon the subject in the later editions of the "Views a-Foot." It will, however, have more especial reference to traveling on foot in England.

The Passage.—There are no regular arrangements made in the packet-ships for those who wish to go to England decently and in tolerable comfort at a moderate price. It will be with more or less difficulty, according as freights are active or dull, that you may obtain a proper "second cabin passage and found." You stand the best chance to do so in the London lines. A special arrangement with the Captain is necessary. A party of three or four may at almost any time, by application to the Captain shortly before a ship sails, engage a state-room, provide themselves with stores, and hire their cooking done, etc.; so that the passage shall cost them but from twenty to thirty dollars. With good messmates, good catering, a liberal gratuity to the cook, steward or ship's servant that waits upon you, and in a *clean* ship, you may make the passage in this way more agreeably than in any other; more so than in the first cabin at four times the expense. The price of the regular first-cabin passage out is $90. *In the steerage,* you pay $10 to $12 for a mere sleeping place, provide yourself with stores, cook for yourself, or hire some fellow-passenger, who does not suffer equally from sea-sickness, to cook for you. You must provide yourself with bedding, cooking utensils, etc. It will cost you about $20. Secure, if possible, an *upper* berth, near the hatchway; be provided with an abundance of old clothes; look out for pilferers; spend an hour each morning in sweeping and keeping clean the steerage; nurse the sick; take care of the women and children; and keep the deck all the time that you otherwise can. You will probably be very miserable, but it will be over after a while; you will have seen a peculiar exhibition of human nature, and will go ashore with a pleasure not to be imagined. You can go to Liverpool or Glasgow by the screw-steamers (second cabin and found), decently and quickly, for from $50 to $75. The same by the mail-steamers, not so comfortably but more quickly. Most disagreeably, but soon over with, in the steerage of some of the steamers for $40.

Returning.—You have the same (and rather increased second cabin accommodations by the London packet), at about 10 *per cent* higher prices. You can live comfortably for two months, and see "the lions" in Paris or London, for the difference between the first and second cabin fare out and home.

Our *Expenses for board and bed,* while in the country in England, averaged seventy-five cents a day. Expenses of short conveyance by rail, coach and boat; fees to showmen and guides; washing, postage and incidentals (properly included as traveling expenses), added to this, made our average expenses about one dollar a day each. How we fared, and with what degree of comfort or luxury we were content, the reader should have already been informed. I have, however, dwelt more upon the agreeable than the disagreeable side of such traveling. We often, on entering a town, looked from one inn to another, in doubt which to select, desiring to avoid unnecessary expense, while we secured quiet and cleanliness. Sometimes we would enter a house and ask to see the rooms and know the charges. No offense was ever taken at this, though once or twice, where we were going to spend a Sunday, and the rooms were not agreeable, or convenient to write in, we proceeded further. We soon, however, were able to guess very well the character of a house by its outside appearance, and could regulate our disbursements with great exactness.

Inns.—The great difference between the large "first-class" inns and the second and third class is, that in the latter the lodgers are so few that one or two servants can take the place of three or four at the former. Frequently the landlord may be porter and Boots, (and will act as guide *commissionaire* or *cice-rone;*) the mistress, cook; and their daughter, waiter and chambermaid. In such cases, generally, no servant's fees at all are expected, and at most a third or half of what is honestly due the servants of the stylish inn will be satisfactory. The small inns are really often more comfortable to the pedestrian than the large ones; because he can be more at his ease; need not care how he appears; can wheel the sofa up to the fire or open all the windows; dine in his slippers, and smoke, if he likes, in the parlor: take command of the house, in short: see for himself that his shoes are greased and his linen washed and drying, his knapsack-straps repaired, lost buttons replaced, and all his rig a-taunto for an early start without delays in the morning.

If you call for anything for your table that the house is not provided with, it will be at once procured from the shops; the cooking is generally good, and the bread always fine. We usually contented ourselves with one hot meal in a day. Two of us were without the habit of drinking tea or coffee, and would often make our breakfast of bread and milk; lunch on bread and cheese and beer, and take a substantial meal at the end of our day's walk. We thought we walked better with this arrangement than any other.

For *less than seventy cents a day* it is possible to travel in England without hardship or injury to health. For how much less I cannot say. I once stopped alone at a house where I dined with the family on boiled bacon and potatoes and a bag-pudding, for which I was charged six-pence; breakfasted on scalded milk and bread for twopence; and was asked sixpence in advance for lodging. I had a good, clean bed and washing conveniences in my room. Add to this twopence for tea, and the day's living is 33 cents. This was in the north of England, and was extraordinary. The usual charge for lodging is a shilling, sometimes ninepence, and sometimes only sixpence. At the first-class inns they will make you pay well in one way or another. Where we did not dine we have been charged threepence each for the use of the public room, that is to say, for sitting in it instead of out-of-doors or in our rooms, while waiting for tea to be prepared. With regard to servants, the best way is to ask the landlord to pay them and charge it in the bill. It relieves you of a great annoyance and in such cases we never found the charge added extravagant.

Equipment.—*Shoes* can be obtained much cheaper in England than America, and, indeed, first-rate shoes are hardly to be had in America; but English shoes, that you would have to buy at the shops, always have a seam across the instep that is very hard upon a foot unaccustomed to it; and for this reason, and to insure a shape to suit you, you had best get them made at home. The leather should be well-tanned and dressed thick kip or cowhide, the best that can be procured; the soles of "English bend," three-eights of an inch in thickness; double this in the heel, which should come so far forward that the break will be perpendicular with the point of the ankle. Give your order, if possible, six months beforehand (I never have known a shoemaker who would get his work done when he promised for any consideration), and go to the *workman* yourself to make sure that he understands what you want, otherwise you will probably receive, just as you are going on board ship, a parcel by express containing a pair of butterfly pumps. Have a distinct agreement that they shall be returned if they do not come in time, and if they do not answer to your order. They should be high enough (6½ inches, including heel, commonly) to well cover the ankle, and lace up with but two crossings over the instep. The laces must be made of the best *leather,* and you should carry half-a-dozen spare ones.

If, finally, the shoes are not large enough to go easily over two woolen socks on your foot, reject them. Get shaker *woolen socks* of an exact fit to your foot, or as large as they may be without danger of folding or rubbing into welts under your shoes. Wear them with the "wrong side" outward. You do not want to wear them double, but your feet will swell so in a long hot day's walk, that you will want that there should have been room enough in your shoes for them to be double before you started. Break your shoes in on the passage.

Gaiters are worn to protect the feet from dust and gravel coming over the top of the shoe. They increase the heat of the feet to that degree that they are best dispensed with. Bathe your feet at every convenient opportunity on the road, and always as soon as you stop for the night, and change your socks and put on slippers.

I took all these precautions and yet suffered a thousand times more, and was delayed more, from foot-soreness than from fatigue. English pedestrians and sportsmen often wear much heavier and clumsier shoes than I have advised.

Knapsack.—We had the India-rubber *army* knapsack, made at Naugatuck, Connecticut. If you get them well "seasoned," so that they will not stick or smell, and with a good *harness,* they will probably be the best that you can procure. Ours were so, and we found them convenient and to wear well.

Clothing you can get in England better than at home. You must dispense with everything not absolutely essential to your comfort; for every ounce is felt in a hot day. We carried in our knapsacks each about as follows:

Four shirts, one pair cloth pantaloons, two pair socks; slippers, handkerchiefs, mending materials, toilet articles, towel, napkin, leather drinking-cup, cap, oil-silk cape, portfolio with writing and sketching materials, knife and fork, candle of tallow (that it may be used to grease shoes with upon occasion), matches, a book, map, pocket-compass, adhesive plaster, cord, shoe-lacings.

Everything selected with care for lightness and compactness, and the whole weighing ten pounds and a-half, including knapsack and straps. We wore upon the road light cloth coats and waistcoats, and linen dusters or blouses, and light cassimere pantaloons. We each carried a strong, hooked hickory-stick, and it will be found best to do so. We usually wore broad-brimmed, pliable felt hats of the best quality; they were excellent both in sun and rain. We also had light linen caps.

For *rainy weather* a cape of the best black oiled silk, 22 inches long before, and 16 inches behind, with a low collar, and buttoning in front, weighing half-a-pound, and folding so small that it could be carried in a coat pocket—a capital and serviceable article. With a loop and a tape it may be gathered tight at the waist under the knapsack, so as not to be lifted by the wind.

A *flask for drink* is hardly worth its carriage in England. A man every way in health should be able to walk a dozen miles or more without wanting to drink. Where good water is constantly to be had, it is refreshing to taste it very frequently, and there are no ill effects to be apprehended from doing so. You will perspire more freely, and I think stand the heat better; but cold water will not quench thirst, except momentarily; on the contrary, I believe it increases it. Malt liquors and spirituous liquors have different effects upon different individuals. Both are disagreeable to me. Most English pedestrians drink very freely of malt liquors, and find them wholesome. On the Continent I would carry a flask for light wine, such as every peasant has to his dinner. Its cost is trifling, and there is nothing which will quench thirst like it. It is not very palatable at first, but exceedingly refreshing, and I believe every way healthful. It has no intoxicating, and very slight stimulating, qualities. I think it would have an excellent effect on the public health, if it could be produced cheaply, and used as freely as tea and coffee now are in the United States.

When you feel very much jaded with a long walk, and hardly able to go any further, if you can swallow a cup of tea and a bit of toast or biscuit, and *pour a wine-glass of spirits into your shoes,* keeping yourself warm during the necessary short halt, you will find yourself good for another hour or two of hard tramping.

Routes and Distances.—Unless you are considerably familiar with the language and history of a Continental nation, I would advise you to spend most of your time in England. It is better to study thoroughly the character of one people, and remain so long, if possible, in their country, that you may feel as if you had lived in it, and made yourself a part of it, than to run superficially over a dozen. It is, however, much cheaper, and in many respects more agreeable to walk in Germany than in England; and a true American, mingling with the peasant people, can hardly fail to do them good, and have his own heart enlightened and expanded by their spirit longing for liberty and universal affection for his country. It is of walking in England, however, that I wish especially to speak.

Your route should be determined by your tastes and objects. If they are as general as ours, and you design to employ the same time in England that we did, I could advise but very slight variation from our route.

With a week's more time, you should see more of North Wales, (though, in general, mountain and lake country *is not England,* and you can get what tourists go to those districts for better nearer at home;) extend your walk into Devonshire, and keep along the south coast to Portsmouth. After visiting the Isle of Wight, the old road to London, running, I believe, through Guildford, is said to be much pleasanter than the more direct way we came. After spending some weeks in and about London, follow up the Thames by Henley, and as near the south bank as you can, to Oxford—then by Stratford-on-Avon, Warwick and Kenilworth to Birmingham; thence, according to your interest, through the manufacturing districts, and by Chatsworth and the Derbyshire moors to York; thence by Fountain's Abbey, through the curious hill-country of West Yorkshire and Lancashire, into Westmoreland; thence either north to Scotland, or by Liverpool to Ireland, crossing afterwards to Scotland from Belfast. Guide-books can be obtained in New York, by the aid of which and a good map, you may, before you leave home, judge how much time you will want to spend in examining various objects of interest, and ascertain distances, etc. You can thus plot off your route and calculate the time at which you will arrive at any particular point. Guide-books are expensive and heavy, and this is their principal use; further, you are liable to pass through a town and neglect to see something for which it is peculiarly distinguished, without you have something to remind you of it.

We traveled at first at the rate of one hundred miles in six days, at last at the rate of about two hundred; sometimes going forty miles, and ordinarily thirty, in a day. We usually did thirty miles in eleven hours, one of which might be spent under a hedge or in a wayside inn, and about one mile an hour lost in loitering, looking at things on the wayside or talking to people that we met; our actual pace was just about four miles an hour.

You can start with twelve miles in a day, and calculate to average twenty-five after the first fortnight.

If you can make anything like a harmonious noise upon any instrument for that purpose, I would advise you to strap it on. You will understand its value by reading the life of Goldsmith. It will make you welcome in many a peasant circle, where you might otherwise have been only a damper upon all naturalness and geniality.

APPENDIX B

Principles of the Mark System, framed to mix Persuasion with Punishment, and make their effect improving, yet their operation severe. By CAPTAIN MACHONOCHIE, R. N., K. H., late Superintendent of the British Penal Settlement at Norfolk Island.

"Our present punishments resemble everything that is most deteriorating in ordinary life: and they deteriorate accordingly. If we would infuse into them those impulses which, under Providential guidance, make other forms of adversity improving, we would make them improving also."

The constituent elements in secondary punishment are labor and time. Men are sentenced to hard *labor* for a given *time:*—but the time is here made to measure the labor—and the first proposal of the Mark System is, that instead of this the labor be made to measure the time. This idea is not peculiar to it. In his letter to Earl Grey the Archbishop of Dublin uses these words: "The best plan, as it appears to me, would be, instead of sentencing men to imprisonment for a certain time, to sentence them to render a certain amount of labor. A fixed daily task may be imposed on them, but with power to exceed this at their own discretion, thereby shortening their period of detention. The effect would be, not only that criminals would thus acquire habits of labor, but of attaching an agreeable idea to labor. By each additional step they took on the tread-wheel they would be walking out of prison—by each additional cut of the spade they would be cutting a way to return to society."

It would be difficult to express the direct primary effect of the system in happier or terser terms; and even when thus stated, the improvement contemplated on existing practice appears immense. But much more when the ulterior consequences are also considered. By substituting a powerful internal stimulus to exertion for that physical coercion which must ever be at best an imperfect external one, while all necessary bondage and suffering as the consequences of crime would be retained, direct "slavery" would be banished from among our secondary punishments. The tendencies of our management would be to good, whereas those of the existing system are "to evil continually." Men would improve under it, instead of becoming worse. And the administration of public justice would acquire a place among the Christian agencies of our land: it is painful to think how far it is at present removed in operation from any such character.

But another view may be also taken of the question thus involved, not less interesting. If we look abroad into ordinary life, we cannot but be struck with the resemblance which our present forms of secondary punishment bear to everything that is in this most enfeebling and deteriorating, and how directly opposed they are to those forms of adversity which, under the influence of Providential wisdom, reform character and invigorate it. Slavery deteriorates—long seclusion deteriorates—every condition, in a word, more or less deteriorates, which leaves no choice of action, requires no virtue but obedience, affords no stimulus to exertion beyond this, supplies the want of nature without effort with a view to them, and restores to prosperity, through lapse of time, without evidence that such restoration is deserved. Yet this is our present system of secondary punishment. What improves, on the contrary, is a condition of adversity from which there is no escape but by continuous effort—which leaves the degree of that effort much in the individual's own power, but if he relaxes, his suffering is deepened and prolonged, and it is only alleviated and shortened if he struggles manfully—which makes exertion necessary even to earn daily bread—and something more, prudence, self-command, voluntary economy and the like, to recover prosperity. To this, as yet, secondary punishment bears no resemblance; but were our sentences measured by labor instead of time—were they to the performance of certain tasks, not to the occupation of a certain time in evading any—the approximation might be made indefinitely close.

Labor being a vague term the system next proposes that it be represented by marks—the earning of so many thousands of which, in a prison or penal settlement, as the case may be, to be made the punishment of all offenses according to their degree. A proportion of these marks to be credited to individuals daily, according to the exertion made in whatever labor is allotted them —all supplies of food and clothing to be charged in them—all misconduct to be punished by fines in them—and only the clear balance to be carried to account towards liberation. By this means both wages and savings' banks would be introduced into prisons —wages to stimulate labor, and give an interest in it, and savings' banks to give a similar interest to habits of economy and self-command. To make the resemblance to ordinary life still closer, and at the same time to promote kindly and social, as opposed to selfish, feeling, it is further proposed that during a portion of their entire period of detention criminals be distributed into parties or families of six, with common interests and accounts, rising or falling together, and thus all interested in the good conduct of each. By this means a strong physical check would be laid on crime in prisons, with a yet stronger moral one; and an apparatus would be gained by which good conduct and exertion would be made popular, and offense unpopular, in the community, and all would be interested in promoting the one and keeping down the other. My experience on Norfolk Island—which was imperfect, because my views were not then sustained, as I trust they yet will be, at home, my powers and apparatus were consequently imperfect, and my results rather indicated tendencies than gave precise conclusions—yet leads me to attach great value to this, as to several other details explained in other papers. But I regard them all only as they seem to me to carry out the principles laid down. If these are right, when once established, the best details to found on them will soon become of themselves apparent. With a near tangible end, like individual reform, in view, no mistakes, however at first great, can be long persisted in.

Severity, then, with a directly benevolent purpose—modeled with a view to recover criminals as well as punish them—controlled and guided by the enlightened pursuit of this noble end, made as great, for the benefit both of the individual and the community, as is compatible with it, but neither greater nor other than strictly subordinate to it—this is the guide here sought to be introduced into secondary punishment: and unless it is attentively considered, it will be found difficult to believe the number of new views that it will open up of interest and promise. It will adjust the controversy between harshness and lenity which has long divided reasoners on the subject—the one impulse having authorized the most distressing cruelties, while the other has occasionally led to indulgences scarcely less injurious in their ultimate consequences to both the criminal and society, enfeebling the one, and leading the honest laborer, in the other, painfully to contrast his own position with that of the convicted felon. It will thus solve many preliminary difficulties, and conduct to many important conclusions. It will give a new spirit to punishment by giving it a new direction. By raising its object it will raise its administration. It will be difficult to be either cruel or careless with such an object as individual reform in view, and *while wielding an agency offering a reasonable probability of attaining it.* (The last is of great importance: we become indifferent, in spite of ourselves, when engaged in a hopeless task.) It will assimilate this branch of our administration to those ways of Providence to men which must always be our surest guides when we seek to influence them. It will thus imitate the highest wisdom, and thereby enable us to obey the highest precept. We may love while we chasten, and be substantially kind even when enforcing the strictest commands of punitive law. It will succeed with little effort, because it will study the human nature implanted in us, instead of trampling its impulses under foot. It will further conduct to great economy as well as efficiency, partly through this cause, partly because the virtues of industry and self-command which it will be its great aim to foster will equally bring about both results. The practical change may be thought a small one on which to found such anticipations—the change from measuring labor by time to that of measuring time by labor—or, in other words, from giving our criminals time-sentences to allotting them tasks:—but the one course is the direct reverse of the other, and the difference may be thus the whole difference between right and wrong, success and failure. It seems, indeed, even impossible to follow out the chain of reasoning suggested without coming to this conclusion. When men are smitten with adversity in ordinary life, and thus *punished* for previous follies or misconduct, they are not condemned to this adversity for a certain *time,* but until they can retrieve their position. They suffer under this *task;* they sorrow over it (but without resentment); they struggle with it: their characters improve under the various efforts and emotions called out by it; (both deepened if they have others to care for as well as themselves;) frequently they rise even higher than before;—and society is instructed by such examples in every way—it shrinks from the preliminary sufferings exhibited in them, and emulates, in due proportion as its own case may require, the manly struggle that has at length overcome them. And so it might be with our punishments, if we would model them on the same type. They are now for the most part barbarous in every sense, in their want of skill and adaptation to high purpose, and in the crime and misery they thus gratuitously produce. We might make them beneficent in every sense, merely by copying the wisdom that is around us;—and when this is fully understood, it is not to be imagined but that every lover of his kind will take even an eager interest in bringing about the change. The real difficulty is to influence to the inquiry.

I must add, that in this condensed statement of the principles of his system, Captain Machonochie has made no allusion to a very important part of it—the *ante-criminal* part, if I may so express it. He proposes, as a preventive measure, the establishment of Industrial Schools, to which the children of the poorer classes or vagrants should be encouraged to come and give their cheerful and active labor, by receiving marks exchangeable for a good, substantial, but coarse, meal in the middle of the day, and some other food to carry home at night. The employments to be as much as possible rural and agricultural, and in every case at least laborious, fitting those subjected to them to face hard work in after life.